University of Cambridge Department of Applied Economics

OCCASIONAL PAPER 25

Soviet Planning Today

Proposals for an Optimally Functioning Economic System

University of Cambridge Department of Applied Economics
Occasional Papers

Soviet Planning Today

Proposals for an Optimally Functioning Economic System

by MICHAEL ELLMAN

CAMBRIDGE
AT THE UNIVERSITY PRESS
1971

Published by
the Syndics of the Cambridge University Press
Bentley House, 200 Euston Road, London N.W.1
American Branch: 32 East 57th Street, New York, N.Y.10022

© Cambridge University Press 1971.

Library of Congress Catalogue Card Number: 72–145613

ISBN: 0 521 081564

Set in cold type by E.W.C. Wilkins & Associates Ltd,
and Printed in Great Britain by Alden & Mowbray Ltd,
at the Alden Press, Oxford

Contents

List of Text Tables and Figures

TABLES

FIGURES

Preface

The Central Economic Mathematical Institute of the USSR Academy of
Sciences is currently working out the theory of an optimally functioning
socialist economy. It has put forward concrete proposals for improving the
economic mechanism and the methods of economic calculation designed to
transform the Soviet economic system into an optimally functioning economic
system. This theory, these proposals, and the work already done by Soviet
researchers, are of great interest, for the understanding both of Soviet planning and of the doctrines taught by economists in the capitalist countries,
and for comparing with analogous work in other countries, and the purpose
of this paper is to describe and explain them.

This paper consists of three parts. The first part, chapters 1–5, explains
the theory of the optimally functioning socialist economy. The second part,
chapters 6 and 7, describes some of the non-optimalities of the existing
planning system. The third part, chapters 8–10, is concerned with evaluating
the usefulness of the theory of the optimally functioning socialist economy
as a guide to what is necessary for overcoming the problems of the Soviet
economy. Chapter 8 contains a detailed study of the system of enterprise
incentive funds in order to provide the necessary background against which
the relevance of the ideas of the Central Economic Mathematical Institute
on the appropriate local optimality criterion to use in an optimally functioning economic system, and its three level planning scheme, can be assessed.
It is important to bear in mind that the enterprise incentive fund system
actually introduced by the September (1965) Plenum was not in accordance
with the ideas of the Central Economic Mathematical Institute, and its problems are not a criticism of the proposals of this institute. On the other hand,
analysis of this system does enable the reader to consider the question of
whether this institute's proposals are more or less relevant to the real problems involved in the use of profit as a measure of efficiency, than other
proposals that have been put forward.

This paper is intended as a selective rather than exhaustive study of the
subject. When considering the usefulness of the ideas of the supporters of
the theory of the optimally functioning economic system for improving the
economic mechanism, I have selected for examination the use of profit as a
measure of efficiency. I have not considered, for example, to what extent
payment to the state by the enterprises for the use of capital equipment has
led to an increase in efficiency. In the same way, when considering whether
the supporters of the theory of the optimally functioning economic system
are able to improve the methods of economic calculation, I have selected for
discussion two applications of their ideas which seem to me of particular

interest. Similarly, I have not included a study of the relationship between the work of Kantorovich and that of von Neumann, the pioneer in the field of linear theory. A pair of linear programmes is equivalent to a game, and hence it is possible to derive the theorem of the characteristics of an optimal plan from von Neumann's 1928 proof of the existence of a saddlepoint for certain games. In addition, in a comment on his growth model, published in 1938, von Neumann drew attention to the duality of the monetary and technical variables. Nevertheless it is still true that if one is interested in linear programming as a technique for generating numerical optical solutions to problems of the organisation of production, then Kantorovich is the pioneer, with A.N. Tolstoi as his predecessor.

Similarly this paper is not a complete study of the subject. It could not be; the discussion on which it is a report is still continuing. I have brought the story up to November 1970, and hope that the reader, having read the paper, will find it easier to understand subsequent developments.

I am deeply indebted to Dr. A. Zauberman of the London School of Economics, who introduced me to the study of Soviet economic thought and to whose encouragement I owe a great deal; to Dr. V.S. Dadayan of the *kafedra* of mathematical methods of analysis of the economy of the Economics Faculty of Moscow State University who supervised my work in Moscow; to my friends at Glasgow University for stimulating discussion of Soviet planning and political economy; and to Dr. M. Cobb who carefully read through several drafts of this paper. I also benefited from helpful conversations with Dr. C. Feinstein, who kindly read the entire draft. At various stages in its life part or all of the draft was read by Dr. C. Bliss, Professor R. Davies, Mr. J. Eatwell, Professor A. Ehrlich, Dr. G. Heal, Professor J. Meade, Dr. L. Pasinetti and Professor J. Robinson, to all of whom I am grateful. Parts of the paper were published as articles in *Economica*, *Economics of Planning*, the *Economic Journal*, and the *Scottish Journal of Political Economy*, and I am grateful to the editors of these journals for permission to reprint this material.

My biggest debt is to Patricia Ellman for continued support, encouragement and understanding, without which this study would never have been written.

My studies in Moscow were financed by the British Council, and my work at the DAE since January 1970 has been financed by the Social Science Research Council.

The text contains both footnotes and references. The references (most of which are to works in Russian) are for the benefit of those readers who would like to refer to the original sources.

Michael Ellman   Department of Applied Economics
                                  November 1970

Glossary

The administrative economy. *The term used by the author to describe the economic mechanism which has existed in the USSR since 1929. The distinguishing feature of the administrative economy is current planning.*

Capital. *The value of the capital goods of an enterprise or association as valued in its accounts.*

CC   *The Central Committee of the party.*

CPSU *The Communist Party of the Soviet Union.*

Current planning. *The system under which enterprises receive instructions as to which products they should produce in the current quarter, half year or year, and quotas for the materials which are to be used to meet the production targets, and other instructions concerning their activities in the current quarter, half year or year. To be contrasted with perspective or medium term planning, which is concerned with compiling and implementing five year plans, and regional planning.*

The efficient allocation of resources. *The rational organisation of the productive forces.*

Gosplan. *The State Planning Commission, the central planning organ.*

Gossnab. *The State Committee on material-technical supply, the central organ for the planning of supply, i.e. the allocation of commodities to enable ouput plans to be implemented.*

Khozraschet. A word which describes an economic unit which has its own profit and loss account and is run in a business like way. Used by extension in phrases such as 'full khozraschet' to describe the choice of inputs and outputs by enterprises or associations themselves, flexible prices, and payment for the use of natural resources and capital goods.

The *khozraschet* economy. *The term used by the author to describe the economic mechanism of a socialist economy without current planning, i.e. an economic mechanism similar to the New Economic Mechanism in Hungary.*

The Lausanne school. *Group of economists who studied the general equilibrium of the economy and provided a mathematical proof of the doctrine that competition ensures the efficient allocation of resources.*

NEP   *The New Economic Policy is the term used to describe the econ-
        omic mechanism which existed in the USSR in the 1920s, an econ-
        omic mechanism based on a compromise between the party and the
        peasants.*

Indirect Centralisation. *Guiding enterprises to socially rational decisions
        by establishing appropriate rules of enterprise behaviour (e.g.
        profit maximisation or the present value criterion) and appropriate
        values of, or rules for determining, the economic parameters (prices,
        the rate of interest). To be contrasted with direct centralisation,
        where the authorities try to ensure that enterprises take socially
        rational decisions by issuing them with detailed instructions, and
        decentralisation, where decisions are made by enterprises whose
        decisions are entirely independent of the wishes of the authorities.*

The productive forces. *The technology, skills, and resources available to
        society.*

The productive relations. *The relations between people in the process of
        production, e.g. the exploitation of the workers by the capitalists
        under capitalism.*

The rational organisation of the productive forces. *The efficient allocation
        of resources.*

The reform. *The economic reform announced at the September (1965) Plenum
        of the CC, and subsequently implemented by stages.*

SOPS   *The Council for the Study of the Productive Forces, the central
        organ for regional planning.*

TSEMI   *The Central Economic Mathematical Institute of the USSR Academy
        of Sciences.*

TsSU   *The Central Statistical Administration.*

The 20th Congress *The 20th Congress of the CPSU was held in 1956. At
        this Congress the First Secretary made a report 'On the personality
        cult and its consequences'.*

The 22nd Congress *The 22nd Congress of the CPSU was held in 1961. At
        this Congress a resolution was passed to remove the body of
        J.V. Stalin from the Lenin Mausoleum.*

Introduction

The theory of the optimally functioning socialist economy which was put forward in the 1960s by TSEMI,[a] and the proposals for improving the economic mechanism and the methods of economic calculation associated with this theory, are the (main) form which discussion of the importance of the efficient allocation of resources for a socialist economy is taking at the present time in the Soviet Union. The historical background to this discussion is as follows.

The central doctrine of the Lausanne school, which was argued by Walras and Pareto, and provided with a neat mathematical basis by Koopmans and Debreu, is that:

> '*Production in a market ruled by free competition is an operation by which services can be combined and converted into products of such a nature and in such quantities as will give the greatest possible satisfaction of wants within the limits of the double condition, that each service and each product have only one price in the market, namely that price at which the quantity supplied is equal to the quantity demanded, and that the selling price of the products be equal to the cost of the services employed in making them.*'[1]

Applying this argument to a socialist economy, before such an economy existed, Barone argued that a socialist economy would have to use such instruments as prices, rent and profits in order to achieve the efficient allocation of resources.[2] Applying this argument to the actual experience of the first socialist economy, von Mises argued that Soviet experience corroborated the doctrine that without private ownership of the means of production the efficient allocation of resources was impossible.[3] Some years later Robbins argued that a planned economy would be unable to solve centrally the millions of equations that have to be solved for the efficient allocation of resources, would be unlikely to adopt market socialism, and would probably

> 'fall back on frankly authoritarian planning. They would attempt to manage production as a whole as the general staff manages an army at war. They would probably retain the price mechanism as an agency for distributing consumer goods, supplementing it when anything went wrong by the

(a) The emphasis in Soviet discussion on the need not only for 'optimal *planning*' but also for 'optimal *functioning*' results from the awareness that it is not much use calculating optimal plans if the economy functions in such a way that the optimal plans are not implemented and non-optimal decisions are made.

device of rationing, as in Russia at present. But for the rest they would dictate production from the centre, choosing what kinds of goods and qualities seemed to them most desirable. Such decisions, as we have seen, could not be based on an accounting system with any very precise meaning. The planning authorities would have no way of discovering with any accuracy whether the ends they chose were being secured with economical use of means. In particular lines of production they could no doubt errect an apparatus which, from the technical point of view, would be very imposing. The Pharoahs did not need a price system for the errection of pyramids. But at what sacrifice of other goods its products could be secured, at what economic as distinct from technical efficiency it functioned, could not be ascertained. The system would require the complete regimentation of individuals considered as producers. As consumers they could choose between the commodities available. But on the choice of commodities to be produced they would have little influence. They would have to take what it was decided to produce. And what it was decided to produce would be the resultant, not of the conflicting pulls of prices and costs, but of the conflicting advice of different technical experts and politicians with no objective measure to which to submit the multitudinous alternatives possible.

Is it certain that such a system would be more efficient than capitalism? Is it certain that the friends of liberty and progress who are also friends of planning have sufficiently considered the compatibility of these aims?' [4]

The desirability of organising the Soviet economy in such a way as to ensure the efficient allocation of resources was argued on the eve of the creation of the administrative economy by Yushkov. [5] Yushkov, aware of the doctrines of the Lausanne school, was primarily concerned with ensuring the efficient allocation of scarce investment resources. A decade before Kantorovich's theorem was proved, Yushkov recognised the importance of prices which could serve as a guide to decision making, argued for payment for the use of capital goods and natural resources, and emphasised the importance of *khozraschet*. The improvement which the use of techniques for the efficient allocation of resources could bring about in the methods of economic calculation was argued in a study published in 1939 by Kantorovich. [6] Some years before Dantzig, Kantorovich argued that a large number of practical problems of the organisation of production had a common mathematical structure and that it was possible to calculate optimal solutions to them which were substantially more efficient than those arrived at by the usual planning methods. No attention seems to have been paid to these works when they appeared. Stalin made his attitude clear in *Economic problems of socialism in the USSR* (1952), the booklet which contains his response to the issues raised in the discussion of the draft textbook of political economy. Stalin rejected the view that economics should be primarily concerned with the rational organisation of the productive forces, with economic policy or the improvement of the methods of economic calculation. (He turned the political economy of socialism into the false consciousness of Soviet society.)

The issue is once more a topical one. The advocates of an optimally functioning economic system consider that both the economic mechanism and the methods of economic calculation should be such as to ensure the efficient allocation of resources, and they have put forward concrete proposals to this end. Their ideas have given rise to an extensive discussion in the course of which they have come under heavy fire from those who consider that their theoretical views are incorrect and their policy recommendations harmful. Strumilin, the doyen of Soviet economists, has even made an ominous comparison between some of the views now being put forward by the advocates of an optimally functioning economy and the views of Groman and Bazarov. [a] [7]

(a) Groman and Bazarov were prominent, but non-Bolshevik, economists of the 1920s. Groman was tried and found guilty of wrecking activities in 1931. Bazarov was arrested in 1930, and then disappeared.

1. The use of mathematics in Soviet economics - an historical survey

'It would be difficult to name another branch of knowledge, with the possible exception of biology, that suffered more from the personality cult
than economics.'

Report of the 1964 round table of
economists and mathematicians.[1]

During the 1920s vigorous discussion of the problems involved in the
rapid socialist industrialisation of backward Russia took place among
Soviet economists. Much of the 'new' Western economics of the post World
War II period, such as the discussion of the economic problems of the
developing countries, growth models and input-output, was simply the repetition and development of the fruitful Soviet work of the 1920s.[2]

During this heroic period the use of mathematical methods was widespread. Indeed, in an article published in 1928, L.P. Yushkov discussed
what later became a central problem of the theory of the optimally functioning economic system, how to create a system of planning that would provide
the 'semi-automatic optimality' of the development of the national economy,
combining optimal national economic development with maximal operational
independence for the separate parts of the economic system.[3] After 1929,
however, conditions changed. In a speech on agrarian policy delivered in
December 1929, at the time of the bitter struggle to impose collectivisation
on the peasants, Stalin criticised those 'Soviet' economists who had failed
to support his policies, and in some cases had even supplied arguments for
his opponents. He criticised Chayanov, Groman and Bazarov by name, and
referred to TsSU's pioneering balance of the national economy for 1923–4 as
a mere 'game with figures'. The only economist mentioned favourably in this
speech was Nemchinov, who had supplied Stalin with useful statistics on
agriculture.[4] Subsequently many able economists, such as Kondratiev,
Groman, Feldman, Chayanov, Preobrazhensky and Vainshtein, were arrested,
and exiled or sent to prisons and concentration camps, some never to return.
The censorship during the period of the personality cult was far stricter
than under NEP. Stalin appears to have adhered to this sceptical view of
the usefulness of economists for the rest of his life. In a work written at
the end of his life Stalin decisively rejected the view that the function of
political economy 'is to elaborate and develop a scientific theory of the
productive forces in social production, a theory of the planning of economic
development ... The rational organisation of the productive forces, economic planning etc. are not problems of political economy but problems of
the economic policy of the directing bodies. These are two different

provinces, which must not be confused ... Political economy investigates the laws of development of men's relations of production. Economic policy draws practical conclusions from this, gives them concrete shape, and builds its day to day work on them. To foist upon political economy problems of economic policy is to kill it as a science.'

As Yaroshenko, one of the participants in the discussion of the draft textbook of political economy to which Stalin was reacting, put it, in a passage quoted by Stalin, 'healthy discussion of the rational organisation of the productive forces in social production, scientific demonstration of the validity of such organisation' is to be replaced by 'scholastic disputes as to the role of particular categories of socialist political economy – value, commodity, money, credit etc.' [a]

Their task confined in this way, Soviet political economists were mainly engaged in agit-prop, and in particular with demonstrating the virtues of socialism in general and of the latest statement by Stalin in particular, and with the sins of capitalism (the height of research was to find a hitherto unused quotation from one of the classics of Marxism–Leninism); and the economic practitioners (engineers and politicians) made decisions on the basis of rules of thumb (as was done in contemporary British and American firms). When in spite of all these obstacles, serious contributions to economic analysis were published, such as the well known works of Kantorovich and Novozhilov,[5] they were ignored.

After the 20th Congress the situation improved, and the study by economists of the rational organisation of the productive forces revived. From 1957 onwards Academician Nemchinov, who had proved his usefulness and reliability in the 1920s, repeatedly advocated the use of quantitative methods of analysis of economic phenomena.[6] As a professor at the *kafedra* (department) of political economy of the Academy of Social Sciences attached to the CC from 1947–1957, a member of the Presidium of the USSR Academy of Sciences from 1953–1962, and the Chairman of SOPS from 1949–1964, Academician Nemchinov was well placed to get things done. Using the 1950 British input-output table as a basis, he began popularising the idea of input-output in the USSR.[7] By emphasising its Russian roots, Marxist orthodoxy and usefulness for planning, Nemchinov was able to persuade TsSU to compile an input-output table for the USSR for 1959, which was published in 1961. He himself organised a team of enthusiastic young economists who compiled a regional input-output table. Nemchinov also provided an institutional framework for this new development in Soviet economics, the economical-mathematical laboratory of the USSR Academy of Sciences, which was founded in 1958, and which subsequently grew into

(a) All these quotations are from Stalin's essay, Concerning the errors of Comrade L.D. Yaroshenko, in J.Stalin, *Economic problems of socialism in the USSR* (Moscow 1952). The subjects which Yaroshenko thought political economy should discuss (the rational organisation of the productive forces, economic planning, formation of social funds etc), but which Stalin regarded as outside the competence of academics, are precisely those which the present day theory of the optimally functioning economic system discusses.

2

the Central Economic Mathematical Institute. Not only Nemchinov, but also other economists who had made contributions to Soviet economics before 1929, such as Novozhilov, Vainshtein and Konius, played a prominent role in the development of the economic-mathematical direction within Soviet economic science after the 20th Congress.

In 1959 there was published under the editorship of Nemchinov a volume entitled *The use of mathematics in economic researches.*[8] This book contained an extensive work, practically a book in itself, by Novozhilov, on the problems of rational decision making in a socialist economy, together with a reprint of Kantorovich's pioneering paper of 1939 on linear programming, and a number of other articles. In 1961 and 1965 two further volumes with the same title and the same editor appeared.[a]

Also in 1959 Kantorovich's famous and very influential book *Economic calculation and the best use of resources* edited and with a preface by Nemchinov, was published. (This book had been basically written in the first half of the 1940s, and papers containing its main theses were read at the Leningrad Polytechnical Institute in 1940 and at the Institute of Economics in 1943, but its publication had to wait for more propitious times.)[10] The purpose of this book was to explain to economists in a simple non-mathematical way, the relevance of linear programming for economic planning in the USSR. In spite of the fact that the book contains numerous references to party documents, Marx, and the labour theory of value, it was greeted by hostile reviews.[11] In April 1960 a conference was held in Moscow to discuss the use of mathematical methods in economic research and planning. Its proceedings were published in a number of volumes.[12] A wide discussion took place, with numerous points of view expressed. Whereas at first the mathematical economists were a small minority, struggling to put their views forward against the opposition of entrenched political economists, the position rapidly changed. In 1963 TSEMI was created and began putting forward proposals to improve the planning system by the large scale application of mathematical methods and computers. In 1964 a decision of the CC and Council of Ministers provided for the establishment of a Unified Automated System of Management. At the 1964 round table of economists and mathematicians it was the political economists who were on the defensive, and the report of this meeting was edited in a way critical of the political economists. In 1965 the Lenin prize was awarded to Kantorovich, Novozhilov and Nemchinov. At the 1966 debate on optimal planning TSEMI put forward far reaching proposals for reforming the economic mechanism, and challenged the position of political economy. The support which TSEMI received from official quarters in the early 1960s reflected the hope that the application of mathematical methods and computers would enable the problems of the planning system to be overcome, and a substantial increase in efficiency achieved. Subsequently, in particular after the 1968 events in Czechoslovakia had shown what incorrect

(a) The 1965 volume contains an important paper by Kantorovich and Makarov on perspective planning.

theoretical views could mean in practice, the wind started to blow in the other direction, and TSEMI had to drop some of its more extreme pretensions.

Four main themes can be distinguished in the lengthy debate which accompanied the rise of 'economic cybernetics' (the usual term for the use of mathematics in economics in the USSR). First, many of the old school of political economists regarded the 'mathematical' theory of prices, in which prices are numbers which help a decision maker to arrive at optimal solutions, as contrary to the labour theory of value. Secondly, the idea that it is helpful to regard national economic planning as an extremal problem, and that the task of economic planning consists of choosing a set of numbers, the intensities at which the activities will be operated, was opposed by traditionally minded political economists, who emphasised the social, political and technological aspects of planning which they regarded as requiring conscious decisions by the planners rather than the solution of some mathematical problem. Thirdly, there arose the intellectual and organisational question of the relationship between the new discipline of economic cybernetics and the traditional subject of political economy, which continued to be taught and to be an integral part of the Marxist–Leninist world outlook. Fourthly, there arose the question of the quality of the traditional planning methods.

When the models of Kantorovich and Novozhilov were first expounded they were attacked because, as Boyarski, the director of TsSU's research institute, put it, 'in the place of value in the Marxist sense he [Kantorovich] places the relationship of cost on the "last" unit of this or that product and against his will reproduces several propositions of so-called "marginalism".'[13] The discussion of the relationship between Marxism and mathematical economics gave rise to a wide debate, both inside and outside the Soviet Union.[14] In this connection the following observations are relevant.

The problems investigated by Marx and those investigated by Soviet economic cyberneticians are entirely different. Marx was concerned with an analysis of the productive relations of capitalism, with the conflict between social groups, with discovering the laws of motion of capitalism. Soviet economic cyberneticians are concerned with the rational organisation of the productive forces of a socialist economy. As Kantorovich has clearly explained:

'Marxist analysis of the capitalist economy aimed at a more general, fundamental investigation of capitalist production and the study of its basic laws, and for this reason could, of course, abstract from all the temporary transient factors and influences.

Economic calculation (and analysis) in a socialist economy serves as a basis for practical solutions and for this reason it must be more accurate and detailed. It must take into consideration the concrete situation including temporary and accidental circumstances.'[15]

The analysis of long run equilibrium growth paths and the analysis of the factors determining the prices of particular goods at particular times involve very different considerations, and it is scarcely surprising that

4

different conceptual apparatuses are required.

Marxists have always objected to the marginal productivity theory of distribution because it attempted to explain the distribution of income under capitalism by technological factors (the marginal products of the factors of production) rather than by social ones (i.e. exploitation). Soviet economic cyberneticians are not developing an apologetic theory to justify capitalist consumption but are concerned with raising the efficiency of socialism.

The charge that his ideas about how prices could be used to raise the efficiency of socialist planning amount to a surrender to 'marginalism' has been answered by Novozhilov in the course of a survey of general equilibrium models. Novozhilov argued that the inadequacies of these models are very important.

'They are clearly connected with the bourgeois world outlook. But marginal measurements (marginalism) are not among them. On the contrary marginal measurements (marginalism) are related to what one might call the rational kernel of the models of Walras and Neumann – to posing an extremal problem for the national economy as a *whole*. Posing the problem of the general optimum with respect to capitalism is unreal and has an apologetic sense. But if we drop the unreal assumptions of these models, there remains the proposition that prices are one of the means necessary for finding and implementing the general optimum. This proposition is analogous to the mathematical method of finding a relative extremum with the help of special *multipliers*. This idea received a clear expression in models of general economic equilibrium.* Linear programming uses this function of prices in practice for the solution of particular economic problems, using special "shadow prices".

Under certain simple conditions these multipliers have a marginal significance. When the number of limited resources is more than one, however, we cannot determine the efficiency of each of these resources on its own,** and therefore we cannot say, that the multipliers corresponding to the optimal plan reflect the marginal efficiency of the utilisation of the corresponding resources. Hence treating the multiplier prices as marginal quantities is possible only at the initial stage of analysis of the problem of optimal planning, when it is necessary to pose the problem in the simplest possible conditions. To suppose that the method of multipliers is the property of bourgeois economic science, however, has not the slightest foundation, although the representatives of bourgeois economic science consider it so.

The poverty of content of the models of Walras and Neumann becomes clear if one compares them with concrete models of the national economy, the Soviet perspective plans. The idea of the optimum lies at their base. In particular the problem of maximising the rate of growth of the socialist

* Cassell, *Theoretische Sozialökonomie* (Leipzig 1921) S.75.

** On this see V.V. Novozhilov, *Trudy Leningradskogo Politekhnicheskogo instituta* 1946 No.1 p. 329.

economy was posed already at the XVth party congress [1927]. At this congress the principle of the optimal relationship between accumulation and consumption was put forward, which provided the most rapid growth rate for a long period. In practice this problem was resolved on the basis of utilising precisely those factors of development from which the Neumann model abstracts, the improvement of the productive relations, technical progress, the growth of the material and cultural level of the working people and so on. History shows that these factors had an immense significance. You see, despite the inadequacies in the practice of price formation, the growth rate of the national economy of the USSR would be inaccessible under capitalism.

It would however be incorrect to underestimate the role of prices in the socialist economy. Much depends on the correct measurement of costs and benefits, such as the compilation of optimal plans, the efficiency of *khozraschet*, distribution according to work, and so on. This means that the correct determination of prices allows us to utilise still more the advantages of the socialist system over the capitalist system, than is possible with incorrect price formation.'[16]

It is true that the emphasis on the efficiency function of prices, on the usefulness of prices as guides to the efficient allocation of resources, by the economic cyberneticians, is the repetition of an argument much emphasised by the Lausanne school. The conception of prices as guides to efficient decision making was not originated by Walras, however. It is simply a generalisation of the Ricardian concept of comparative costs as a guide to rational decision making in international trade. Emphasis on the allocative function of prices is a wholly understandable reaction to the problems of the administrative economy (some of which are discussed in chapters 6 and 7 below). In addition, some of the economic cyberneticians (for example Val'tukh)[17] have warned against an illegitimate extension of the concept of scarcity prices from non-reproducible to reproducible commodities. Moreover, some Soviet specialists are well aware of the limitations of the information embodied in prices. This information, Novozhilov has argued, is adequate for 'the decentralised fulfilment of a given plan on the basis of *khozraschet* and for small alterations to the plan, but inadequate for important alterations to the plan, still less for the compilation of perspective plans.'[18]

The most penetrating criticism of the work of Kantorovich and his followers has come not from those who criticised 'marginalism' but from mathematical economists who put forward solid arguments on specific questions, such as Gerchuk who criticised exaggerated ideas in some circles about the applicability of linear programming,[19] and Lur'e who criticised the idea that the rate of interest to be used in planning should be identified with the marginal product of capital in an aggregate production function, and put forward an alternative way of determining it.[20]

In some quarters the work of Kantorovich and Novozhilov is regarded as a vindication of 'Western economic theory', and a powerful critique of

Marxism which has not yet discovered the elementary truth that the efficient allocation of scarce resources among competing ends is the central question in economics. Novozhilov has commented on this argument, as formulated by Campbell, as follows:

'In this connection it is necessary first of all to introduce an important correction in Campbell's story about the fate of economic science in the last half century. There is a gap in it. It does not take into account that at the beginning of this period there took place the most important test in history of an economic theory. There arose socialism. Marxist theory foresaw this fact, explained it as a law governed stage of development. Western "theory" not only did not foresee it, but up to this very day cannot satisfactorily explain how it could take place and how a planned economy is possible.' [21]

Which is the scientific theory, the one that foresaw the coming of socialism or the one that is baffled by it?

In so far as the economic cyberneticians confine themselves to the development of improved methods of economic calculation there is no real conflict between their ideas and orthodoxy (although it is still necessary to wage a difficult struggle to get the improved methods of economic calculation adopted on a large scale). In so far as the economic cyberneticians draw conclusions from the study of the rational organisation of the productive forces for the economic mechanism, it is undoubtedly true that their ideas about the economic mechanism are at variance with orthodox ideas about the economic mechanism. (In this connection one should bear in mind that orthodoxy is not immutable.) The reasons why this should be so are explained in chapter 4.

From a Marxist point of view, the main weakness of the work of the economic cyberneticians is that it concentrates on the rational organisation of the productive forces, and neglects the need to develop the productive relations.

The idea that national economic planning can fruitfully be represented by an extremal problem, by the selection of an optimal intensity vector, which given the technology matrix maximises some objective function, seemed at first sight very odd to many Soviet economists. The notion that planning consists merely of picking a 'set of numbers' was criticised by Nemchinov in his preface to Kantorovich's book. The treatment of national economic planning as an extremal problem subsequently became one of the basic assumptions of the theory of the optimally functioning economy, a theory which is discussed in chapter 2. The way that Kantorovich expanded his interpretation of the economic significance of the linear programming problem from certain problems of the organisation of production to the national economy as a whole, is considered in chapter 3.

A major issue resulting from the emergence of economic cybernetics was the organisational and doctrinal fate of political economy. Before the emergence of economic cybernetics, political economy, which is an integral part of the official doctrine of the USSR — Marxism—Leninism — and disseminated at all levels from evening classes for workers via *Pravda* editorials to the Academy of Social Sciences attached to the Central Committee of the party, had held an unchallenged position as the theoretical basis of the economic policy of the Soviet state. Many political economists did not take kindly to this new discipline, economic cybernetics, with its affinity to the doctrines of the Lausanne school and its evident aspiration to replace political economy. Already in Boyarski's review of Kantorovich's book we read that mathematics has a role to play in economics provided that it is subordinated to economic science (i.e. to Marxism—Leninism). At the November 1966 debate on optimal planning the rivalry between economic cybernetics and political economy was clear. At the meeting Academician Fedorenko, the Director of TSEMI, distinguished between two approaches to economics, the descriptive and the constructive. He suggested that the time had come to abandon the descriptive approach, implicitly identified with political economy, in favour of the constructive approach, i.e. the theory of optimal planning, which alone could serve as a source of useful ideas on how to improve the planning and management of the economy. The distinguished mathematical economist A.L. Lur'e, added that it would not be so bad if the political economists were in fact descriptive (description is a useful activity), the trouble was that they were often destructive, hindering the analysis of such important problems as how to raise efficiency and how to utilize such levers as profit and rent.[a]

Fedorenko's argument, not surprisingly, aroused much controversy. Professor Tsagolov in rebuttal argued that to distinguish between a descriptive political economy and a constructive political economy was incorrect. There was only one political economy, which was not a mere descriptive science because it formulated the laws characterising the essence of socialism (the basic law of socialism, the law of planned proportional development and so on). In addition there were some suggestions for improving economic practice. It was in this pigeon hole that he placed research on optimal planning. The compilers of the record of this debate in the journal of TSEMI indignantly note that to accept this subordinate role for the theory of optimal planning would mean practically abandoning it as a scientific theory. At the same meeting corresponding member of the USSR Academy of Sciences Pashkov also advocated maintaining the subordination of economic-mathematical modelling to political economy.[23]

The reason why optimal planning challenged the position of political economy is that it is not much use calculating optimal plans if the method of functioning of the economy is such that the optimal plans are not implemented and non-optimal decisions are made instead. In an instructive article published in 1964,[24] Belkin and Birman wrote that:

'Electronics has brought no really tangible benefit to the planning and management of the economy, mostly because the existing practice of

(a) The reason for the low opinion the optimal planners have of political economy is that 'Until recently economic science was often used, not so much as the theoretical basis for the working out of the most efficient economic policy, but for commenting on decisions which had already been taken.'[22]

8

planning and management is not adapted to the devising and particularly the effecting of optimal decisions.

Just one example. It is widely known that the compilation of optimal schemes of freight shipment can yield a quite tangible saving. This is not a complicated task. Many articles and books have been written and not a few dissertations defended, but almost no freight is shipped by the optimal schemes. Why? Simply because the transport organisations are given plans based on ton kilometres. One can establish computer centres, and conceive superb algorithms, but nothing will come of it as long as the transport organisations reckon plan fulfilment in ton kilometres.'

Precisely because the administrative economy often operates in such a way as to frustrate attempts to implement optimal solutions to particular economic problems, an important part of the work on optimisation of the Soviet economy must be concerned with proposals for transforming the existing economic system into an optimally functioning economic system. TSEMI considers that it is impossible to work out such proposals, for example payment for the use of natural resources, without a scientific theory which explains both the need for such categories and how to calculate their numerical magnitude. This is the role which the theory of the optimally functioning economic system aspires to fill, and there naturally arises the question of its relationship with the already existing discipline of political economy. TSEMI's point of view was clearly explained by one of its deputy directors in the November 1966 debate on optimal planning.

'Let us take motor transport. How can it use the index of profit and expand direct contacts, when the tariffs take account neither of the type of freight, nor the capacity of the lorries, nor the limitation of transport? Is it possible for example, to establish the same tariff for the delivery of bread to bakers at the usual time and at the peak with limited transport resources? How is it possible without taking all these aspects into account in prices to harmonise the interests of the enterprises with the interest of the whole national economy?

I have been working on the use of mathematical models in the economy since 1958. I have to recognise, unfortunately, that up till now in the industry in which I am working (motor transport) the real saving from the introduction of the new methods has been considerably less than we expected. But this is not the fault of the officials in transport, and it is not the fault of the models. Because of inadequacies in price formation the minimisation of costs leads to the worsening of practically all the indices of the work of motor transport. The same is observed in other fields.

Precisely for this reason we say: a radical improvement in the practice of planning and management of the national economy is impossible without the creation of a consistent economic theory, in which the system of prices, the principles of incentives, the forms of relationships between the various levels of the national economy etc find their logical explanation.

Some participants in the discussion say that "some of your practical suggestions are very good, we completely accept them". V.P. D'yachenko noted a number of points of contact in the field of practical suggestions, regarding payment for the use of natural resources, taking account of scarcities. But how is it possible to explain the necessity for payment for capital and natural resources and to give methods for their practical calculation starting from the conception of the average costs of an industry as the basis for price formation? In our opinion it is impossible to do this. That is why we are struggling not only for the acceptance of concrete suggestions but also for giving them a precise theoretical basis, which is very important for the construction of a strict and integrated system of an optimally functioning economy.' [25]

The criticism of political economy by the optimal planners appears to have had a positive effect on the work of the Institute of Economics, which is reflected both in its published work and in its research interests. In 1967–70 some of the most interesting studies of the economic reform were produced by the Institute of Economics, at a time when TSEMI was publishing works on optimal prices and methods for iterative aggregation which can scarcely be regarded as a contribution to the understanding of economic reform. Rakitsky's 1968 book on the reform,[26] sponsored by the Institute of Economics, advocates an economic reform which combines an improvement in the organisation of the productive forces with an improvement in the productive relations. Ya.G. Liberman's 1970 book on the reform,[a][27] also sponsored by the Institute of Economics, contains useful suggestions for the further development of the reform, and its criticism of TSEMI's ideas about the role of optimal prices in the economy are not just dogmatic criticisms but powerful and well argued criticisms. Similarly, the Institute of Economics is playing an important role in research on the economic aspects of technical progress.

In a book published in 1968, two years after he made a speech calling in effect for the replacement of political economy by economic cybernetics, Academician Fedorenko stated that:

'In the complex and continually developing system of economic sciences the decisive place belongs to political economy. Marxist–Leninist political economy, which reveals the objective laws of development of economic life, plays an immense role in forming and strengthening the scientific world outlook of Soviet people. At the same time it is the theoretical basis for the actual running of the socialist national economy, for the building of a socialist and communist national economy, for the analysis of world developments and the relationship between our country and other countries.' [28]

Academician Fedorenko envisaged in this book the writing of a fundamental work *The political economy of socialism* a most important part of which

(a) Ya.G. Liberman is not the same person as the E.G. Liberman whose writings have received world wide publicity.

would be the theoretical bases of the system of an optimally functioning economy.[29] In 1970, TSEMI's views on the economic mechanism appeared in a book the first chapter of which was pure orthodoxy.[30]

A *modus vivendi* has been reached, along the lines suggested by Professor Tsagolov at the 1966 debate, in which TSEMI's right to put forward ideas on improving planning practice has been generally accepted, and TSEMI has disavowed its earlier critical attitude to political economy. TSEMI has recognised that only Marxist–Leninist political economy can form the theoretical basis of the economic policy of the party and the socialist state. Political economy is discussed in the press, lectures are given on it in the factories, and it is taught to students throughout the higher educational system. Economic cybernetics is a specialised academic discipline which is taught to future planners.

The favourable evaluation of the work of TSEMI by the Presidium of the Academy of Sciences in 1969 made it clear that the Academy of Sciences now regards TSEMI, which was only founded in 1963, as being one of the two leading economics institutes, and the chairman of the commission looking into the work of these two institutes particularly approved of TSEMI's quest for an optimally functioning economic system.[31]

The attitude of the optimal planners to the traditional planning methods was made very clear at the March 1968 conference on problems of growth and improved planning organised by the scientific council of the USSR Academy of Sciences on the laws governing the transition from socialism to communism. At this conference S. Shatalin, a deputy director of TSEMI, put forward the thesis of the three conceptions of planning. 'The essence of this thesis is the proposition that at the present time there are being worked out and developed three conceptions of planning the national economy. The first conception exists and is realised in the process of working out the national economic plans. This conception, in the opinion of S. Shatalin, is non-scientific, because it starts off from goals for the output of the most important means of production. The second conception is beginning to be introduced into planning. It is based on the utilisation of the input-output model and it starts from goals for final output. Finally, the third conception of planning, which S. Shatalin regards as the only really scientific one, "adequate for the essence of a socialist economy", is the conception of optimal planning.'[32] This thesis has come in for sharp criticism from Professor M.Z. Bor of the economics department of the Academy of Social Sciences attached to the CC.[33] Bor argues that Soviet plans have always aimed at the efficient utilisation of resources, and that they have always had a scientific basis. 'The supporters of the so-called theory of optimal planning, however, in their articles and books treat national economic planning as in essence not scientific but empirical. From this follows their false premise about the necessity for creating a theory of scientific planning under the head "the theory of optimal planning".'

In 1969 Bachurin, a deputy chairman of Gosplan, expressed his irritation at the attitude of the optimal planners to the traditional methods of planning. 'In the opinion of the authors of the system of an optimally functioning economy it turns out that really scientific planning will only become possible with the introduction of the system of working out an optimal plan suggested by them. From this it follows that the practice of planning in the USSR and other socialist countries as it has existed for many years was based only on intuition, on subjective decisions, and did not have a scientific basis.' [34] He replied to the accusation that Gosplan's methods were unscientific by accusing the supporters of the theory of optimal planning of a lack of orthodoxy, of having a position on some issues similar to that of supporters of 'market socialism'.

In 1970 Kovalev, the head of Gosplan's Chief Computing Centre, strongly attacked 'the nihilistic approach to planning the national economy and especially to centralised planning, which exists among some supporters of the "theory of optimal planning".' [35]

Why the supporters of optimal planning consider that the traditional planning methods are 'unscientific', and that it is necessary to replace them by optimal planning, will become clearer by analysing whether or not the balance method of planning is capable of leading to the compilation of consistent plans.[(a)] Such an analysis is contained in chapter 6.

At the beginning of the 1970s the position of mathematical economics within Soviet economic science is entirely different to that at the beginning of the 1960s. 'Formerly it was necessary to argue, demonstrate, substantiate, convince. Today it would seem that everyone is convinced, openly at any rate they do not argue, and many even help us. Conditions have been created for the development of the economic-mathematical direction in Soviet economic science : there exist scientific institutes and special faculties [within higher educational establishments]; books and journals are published; dissertations are defended; prizes are awarded. But, and this is the chief difficulty, practical contributions are awaited from our work, real benefits are required from us, we are required to give answers to numerous important and difficult questions.' [36]

The kind of answers the mathematical economists are giving to the 'numerous important and difficult questions' of planning and economic management and the extent to which they can be regarded as 'practical contributions' will be considered in chapters 8 and 9 below. First, however, it is necessary to consider the theoretical framework within which they are being offered, the theory of the optimally functioning economy, and some theoretical issues which this theory raises; and then some of the non-optimalities of the administrative economy, a study of which makes very clear why some individuals and organisations lay so much stress on the need for the optimisation of the economy.

(a) The critical attitude of Soviet economic cyberneticians to the traditional planning methods is analogous to the critical attitude of British econometricians to the methods traditionally used by the Treasury for forecasting and controlling the economy.

Summary

The use of quantitative methods in Soviet economics was common in the 1920s. During the period of the personality cult the ideas of economists about the economic mechanism and the methods of economic calculation were not welcome, and decisions were made by engineers and politicians using a limited arsenal of methods of economic calculation. Economists were expected to confine themselves to apologetics.

After the 20th Congress the application of quantitative methods in economic analysis developed rapidly. In the early 1960s the wind blew strongly in support of this new tendency. After 1967 it veered. The ideas of Kantorovich and TSEMI have remained controversial.

At the present time the important questions are, to what extent can the application of mathematical methods help raise the efficiency of economic planning and management? Can TSEMI throw more or less light on how to raise efficiency, stimulate technical progress, and improve the management of enterprises, associations and the national economy as a whole, than other organisations working in this field?

2. Optimal planning and functioning - a theory of economic reform and improved methods of economic calculation

The theory of optimal planning and functioning rests on four assumptions, the existence of a national-economic objective function, the scarcity of resources, the hierarchical nature of the economic system, and the need for an effective system of incentives.[1] The first two of these assumptions derive from linear programming, the third from systems engineering,[a] and the fourth reflects the experience of the Soviet planning system.

This theory arose as a result of a process of interaction between the requirements and problems of the Soviet planning system and the new techniques of planning and control developed in the last four decades by mathematicians, engineers and economists. 'The old system of economic management', a Soviet economist has written,[2] 'was well suited to the attainment of its chief aim, to mobilise resources and concentrate them on the satisfaction of the most urgent needs of the state. It was mainly aimed at the quantitative, extensive, growth of production (this showed itself for example in the practice of awarding bonuses for overfulfilment of the physical indices of the plan) and feebly stimulated raising the efficiency of production (this gave rise to the formerly well known formula: "the fulfilment of the plan at any price"). This has if not a theoretical, then at any rate a historical justification in the specific conditions of that period in which the system arose (the permanent threat from the imperialist states, and also the existence of colossal natural and labour resources together with a chronic deficiency of all or almost all commodities).' The advocates of an optimally functioning economic system would like to replace this system by an alternative one which stimulates efficiency and in which all decisions are made on rational (objective, scientific) grounds. This involves both a replacement of much administrative decision making by the use of market forces, and an all round improvement in the quality of decision making to be brought about by the use of mathematical methods. In this way it is hoped to 'guarantee planning against bureaucratism, voluntarism and so on.'[3] Whereas in the past policy making has tended to be a series of ad hoc, and often contradictory, responses to changing circumstances, lacking any scientific basis, the advocates of an optimally functioning economic system consider that 'Improving the methods of planning and management shouls take place not by way of sporadic alterations of separate parts of the existing system of planning and management, but by way of a definite general line for the improvement of the entire economy of the country as a

---

(a) See for example, M.D. Mesarovic, D. Macho, and Y. Takahara, *The theory of hierarchical, multi-level, systems* (New York & London 1970).

whole and the gradual putting into effect of a single conception objectively reflecting the laws of development of a socialist economy.'[4]

The theory of the optimally functioning economy has been developed by TSEMI, with support from Academician Kantorovich of the Institute of Mathematics of the Siberian branch of the USSR Academy of Sciences, the Institute of Economics and the Organisation of Industrial Production of the Siberian branch of the USSR Academy of Sciences (of which the director is corresponding member of the Academy of Sciences Aganbegyan). Professor Novozhilov of the Leningrad branch of TSEMI, and some of the research workers in the various industrial research institutes, such as I.Ya. Birman, head of the department of economic-mathematical methods of the Central Scientific Research Institute for Technical-Economical Research in the Building Materials Industry. This statement, however, is something of an oversimplification, because even among supporters of this theory there exist 'various, and on some points mutually exclusive opinions. It could not be otherwise as this is a developing theory.' Within TSEMI there are disagreements between those who do, and those who do not, regard profit as a suitable local optimality criterion, between those who approach the question of multi-level optimisation from algorithms of iterative aggregation and those whose work is based on the approximation approach. The supporters of this theory recognise that 'The conception of an optimally functioning economy is not at the present time a fully worked out theory.'[6] Moreover this incomplete theory, whose adherents disagree among themselves, is far from finding complete acceptance among Soviet economists and specialists in industrial management, let alone among the officials of the central economic organs or among policy makers. The two day debate held in November 1966 showed that many economists, for example Professor Tsagolov of the economics faculty of Moscow State University, had a lukewarm, or even downright hostile, attitude towards optimal planning. Leaving aside the criticism of some economists, within the wider field of industrial management the point of view of TSEMI is not identical with that of the Institute of Cybernetics of the Ukrainian Academy of Sciences headed by Academician Glushkov, nor with that of the Institute of Management Problems (automation and remote control) headed by Academician Trapeznikov.[7] Moreover, many of those who support the idea of 'optimal planning' have an understanding of what this term means very different to that of TSEMI. Today it is no more possible to write that 'Soviet economists think ...' than it is possible to write that 'British (or American) economists think ...' The theory of optimal planning has not been of interest solely to a small coterie of mathematical economists. In an important theoretical article in *Pravda* on economic reform, Allakhverdyan, a deputy director of the Institute of Economics and the author of several books on the Soviet financial system, based himself at one point on the theory of optimal planning.[8]

Many of those who advocate optimal planning and functioning regard it as a hierarchical or multi-level process, the first step in which is the elaboration of long term forecasts of the development of the economy, concerned in particular with long term tendencies in technology, natural resources, consumption, and population. (A considerable volume of research has been undertaken in recent years, at TSEMI and at other institutes, on forecasting.) The next stage is the elaboration of a national economic perspective plan. (A major application of mathematical methods in Soviet planning has been the calculation, by Gosplan's research institute, of planning input-output tables,[a] which have been used during the work on compiling the five year plan, to calculate the effect on the economy of alternative paths of development. This is discussed in chapter 6.) The separate industries each compile optimal perspective plans, whose variables are such questions as the location of enterprises, the capacity of enterprises, the technology to be used, and the best use of deficit materials for which there are substitutes. Up till now 'The most tangible results in the field of the introduction of economico-mathematical methods into the practice of planning has been achieved in the optimisation of the perspective plans for the development and location of industries.'[9] (A survey of Soviet work in this field will be found in chapter 9.) The separate enterprises or associations each compile optimal perspective plans and use the methods of operational research to ensure that their current plans are optimal.[b]

As far as current planning is concerned, TSEMI's general theoretical framework is a fairly conventional application of general equilibrium theory to a planned economy. The central planners work out a highly aggregated plan for the outputs and prices of the chief commodities. Each industry, on the basis of the planned quantity and price of its output, and on the basis of its own optimality criterion, works out a plan for the output and price of its key products. Each enterprise receives from above plans for the output of its key products, plans for the supply to it of its key inputs, and certain financial parameters, such as prices for key goods, wage rates, payments for the use of natural resources and capital goods, and the rate of interest on bank loans. Subject to these obligations, the enterprise is free to maximise the local optimality criterion. As far as concrete policy measures are concerned, TSEMI emphasises the importance of developing wholesale trade in producer goods (as opposed to their rationing), the grouping of enterprises into associations, and an increased flexibility of prices, for example by establishing three groups of prices, fixed, limited and contractual. The fixed prices would be for the most important goods and would be fixed by the centre uniformly for the entire country. The limited prices would be maxima established by the centre. Transactions at prices below the maxima would be permitted. The contractual prices would be free prices established

(a) A 'planning' input-output table is one which refers to a future year, an 'accounting' table is one which refers to a past year. In previous publications the terminology 'ex ante' and 'ex post' was used.

(b) The efforts of the mathematical economists in the Soviet Union to introduce modern planning techniques into the work of the central planning organs are analogous to the efforts of British econometricians to introduce econometric models into the work of the Treasury. The attempt by the mathematical economists to introduce these methods into the planning of enterprises is analogous to the work which has been done by consultants and by the Ministry of Technology in disseminating modern management techniques.

by agreement between buyer and seller. As far as retail prices are concerned, TSEMI advocates equilibrium prices, in order to eliminate shortages and queues.[10]

The economic cyberneticians completely reject the idea that the transition from the administrative economy to an optimally functioning economy will be a once and for all process. They conceive of it as a process stretching over many years in which the economic mechanism and the methods of economic calculation are steadily improved, a process which some might be tempted to call 'piecemeal social engineering', but which Volkonsky describes as the 'deepening of optimisation'.[11]

In advocating both an improvement in the methods of economic calculation and an improvement in the economic mechanism, TSEMI is following in the steps of the late Academician Nemchinov, who not only played a major role in the rise of economic cybernetics in the USSR, in encouraging the use of mathematical methods in planning, but also played a major role in the discussion which preceded the publication in *Pravda* in September 1962 of the much publicised article by E.G. Liberman, and himself published in *Kommunist* (1964 No. 5) a powerful statement of the case for economic reform.

The theory of optimal planning and functioning provides a theoretical framework for a large volume of research, ranging from the construction of regional input-output tables to work on rent payments for the use of natural resources, from the introduction of computers into the work of the planning and statistical organs, the ministries and the enterprises, to work on measures for preventing inflation if the flexibility of prices is increased. Although TSEMI is the leading organisation in this field, work on optimal planning is being done in a large number of institutes. For example, the Institute of Economics of the Estonian Academy of Sciences has done a great deal of research on regional input-output, the Chief Computing Centre of Gosplan USSR has calculated numerous planning input-output tables in physical terms, and the Institute of Mathematics of the Siberian branch of the Academy of Sciences, together with some metallurgical institutes, has introduced optimal production scheduling into the work of the steel industry.

The USSR Academy of Sciences has set up a Scientific Council to direct and coordinate research on the optimal planning and management of the economy. This Council has 89 members and 29 sections, 13 devoted to particular planning problems and 16 to the problems of particular economic regions. The sections concerned with planning problems include one concerned with long term forecasting, another with the use of economic-mathematical methods for the study of the economies of foreign countries, and another on transport problems. The Council is coordinating a large volume of research on optimal planning.

In 1970 an editorial article in the journal of TSEMI explained that:

' "The construction of communism" it is stated in the Theses of the CC CPSU *On the 100th anniversary of the birth of Lenin* "is our general

17

perspective ... Going along the Leninist path, the CPSU sees the chief task of the building of communism as the creation of its material-technical base". One of the decisive preconditions for the fulfilment of this grandiose task is the transformation of the existing economy of the country into an optimally functioning one. This means the achievement of such a high level of the organisation and planning of social labour that the fullest possible utilisation of all resources in the interests of raising the living standards of the working people, and also satisfying other requirements of society, would be provided.

Only a country with a socialist planned economy has the objective possibilities for the real optimisation of the management of the national economy. In this is the principal advantage of the socialist system over the capitalist.

Transforming objective possibilities into reality does not take place and can not take place, however, automatically. It requires a gigantic organisational work ...'[12]

The theory of the optimally planned and functioning economy is a controversial theory, which is vulnerable to criticism on a large number of grounds, of which the following are of particular importance.

An economic system is part of a social order, yet TSEMI's approach is derived not from the study of society but mainly from linear programming and systems engineering. It is true that TSEMI's fourth assumption is the need for an efficient system of incentives. It is also true that I.Ya. Birman has recognised that 'strictly centralised planning and management, when all the details are calculated and planned in one centre, is hardly desirable, even if it were feasible. Economic activity is the activity of people, and it is foolish to deprive them of the possibility of showing initiative, independence and creativity.'[13] Similarly Novozhilov has more than once argued that the optimisation of planning is concerned not only with choosing the best from all the feasible plan variants, but also with improving the productive relations of socialism. Nevertheless, it remains true that none of TSEMI's work has thrown any light on the crucial questions of how to enlist the support of workers, engineers, managers, and scientists for raising efficiency, and how to develop the productive relations of socialism.

The two assumptions of the theory of the optimally functioning economy derived from linear programming — the existence of a national-economic objective function, and the scarcity of resources, are controversial. An exposition and critique of these assumptions is contained in chapters 3, 4 and 10 of this study.

What does it mean to talk about an 'optimal plan' in a society with conflicting social groups? Soviet writers on optimal planning usually avoid this question, and concentrate on methods for solving extremal problems given the constraints and the objective function. As one writer on optimal planning puts it: 'It should be emphasised that at every given moment the aim of production and the criterion of optimality must be given from outside, from beyond the boundaries of the model of the national economy (who should formulate this criterion and the system of constraints is a special question which does not relate to our theme).'[14] The same point has been made by another writer on optimal planning. Optimal planning cannot give 'final recommendations about the further development of the country. It will give only sensible variants of development in a convenient and clear form. A final decision, within the limits of the real possibilities, must be taken before by the competent organs.'[15] Academician Glushkov has explained that 'The essence of optimal planning and management is that, of the infinite number of variants of development of our national economy *within the direction of the solution of the general tasks posed by the party*, to choose at every given moment the best variant, which provides for the solution of those tasks in a historically short period.'[16] The problem has been recognised by Volkonsky, a research worker at TSEMI, who read a paper entitled 'On the possibilities and difficulties of applying the concept of the optimum to society as a whole' at a conference on economic-mathematical models in April 1969. This paper has remained unpublished, but its delivery has been described as follows:

'The speaker based his theses on the fact that there exists a contradiction between the necessity to work out the principles of optimal, or rational from the point of view of society as a whole, decisions, and the fact that the interests of members of society and of various social groups diverge. In this connection he made an attempt to describe several systems, regulating the life of society, and enumerated the concepts and categories which, in his opinion, are necessary for the discussion of optimality. Among these the speaker included the democratic mechanism for the self-regulation of social life, the "value" orientation of society, the role of science (i.e. of the specialists) and so on.'[17]

These are crucially important questions, wide discussion of which could be most illuminating. It is no accident that Volkonsky's paper had a 'lively' reception. Similarly, the Hungarian economist Academician Friss has pointed out that national economic perspective plans must be based on certain political decisions, and if these political decisions, on which the general conception of the plan is based, are incorrect, then the plan

'may be satisfactory from the point of view of techniques of planning, but it will not be a good let alone an optimal plan.

How is it possible to ensure the correctness, the scientific well foundedness of the considerations, the conception, which are the starting point of the planning work? First, the organ which takes the decisions should have the trust of society, act on its behalf, with its authority, because the question concerns the fate of society. Secondly, it is necessary to attract the widest possible circle of experts, specialists, scientists and deputies to the task of working out the conception, the variants of the plan, to the preparatory work for the taking of decisions. Thirdly, it is necessary to strive for wide democratic control over the taking of decisions by means of bringing in the masses.'[18]

It is easy to write about indirect centralisation, about calculating optimal prices which will guide profit maximising enterprises to socially rational decisions. Such prices do not in general exist, and in practice it is difficult to see how the problems of information and aggregation could be overcome.[a]

Would the decisions that were left in the hands of the central planners be any more efficient than those being made at the moment? Some years ago in Yugoslavia it was fashionable to argue that while current decisions should be left to the enterprises themselves, investment should continue to be planned, a doctrine popular with some economists. Experience has shown, however, that many of the investment decisions taken by the planners were wasteful.[19] Volkonsky suggests dealing with the frequently arbitrary nature of the decisions made by the planners by making them take exams in economic-mathematical methods.[20] Chernyavsky, who is head of a sub-department of Gosplan, suggests that the less qualified officials should give way to better qualified ones.[21] In effect what some of the mathematical economists are suggesting is that many of the existing planning and economic officials be replaced by the mathematical economists and their pupils. Only in this way, it is argued, can rational decision making be achieved. The existing economic and planning officials are unlikely to view this process with favour.

Summary

The theory of optimal planning and functioning is a theory of economic reform and improved methods of economic calculation, which was developed in the 1960s by TSEMI. It is based on ideas derived from linear programming, systems engineering and the experience of Soviet planning. It is a theory which is vulnerable to criticism on a number of grounds, ranging from the meaning of an 'optimal plan' in a society with conflicting social groups, via the feasibility of indirect centralisation, to the difficulty of ensuring the economic rationality of decisions made by planning officials. This theory provides a framework for a large volume of research.

(a) The concept of indirect centralisation was developed by the late Professor Novozhilov. For a Western study of an indirectly centralised economy see the paper by Arrow and Hurwicz in Pfouts R. (ed) *Essays in economics and econometrics* (Chapel Hill n.d.).

3. What is the most useful economic interpretation of the linear programming problem?

'There are two ways of increasing the efficiency of the work of a shop, an enterprise, or a whole branch of industry. One way is by various improvements in technology; that is, new attachments for individual machines, changes in technological processes, and the discovery of new, better kinds of raw materials. The other way — thus far much less used — is improvement in the organisation of planning and production. Here are included, for instance, such questions as the distribution of work among individual machines of the enterprise or among mechanisms, the correct distribution of orders among enterprises, the correct distribution of different kinds of raw materials, fuel and other factors.'

L.V. Kantorovich (1939) [1]

In his seminal work *Mathematical methods for the organisation and planning of production* (1939) Kantorovich argued that the economic interpretation of the new method of solving a class of extremal problems which he had discovered was that it was concerned with one of the two ways of raising efficiency in production planning. One way of raising efficiency, he argued, was concerned with replacing obsolete methods of production by new, more advanced technologies. The other way of raising efficiency was by reallocating resources between existing technologies. It was to this latter type of problem that his new method was relevant.

The distinction which Kantorovich appears to have had in mind can be illustrated in the following way. Compare two factories A and B, which start off with identical resources and identical technologies. It is perfectly possible that factory A where resources are always allocated efficiently (i.e. where given the available resources and technology the output produced is always on the efficiency frontier) produces less in period 5 and all subsequent period than factory B where resource allocation is inefficient (in the sense that the output produced is less than that which would have been possible with a better organisation of production) but where technical progress is taking place. Such a situation is shown in table 3.1.

Table 3.1 *Allocative efficiency and technical progress*

Time	Factory A			Factory B		
	Resources	Technology	Output	Resources	Technology	Output
1	b	A^1	x	b	A^1	x'
			$x > x'$			
5	b	A^1	x	b	A^5	x''
			$x < x''$			

21

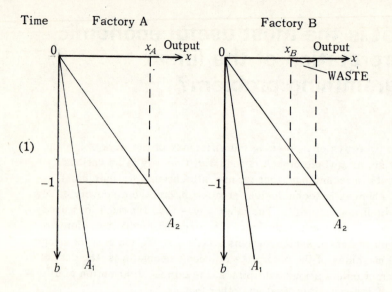

$$x_A > x_B$$

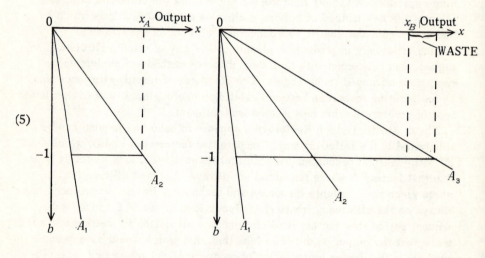

$$x_A < x_B$$

i.e. the 'inefficient' factory has a greater output than the 'efficient' factory.

Fig. 3.1 *Allocative efficiency and technical progress*

The two goods case can be represented diagrammatically as in figure 3.1.

Kantorovich's new method, he appears to have been arguing in 1939, was relevant to the problem of increasing efficiency by eliminating waste, but not relevant to the problem of increasing efficiency by introducing new techniques of production.

This sharp distinction between the two ways of raising efficiency in production planning, which was originally made by Kantorovich, and subsequently emphasised by Gerchuk[2] and Vainshtein,[3] seems to the present writer to have been a very useful one, for two reasons. First, interpreting linear programming as being concerned with one of the two methods of raising efficiency in production planning enabled Kantorovich to delineate the areas where its application could bring about useful gains in efficiency — production scheduling, the organisation of transport, the cutting of sheets of materials, the utilisation of arable land. The application of linear programming to raising efficiency throughout the world since then has been most useful precisely in those fields pointed out by Kantorovich in 1939. Secondly, although it is possible to expand programming models to include such questions as the optimal allocation of resources to research and development, it is as yet unclear whether this helps raise efficiency or increase understanding, or whether it merely hampers understanding to treat the creation of new technologies, training the labour force and geological exploration in this way, although it is abundantly clear that the application of linear programming to those areas where it is applicable according to Kantorovich's 1939 interpretation does enable efficiency to be increased.

Subsequently Kantorovich reinterpreted linear programming as a model of national economic planning, both current and perspective. This interpretation can be presented as follows. Consider an economy in which production takes place in discrete time periods. The problem of drawing up an optimal plan for any period is the problem of maximising the volume of output, given the technology which exists, the resources which are available, and the required relative outputs.

The technology can be represented by the matrix

$$
\begin{matrix}
a_{11} & a_{12} & \cdots & a_{1n} \\
\cdots & \cdots & \cdots & \cdots \\
a_{m1} & a_{m2} & \cdots & a_{mn}
\end{matrix}
$$

where a_{ij} is the amount of the ith commodity produced (if $a_{ij} > 0$) or used up (if $a_{ij} < 0$) by the jth activity when it is operated at the unit level. Each column provides information about a particular activity. Each row provides information about the utilisation of a particular commodity in the system. A plan $p = (\lambda_1, \lambda_2 \ldots \lambda_n)$ is a list of numbers characterising the intensities at which the activities are operated in the planned period. With a plan $p = (\lambda_1, \lambda_2 \ldots \lambda_n)$ the various commodities are produced in quantities

$$
x_i = \sum_{j=i}^{n} a_{ij} \lambda_j \qquad i = 1 \ldots m
$$

if $x_i > 0$ the ith commodity is an output

if $x_i = 0$ the ith commodity is an intermediate good, and
if $x_i < 0$ the ith commodity is an input.

It is required that

$$x_i \geqslant b_i$$

where b_i is the quantity of the ith good available at the start of the process of production (if $b_i < 0$) or the quantity of the ith good required at the end of the process of production (if $b_i > 0$); (i.e. the resources used up in the process of production must not exceed the resources available, and final products must be produced in not less than the required quantities). Note that the technological assumptions are such as to rule out increasing returns to scale, indivisibilities and externalities.

The mathematical formulation is:

Given the real numbers

$$a_{ij}\,(i = 1 \ldots m,\, j = 1 \ldots n)\,,\ b_i\,(i = 1 \ldots k)$$
$$r_i > 0\,(i = k + 1,\, \ldots k + q;\, m = k + q)$$

(i.e. given the technology, the resources and the requirement that the system be productive)

It is required to find a vector $p = (\lambda_1,\, \lambda_2 \ldots \lambda_n)$, i.e. a plan, such that

$$\lambda_i \geqslant 0 \qquad i = 1 \ldots n \tag{1}$$

(i.e. no activity be operated at a negative level)

$$x_i \geqslant b_i \qquad i = 1 \ldots k \tag{2}$$

(i.e. the quantities of inputs used up in the process of production may not exceed the inputs available at the beginning of the process of production. $x_i,\, b_i < 0$)

$$\frac{x_{k+1}}{r_{k+1}} = \ldots \frac{x_{k+q}}{r_{k+q}} = z \tag{3}$$

(i.e. the outputs must be produced in fixed proportions)

$$z = \max \tag{4}$$

(i.e. the volume of output is maximised).

A plan which satisfies (1) and (2) and (3) is called feasible, and one which satisfies (1) − (4) optimal.

Now consider the problem of compiling an optimal plan not just for one period but for many periods. This is a natural extension of the previous problem. The problem of drawing up an optimal perspective plan is the problem of choosing an intensity vector for each of the time periods in such a way that there is no other feasible intensity vector the output associated with which is greater than the output associated with the optimal intensity vector, subject to the technology which exists in each period, and the resources available at the commencement of the process of production.

In the dynamic case the technology can be represented by the T matrices

$$A^t \qquad (t = 1 \dots T)$$

where a_{ij}^t is the amount of the ith commodity produced by the jth activity in the tth period (if $a_{ij}^t > 0$) or used up by the jth activity in the tth period (if $a_{ij}^t < 0$) when the jth activity is operated at unit level. As before the intensities must be non-negative, the resources used up must not exceed those available at the start of the process of production, and no output may be produced in less than the required relative quantities. A plan $p^t = (\lambda_1^t, \lambda_2^t \dots \lambda_n^t; t = 1 \dots T)$ is optimal if there does not exist an alternative feasible plan $p'^t = (\lambda_1'^t, \lambda_2'^t \dots \lambda_n'^t)$ in which all the outputs are produced in greater quantities, i.e. a plan p^t is not optimal if

$$x_i^t = \sum_{j=1}^{n} a_{ij}^t \lambda_j^t < \sum_{j=1}^{n} a_{ij}^t \lambda_j'^t = x_i'^t \qquad \begin{array}{l} i = k+1, \dots k+q \\ t = 1 \dots T \end{array}$$

where x_i^t is the output of the ith commodity in the tth period with plan p^t, and $x_i'^t$ is the output of the ith commodity in the tth period with the feasible alternative plan p'^t.

This new, enlarged, interpretation of the economic significance of the linear programming problem has come in for criticism on two main grounds, the first concerned with its maximand, and the second with its choice of variables to optimise.

Kantorovich's maximand has been much criticised. Whereas Koopmans[a] defines an output vector x as efficient if there is no other feasible output vector x' such that $x' - x$ is either positive or semi-positive, Kantorovich assumes that the relative output pattern has been fixed by the planners, so that the problem is to choose between output vectors x, x', x'', where

$$\frac{x_i}{x_j} = \frac{x_i'}{x_j'} = \frac{x_i''}{x_j''} \qquad i,j = k+1, \dots k+q$$

An output vector x is preferable to any other feasible output vector x' if $x > x'$, i.e. if $x - x'$ is positive. Kantorovich's maximand is unique, Koopmans' is not. (Koopmans has to introduce additional criterion, Pareto-optimality, to select the optimal output, given the distribution of income, from the efficient outputs.) For an individual factory in the administrative economy it makes perfectly good sense to assume that the assortment pattern is given (by the planners), but for the whole economy it makes much less sense. The criticism of Kantorovich's maximand has given rise to a prolonged debate in the Soviet Union on the appropriate objective function in national economic planning.[4] It is far from clear how to construct a national economic objective function which represents anything more than a formulation which the research workers who do the calculations regard as

(a) Koopmans' main writings in this field are, T.C. Koopmans, Analysis of production as an efficient combination of activities, in T.C. Koopmans (ed) *Activity analysis of production and allocation* (New York 1951) ; T.C. Koopmans, The efficient allocation of resources, *Econometrica* 1951; and T.C. Koopmans, *Three essays on the state of economic science* (New York 1957) essay 1.

25

generating acceptable answers. Furthermore, the idea that this approach helps the solution of such questions as the division of the state budget between, say, defence and medical care, remains to be demonstrated.

Kantorovich's choice of which quantities to take as exogenous and which variables to optimise, has also come under fire. In their classic paper entitled 'Optimal models of perspective planning' which was written, inter alia, to refute the notion that linear programming is purely static and to demonstrate its applicability to dynamic problems, Kantorovich and Makarov write:

> 'The expenditure norms in the activities, in particular when one is making forecasts for future years ... in reality are stochastic quantities, known only with a certain probability, or more precisely for which one can give only a certain probability distribution.
>
> Therefore the problem of compiling the plan should be treated as a problem in stochastic programming.'[5]

In other words, technical progress is to be treated as an exogenous factor and the main problem of perspective planning is the best allocation of resources between activities that happen to be in existence, for which one estimates probability distributions. Schmookler has commented on this type of argument as follows:

> 'With few exceptions generations of economists regarded technical progress analytically as an exogenous variable. Not knowing its precise linkages, they could not make of it a dependent variable in their analysis. With the passage of time, however, economists came actually to believe that its causes lay in other domains of human behaviour and therefore should in principle be treated the same way as earthquakes. Now there undoubtedly is some exogenous component in technical change, but there is also an endogenous one (a fact which was recognised, to cite just a few examples, by Smith, Mill, Marshall and Hicks). What is more, recent evidence suggests that the endogenous component is usually dominant, at least in modern economies ... The production of new technology is itself an economic activity. It represents in essence the mobilization of society's creative energies to relieve the scarcities which existing resources and products cannot. Far from being an exogenous variable, it is one of the most interesting endogenous variables of them all.'[6]

Conclusion

The original economic interpretation of the linear programming offered by Kantorovich was that it was concerned with one of the two ways of raising efficiency in production planning. This interpretation was a very fruitful one. It enabled Kantorovich to delineate an important class of economic problems to which his new method was relevant, and the subsequent application of this method to these problems throughout the world has led to useful increases in efficiency. Subsequently Kantorovich offered an enlarged interpretation of the economic significance of his method, according to which it represents the process of national economic planning, both current and perspective. This new interpretation, unlike the old one, has not so far led to the calculation of numerical optimal plans the implementation of which has led to useful increases in efficiency. The expansion of his interpretation to current national economic planning appears to have been motivated largely by a desire to demonstrate the relevance of the optimality conditions for the economic mechanism. The extension of his interpretation to perspective national economic planning appears to have been motivated largely by a desire to demonstrate the usefulness of a rate of interest in investment planning. These demonstrations are considered in the following chapter.

4. How the study of linear programming leads to proposals for reforming the economic mechanism

'The rather inappropriate mathematical methods which have been employed (at all levels of mathematisation) by the school of Cournot and Walras – and Marshall – ... caused it to appear that the price system is just one way of organising an economy efficiently; that it is, in a sense, exterior to the economic problem, something that is brought in from outside. What the linear theory has shown – and this, speaking as a theoretical rather than a practical economist, seems to me to have been its greatest service – is that, so long as the convexity assumptions hold ... the price mechanism is something that is inherent. It does not have to be invented, or brought from outside. It belongs.'

J.R. Hicks[1]

'The most important achievement of world economic mathematical science is the strict proof that, on fairly wide assumptions, such a system of prices [i.e. equilibrium prices] exists, and that it is possible to establish a system of decentralised optimal control on the basis of market relationships.'

V.A. Volkonsky[2]

The purpose of this chapter is to explain how the study of linear programming has led some Soviet economists to nine important policy conclusions:

(1) Prices have a major role to play in a planned socialist economy as guides to efficient resource allocation.

(2) The price formation method traditionally employed is inadequate.

(3) The price formation formula traditionally employed is inadequate.

(4) Rent payments for the use of land and other natural resources have a major role to play in a planned socialist economy as guides to efficient resource allocation.

(5) A charge for the use of capital goods has a major role to play in a planned socialist economy as a guide to efficient resource allocation.

(6) A charge for the use of scarce types of labour (or subsidies for the use of surplus types of labour) has a major role to play in a planned socialist economy as a guide to efficient resource allocation.

(7) The appropriate criterion for guiding and evaluating the work of enterprises in a planned socialist economy is profit.

(8) Investment appraisal decisions should make use of a rate of interest to make costs and benefits at different times comparable.

(9) Devolution of decision making has a useful role to play in a planned socialist economy.

In the course of working out a solution to a problem in the organisation of production presented to the Institute of Mathematics and Mechanics of Leningrad State University in the 1930s, Kantorovich discovered a new method of solving a certain class of extremal problems.[3] Assuming that a feasible plan exists, and the problem is not set in the Land of Cockaigne, then the following theorem characterises the optimal plans calculated in accordance with this method.

Theorem.[4] For a feasible plan $p = (\lambda_1 \ldots \lambda_n)$ to be optimal it is necessary and sufficient that multipliers $c_1 \ldots c_m$ exist such that

$$c_i \geqslant 0 \qquad i = 1 \ldots m \tag{1}$$

(i.e. the multipliers are non-negative)

$$\exists\, c_i > 0 \qquad i = k + 1, \ldots k + q \tag{2}$$

(i.e. at least one of the outputs has a positive valuation)

$$\sum_{i=1}^{m} a_{ij}\, c_i \leqslant 0 \qquad j = 1 \ldots n \tag{3}$$

(i.e. for every activity the valuation of the outputs is less than or equal to the valuation of the inputs)

$$\sum_{i=1}^{m} a_{ij}\, c_i = 0 \qquad \text{if } \lambda_j > 0 \qquad j = 1 \ldots n \tag{4}$$

(i.e. for the activities used, the valuation of the outputs is equal to the valuation of the inputs used up)

$$c_i = 0 \qquad \text{if } x_i > b_i \qquad i = 1 \ldots k \tag{5}$$
$$\text{or } x_i > r_i z \qquad i = k + 1, \ldots k + q$$

(i.e. the valuation of factors of production which do not limit production and of outputs produced in excess of requirements, is zero).

Policy conclusions (1) to (7) above are derived from this theorem.[a] In view of the economic importance of these conclusions, the

---

(a) These multipliers are the variables of the dual problem. Kantorovich proved that a necessary and sufficient condition for the existence of an optimal solution to the problem

$$\begin{array}{ll} \text{Max} & cx \\ \text{ST} & Ax \leqslant b \end{array}$$

was the existence of multipliers y with the properties stated above. The duality theorem states that if either of the problems

$$\begin{array}{ll} \text{Max} & cx \\ \text{ST} & Ax \leqslant b \end{array} \quad \text{and} \quad \begin{array}{ll} \text{Min} & by \\ \text{ST} & Ay \geqslant c \end{array}$$

has a solution then both have a solution and the values of the two programmes are the same. If either programme is not feasible then neither has an optimal solution. From the economic point of view it is the properties of the multipliers, that is of the variables in the dual problem, that are important.

From a geometrical point of view these multipliers are the coefficients of the variables in the equation of the hyperplane which touches the cone of feasible outputs at the efficient point.

way that the policy implications of this theorem were explained by Kantorovich and his followers is examined in detail below.

Linear programming and prices

In *Economic problems of socialism in the USSR* (1952) Stalin repeated the familiar Marxist—Leninist argument that price-market relationships in a socialist economy are a relic of capitalism, the persistence of which in a socialist economy is due to the existence side by side with the socialist sector of a cooperative sector (the collective farms), and that these price-market relationships are destined to wither away under communism. 'At present the collective farms will not recognise any other economic relation with the town except the commodity relation — exchange through purchase and sale. Because of this, commodity production and trade are as much a necessity with us today as they were thirty years ago, say, when Lenin spoke of the necessity of developing trade to the utmost.

Of course, when instead of the two basic production sectors, the state sector and the collective farm sector, there will be only one all-embracing production sector, with the right to dispose of all the consumer goods produced in the country, commodity circulation with its "money economy", will disappear, as being an unnecessary element in the national economy.'[a] Seventeen years later, writing in the journal of TSEMI, three Soviet economists argued that the existence of the price mechanism under socialism is not a result of the coexistence of two forms of ownership which is doomed to disappear under communism, but an integral part of an optimally functioning economic system.[5] From a mathematical point of view this is simply an application of the Kantorovich theorem, the multipliers c_i being regarded as prices. The purpose of this section is to explain how Soviet mathematical economists have presented the case for regarding price-market relationships as an integral feature of an optimally functioning economic system to their non-mathematical colleagues.

Kantorovich has explained the usefulness of prices in a planned socialist economy by means of examples such as the following.[6] Consider the following planning problem. Two articles have to be put into production, No. 1 and No. 2. The requirements for both are unlimited but it is necessary that they should be produced in a fixed ratio, e.g. twice as much should be produced of article No. 1 as of article No. 2.

Each of these goods may be put into production at factories of types A, B, C, D and E. The number of factories of each type and the production capacity/month for articles No. 1 and No. 2 are given in table 4.1.

(a) J. Stalin, *Economic problems of socialism in the USSR* (Moscow 1952) p. 20.
Stalin did offer another reason for the operation of the law of value under socialism, the existence of a retail market (ibid p. 23) but his emphasis was on the reason given in the text. (Stalin also suggested, with particular reference to a future socialist Britain, that foreign trade might be another reason for the existence of prices under socialism. See ibid pp 14—15.)

Table 4.1   *Data for production scheduling problem*

(1)	(2)	(3)	(4)	(5)	(6)
		Production capacity of each factory		Opportunity cost[a] of article	Opportunity cost of article
Type of factory	No. of factories	for article No. 1	for article No. 2	article No. 1	article No. 2
A	5	100 000	15 000	0.15	6.7
B	3	400 000	200 000	0.5	2
C	40	20 000	2 500	0.125	8
D	9	200 000	50 000	0.25	4
E	2	600 000	250 000	0.41	2.4

The entries in columns 1–4 contain the original data of the problem. The entries in column (5) are derived by dividing the entries in column (4) by the corresponding entries in column (3). The entries in column (6) are obtained by dividing the entries in column (3) by the corresponding entries in column (4).

The problem is to compile production plans for the factories in such a way as to maximise output, given the desired assortment pattern. How can we solve this planning problem? One way would be to satisfy approximately the required assortment pattern within each group of factories, as is done in the plane represented by table 4.2.

Table 4.2   *A feasible plan*

Type of factory	Article No. 1		Article No. 2	
	No. of factories	Aggregate output	No. of factories	Aggregate output
A	1	100 000	4	60 000
B	2	800 000	1	200 000
C	10	200 000	30	75 000
D	2	400 000	7	350 000
E	1	600 000	1	250 000
		2 100 000		935 000

It is possible to compile another plan which in the output of both the first and the second article is smaller — an inferior plan. This is set out in table 4.3.

There is a great variety of feasible plans. How can we choose the optimal one?

Suppose that we turned all the factories over to producing article 1, we would produce (from table 4.1) $5 \times 100\,000 + 3 \times 400\,000 + 40 \times 20\,000 + 9 \times 200\,000 + 2 \times 600\,000 = 5\,500\,000$ units of article No. 1. But we also

(a) Kantorovich refers to these opportunity costs as 'relative labour content'. They are the rates of transformation of one output into another.

31

Table 4.3   *An Inferior Plan*

Type of factory	Article No. 1		Article No. 2	
	No. of factories	Aggregate output	No. of factories	Aggregate output
A	–	–	5	75 000
B	3	1 200 000	–	–
C	–	–	40	100 000
D	–	–	9	450 000
E	1	600 000	1	250 000
		1 800 000		875 000

require article No. 2. Consequently, some of the factories must produce article No. 2, as a result of which we will have less of article No. 1. Which factories should we switch over to producing article No. 2?

If we switch factories of type A from producing No. 1 to producing No. 2, for every unit of No. 1 sacrificed we gain 0.15 units of No. 2; if we switch factories of type B for every unit of No. 1 sacrificed we gain 0.5 units of number 2; if we switch factories of type C for every unit of article No. 1 sacrificed we gain 0.125 units of article No. 2; similarly we gain 0.25 with type D and 0.41 with type E. It makes most sense to switch factories of type B over from producing article No. 1 to No. 2 because it is in factories of type B that the opportunity cost of article No. 1 is highest.

If we use the three B factories to produce article No. 2 then

$$\underline{\text{Output of 1}}$$
$$5\,500\,000 - 1\,200\,000 \;=\; \underline{4\,300\,000}$$

$$\underline{\text{Output of 2}}$$
$$3\,200\,000 \;=\; \underline{600\,000}$$

We will have to switch over some more factories. The second highest opportunity cost is in factories of type E. Therefore we switch over the two E factories.

$$\underline{\text{Output of 1}}$$
$$4\,300\,000 - 1\,200\,000 \;=\; \underline{3\,100\,000}$$

$$\underline{\text{Output of 2}}$$
$$600\,000 + 500\,000 \;=\; \underline{1\,100\,000}$$

We still have not met the required assortment pattern. The third highest opportunity cost is in factories of type D. Accordingly we switch over three factories of type D.

$$\underline{\text{Output of 1}}$$
$$3\,100\,000 - 600\,000 \;=\; \underline{2\,500\,000}$$

$$\underline{\text{Output of 2}}$$
$$1\,100\,000 + 150\,000 \;=\; \underline{1\,250\,000}$$

This is the optimal plan.

Table 4.4 *The Optimal Plan*

Type of factory	Article No. 1		Article No. 2	
	No. of factories	Aggregate output	No. of factories	Aggregate output
A	5	500 000	—	—
B	—	—	3	600 000
C	40	800 000	—	—
D	6	1 200 000	3	150 000
E	—	—	2	500 000
		2 500 000		1 250 000

The optimal plan furnishes an appreciably higher output than the plans in tables 4.2 and 4.3.

We found the optimal plan by comparing opportunity costs. The only type of factory where both articles are produced in the optimal plan is D. There the opportunity cost of 1 unit of article No.2 is 4 units of article No.1. That is, when we switch factories of type D over from producing article No. 1 to producing article No. 2, for every unit of No. 2 gained, 4 units of No. 1 must be sacrificed. In the optimal plan, both articles No. 1 and No. 2 are produced in factories of type D, i.e. in the optimal plan the relative valuation of articles No. 1 and No. 2 is, one unit of article No. 2 is 4 times more valuable than 1 unit of article No. 1. Let the valuation of one unit of No. 1 be a, and of No. 2 be $4a$. Call these valuations (4:1) 'shadow prices'.

These shadow prices can be used as a guide to rational decision making. This can be shown by the following example. Suppose that the previous plan (article No. 1 − 2 500 000 units, article No. 2 − 1 250 000 units) is changed and a new task is set, namely, article No. 1 − 3 000 000 units, article No. 2 − 1 000 000 units. Is this plan feasible? The value of the old plan in shadow prices is

$$2 500 000 \, a + 1 250 000 \times 4a = 7 500 000 \, a$$

The new target is

$$3 000 000 \, a + 1 000 000 \times 4a = 7 000 000 \, a$$

Hence not only is the new plan feasible, but we can adopt a plan which contains more of both outputs. We have used the shadow prices in order to judge the rationality of a possible plan.[a]

The shadow prices can also be utilised to evaluate the rationality of using a proposed new technology. Suppose that a new technology is proposed

(a) This method of evaluating an alternative plan, which is given by Kantorovich, does not work in general. (It works in this case, as explained in the conclusion, because the alternative plan is not one such as c.)

so that a factory of type E can produce 550 000 units of No. 1 and 150 000 of No. 2. Is it rational to introduce this technique of production? The value of the output of a factory of type E in the optimal plan was $250\,000 \times 4a = 1\,000\,000\ a$. The value of output if the new technique is used is $550\,000\ a + 150\,000 \times 4a = 1\,150\,000\ a$. Hence it is desirable to use the new technology.

These examples indicate 'that prices are indispensable also in a planned economy'. In the particular problem examined there was no private ownership of the means of production and the economy was planned, nevertheless 'prices arose naturally and turned out to be necessary and useful'.[7]

Conclusion

The study of linear programming has introduced into Soviet economic thought the idea that prices have a role to play in a socialist economy as guides to efficient decision making which is both permanent and important.[a]

Linear programming and the price formation method

The traditional method of price formation was for wholesale prices to be fixed at irregular intervals (1955, 1967) by state organs. The study of linear programming shows that the optimal prices continually alter in accordance with changes in the conditions of production and in accordance with changes in demand, and lead to proposals for more flexibility in price formation.

'Analysis of economic-mathematical models of planning inevitably leads to the conclusion that efficient planning decisions can receive a correct social evaluation only when there exist *real prices*. By this we mean prices which arise as a result of the action of an objective mechanism, providing social recognition of the cost of production and the usefulness of a given good ... These conditions require a considerable strengthening of the *flexibility of prices*, which it is necessary to use for active influence on the proportions of production and for overcoming the scarcities of particular types of output. Flexible prices allow many tasks of the current regulation of the physical proportions of the economy to be performed considerably better than this is done by the contemporary practice of planning.'[8]

Linear programming and the price formation formula

Traditionally, enterprise wholesale prices were fixed on the basis of costs (i.e. labour and material costs and depreciation) plus a small profit margin expressed as a percentage of cost. A number of Soviet economists consider that it follows directly from part (4) of the Kantorovich theorem that this is incorrect because it ignores capital intensity and the use of scarce natural resources as price forming factors, and hence prices formed on the basis of

(a) Stalin recognised that prices have a useful role to play in a socialist economy as guides to efficient decision making (Stalin op cit pp 23–25). Nevertheless, he regarded this as a transitory phenomenon, which would disappear with the transition from socialism to communism, and not a very important one.

the traditional formula are unable to guide decision makers to optimal solutions.

Terekhov has explained that part (4) of the Kantorovich theorem means that *'for those activities utilised in the optimal plan, the valuation of outputs equals the sum of the valuation of inputs. If the only limited resource is labour, then the valuation of output is determined by the shadow prices of labour inputs.*

In the general case, when various kinds of resources figure in the model, the valuation of output includes: labour costs, material costs (e.g. fuel and energy), differential rent for natural resources (in those cases where they are utilised in production), the hire valuation of machinery and other items of capital equipment. Labour and material costs are usual cost elements, only here they are reckoned at their shadow prices. Differential rent and hire valuations for capital equipment are formed out of net income, created by surplus labour (except for depreciation, which is included in the hire valuations but is a part of the cost of production and not net income). On the whole the valuation of output in the optimal plan is similar to the formula for the price of production: costs of production plus profit, proportional to capital employed ...'[9]

A feature of the reform strongly supported by the optimal planners was a switch in the formula for forming enterprise wholesale prices from cost (i.e. labour and material costs) plus a profit margin expressed as a small percentage of cost, to cost plus a profit margin expressed as a substantial percentage (usually 15 per cent) of the value of the capital employed, a move in line with the suggestions of the optimal planners (and also of those economists who advocated the price of production as a general base for price formation), but not altogether satisfactory from their point of view (because the allowance for the use of capital equipment should take the form of rent charges reflecting the scarcity of particular types of means of production rather than an economy wide average rate of profit).[10]

Linear programming and rent

Traditionally Soviet enterprises have not had to pay for the use of land or natural resources.[a] Rent payments for the use of scarce natural resources were introduced as part of the reform, and the further development of this principle is currently very topical. The optimal planners explained the need for such payments by means of simple examples such as the following.

A farm has three pieces of land of varying fertility.[11] The best piece, size 200 hectares, can yield 25 centners per hectare, the middling one, size 500 hectares, can yield 20 centners per hectare, and the worst piece of land, size 400 hectares, yields 15 centners per hectare. Labour costs per hectare on each piece of land are 3 man days, and the resources

(a) 'An exception is the establishment in 1949 of stumpage payments for uncut timber, which were fixed at 46 kopecks per cubic metre and cover only 25–30 per cent of the costs connected with forestry, and clearly, in no way stimulated the efficient processing of timber.'[12]

available are 3000 man days. For simplicity assume that the non-labour resources (seed, fertilisers, machines) are used in equal quantities per hectare on all three pieces of land, and are available in abundance and do not limit production. The data can be represented by table 4.5.

Table 4.5 *Resources, Costs, Output*

Resources	Expenditure/unit of output			Volume of resources
	Best land	Middling land	Worst land	
Land				
Best (hectares)	0.04	–	–	200
Middling (hectares)	–	0.05	–	500
Worst (hectares)	–	–	0.07	400
Labour (man days)	0.12	0.15	0.2	3000
Output	1	1	1	

Each column indicates the inputs necessary to produce 1 centner of wheat on that type of land. For example, the second column indicates that to produce 1 centner of wheat on the middling land requires $1/20 = 0.05$ hectares of land, and $3/20 = 0.15$ man days. In order to maximise output, the optimal solution is to use 600 man days on the best land, 1500 man days on the middling land, and 900 man days on the worst land. Total output is 19500 centners, and 100 centners of the worst land are superfluous.

Solving the dual problem, the shadow prices are, for labour 5, for the best land 10, for middling land 5, and for the worst land 0.

'Differences in the fertility of the pieces of land results in the fact that varying quantities of labour are expended per unit of output, at the same time that the expenditures of labour per hectare are identical. Utilisation of the middling land rather than the worst saves 0.05 man days per centner of output, and per hectare the saving is 1 man day. The use of a hectare of the best land saves two units of labour in comparison with expenditures on the worst land, and the shadow price of 1 hectare of the best land is twice the valuation of 1 man day of labour.

Hence, *the shadow prices of pieces of land of different fertilities reflect the saving of labour resulting from production on the best and middling pieces of land rather than on the worst piece. With identical expenditures of labour and means of production per unit of sown area the shadow prices indicate the quantity of differential rent I[a] caused by differences in the fertility of the pieces of land.*

In our example, if we let the valuation of 1 man day of labour be equal to 5 roubles, then the differential rent from 1 hectare of the middling land is 5 roubles, and from 1 hectare of the best land, 10 roubles. Including

(a) In Marxist–Leninist political economy differential rent is divided into two categories, differential rent I and differential rent II. Differential rent I is the differential rent created by natural conditions (e.g. location), while differential rent II is differential rent created by man (e.g. applying investment to land).

differential rent in the valuation of output equalises costs per unit of output on pieces of land of different fertility, making them the same as costs on the worst piece of land the utilisation of which is nevertheless required in the plan for the satisfaction of the needs of society ...

At the present time, in point of fact, the direct calculation of differential rent does not take place. Of course, rent is both created and distributed, partly it accrues to the state and partly it remains at the disposal of the enterprises. The extraction of rent, however, takes place not by a direct but by an indirect method, via the system of zonally differentiated procurement prices for agricultural products, income tax on the collective farms, and deductions from the profits of state enterprises. This system is inadequate for equalising the economic conditions in which enterprises are working.

The practice of the economic calculation of land is also unsatisfactory. The methods which are used for this are cumbersome, insufficiently precise, and permit elements of subjectivism. They are usually not connected with the rent created on qualitatively different pieces of land, and land is evaluated by an abstract system of marks.

The direct calculation of differential rent helps the solution of a number of problems. It opens up the possibility of fixing rent payments to the state for those enterprises which use relatively better natural resources and land. This creates real equality in the conditions of enterprises in agriculture and mining regardless of differences in their natural endowments. Their relations with the state can be established more correctly. The payment of rent is a stimulus for the rational utilisation, better maintenance, and safeguarding of natural riches. An objective index for the comparative economic evaluation of land, and also raw material deposits, forests and other natural resources, is created. Rent payments will also serve as an important accounting index in the enterprises' own calculations.'

Linear programming and a charge for the use of capital goods

Traditionally, Soviet enterprises have not had to make any payment for the use of capital equipment. In this section it will be shown how the study of linear programming has led some Soviet economists to advocate the introduction into Soviet planning practice of a charge for the use of capital goods.

Consider the choice between the use of manual labour and of machinery to accomplish a particular task, e.g. the building of a dam, which must be complete in a hundred days.[13] Assume that the task may be divided into four types of operations. For example one type of operation might be movement of earth from A to B. The data of the problem is summaraised in table 4.6.

The meaning of this table is as follows. Take row 1. Assume that this operation is the movement of earth from A to B. Then the first row states that the movement of 2 000 000 kgs of earth from A to B requires 2 000 000/40 = 50 000 man days, or 500 workers/day for 100 days at a cost

Table 4.6   *Data for choice between manual and mechanised methods*

Type of oper- ation	Volume of operations	By hand		By machine		No. of machines necessary to carry out the total volume of operations in 100 days
		Daily output	Cost/ unit	Daily output	Cost/ unit	
I	2 000 000	40	0.6	1 000	0.2	20
II	1 500 000	10	3.0	500	1.2	30
III	200 000	4	7.0	50	1.0	40
IV	40 000 000	200	0.15	10 000	0.05	40
V	2 500 000	20	1.5	500	0.3	50

of $2\,000\,000 \times 0.6 = 1.2$ million roubles. The same volume of work can be accomplished in $2\,000\,000/1\,000 = 2\,000$ machine days, or 20 machines/day for 100 days at a cost of $2\,000\,000 \times 0.2 = 400\,000$ roubles. Similarly for the other operations. In all five types of operation, the use of manual labour is more costly than the use of modernised methods. Unfortunately only 100 machines are available and 180 would be required for the entire work to be carried out by machinery. On which operations should machines be used and on which manual labour? This is a typical problem in optimal planning.

At first sight it might seem that machines should be utilised where they would result in the highest reduction in costs as compared with work carried out by hand, say for type III operations for which the cost is seven times lower. Such a solution, however, is superficial, and will not lead to an optimal plan.

In order to arrive at an optimal solution we calculate for each type of operation by how much the use of machines rather than manual labour will reduce costs/day. The saving/unit of a type I operation is $0.6 - 0.2$ roubles/ unit of operations. As a machine can do $1\,000$ units of type I operations/day, the daily saving by substituting one machine for the corresponding number of workers is $1\,000 \times 0.4 = 400$ roubles. Similarly for type II operations the daily saving is 900 roubles, for type III operations 300 roubles, for type IV operations $1\,000$ roubles and for type V operations 600 roubles. From this it is clear that a machine should first of all be used in operation IV, and then in operations II, V, I and III. To complete type IV operations in 100 days, 40 machines are necessary, for type II operations 30 machines are necessary, and for type V, 50 machines. Thus all the machines are exhausted. A part of type V operations (and all type I and II) has to be undertaken by manual labour.

In this manner the optimal plan of table 4.7 is calculated. We obtained an efficient allocation of machines by comparing the saving resulting from the use of machines in the various operations. In type V operations, where both machines and manual labour are used, the saving/day resulting from the use of machinery is 600 roubles. If an additional machine can be obtained for less than 600 roubles, then it is rational to obtain it. Conversely, if someone offers more than 600 roubles for the daily use of a machine, it is rational

Table 4.7   *The Optimal Plan*

Type of operation	By hand			By machine		
	No. of workers	Volume of operations	Cost (in roubles)	No. of machines	Volume of operations	Cost (in roubles
I	500	2 000 000	1 200 000	–	–	–
II	–	–	–	30	1 500 000	1 800 000
III	500	200 000	1 400 000	–	–	–
IV	–	–	–	40	40 000 000	2 000 000
V	500	1 000 000	1 500 000	30	1 500 000	450 000
Total	1 500		4 100 000	100		4 250 000

to accept the offer. 600 roubles represents the value to the optimal plan of an additional machine. Call this figure the 'hire valuation' of a machine.[a]

If costs are calculated with hire valuation counted as an additional cost, then table 4.8 is obtained.

Table 4.8   *Cost calculations (with hire valuations regarded as costs)*

Types of operations	Full cost when using machines (including hire valuations) in roubles/unit	Cost when working by hand in roubles/unit
I	0.8	0.6
II	2.4	3.0
III	13.0	7.0
IV	0.11	0.15
V	1.5	1.5

It is at once clear that the manual methods are only cheaper for operations I and III, and that for operations type V the two methods are equally costly.

'Hence if in the calculation of cost a correctly determined hire valuation is included in the expenditure on a machine, it is possible to be guided in the choice of equipment by the principle of least cost (principle of profitability) and each operation will be performed by the method showing the lower cost.'[14]

The use of these hire valuations can guide a decision maker to rational decisions, as the following example shows. Suppose that one of the machines

(a) The Russian phrase is *prokatnaya otsenka*. The hire valuation of a unit of equipment is simply the shadow price of a unit of that equipment, the value to the optimal plan of an additional unit of that type of equipment. Kantorovich uses the term 'hire valuation' because this sum is the upper limit of the figure which it would be rational to pay for the hire of that machine, and the lower limit of the figure at which it would pay to hire out the machine. The equivalent Marshallian concept is quasi rent.

The shadow price of a unit of equipment is the marginal product of that type of equipment. By aggregating all the capital goods into one, and assuming substitutability, it is possible to confuse the saving made possible by additional capital goods with the income of property owners ('the marginal productivity theory of profit').

has broken down and needs repairing. The time needed for the repair is 10 days and the cost is 2 000 roubles. It would be possible to repair the machine by a quicker method in 2 days but the cost in that case would be 3 000 roubles (because of the need to pay overtime and use more expensive materials). Is it desirable to use the quicker method? An optimal solution to this problem can be arrived at by the use of the hire valuations. The additional cost of the speedy repair is 1 000 roubles. The saving it leads to is 8×600 roubles $= 4 800$ roubles. Therefore the use of the quicker (but more expensive) method is justified.

The hire valuations can also be used to work out the effect on costs of a change in the working day. Consider the proposal to reduce the working day from 8 to 7 hours. Assume that as a result labour costs/hour rise 14 per cent (daily wages remain constant) and the hourly productivity of a machine rises by 5 per cent (as a result of fuller utilisation owing to increased attention and the possibility of working at higher speeds). What is the economic effect of such a change? Take type V operations. Daily expenditure is now $150 \times 1.14 = 171 + 600$ roubles hire valuation $= 771$ roubles. Output is $500 \times 1.05 = 525$ units of type V operations. Costs per unit are $771/525 = 1.47$ roubles instead of 1.5 roubles. That is, the reduction in the working day actually reduced costs.

'Hire valuations correspond to the principle of payment for capital which is being put into practice at the present time as part of the new system of planning and management of the national economy.[a] The state no longer provides the enterprises with machines and other capital goods free as it did formerly, but hires them out, receiving in exchange for their use a definite rental payment. If this payment is fixed on the basis of the shadow prices then it is determined by the national economic efficiency of the given type of equipment (the increase in total final product of the national economy, or the saving in the whole mass of living labour, from the use of a unit of that equipment). In this case the enterprise will order equipment only in that quantity and use it in that regime, in which the total effect from its use will be no lower than the national economic effect. Otherwise the given process of production will be loss making.

Payment for capital at the level of its national economic efficiency is an economic instrument for overcoming methods of economic management such as those under which at many enterprises equipment which has been ordered and received remains uninstalled for many months, lathes and

(a) Strictly speaking this is doubtful. Whereas the theory leads to the view that enterprises should pay to the state sums equal to the quasi rents produced by particular capital goods, in fact an arbitrary rate of interest is charged, which is the same for all the capital goods within an industry, and which varies between industries in order to avoid turning low profitability industries into loss making ones.

What does correspond more to the theory are the fixed payments which have been introduced in the economy to take account of specially favourable circumstances facing some enterprises.

machines stand idle, or are only half utilised, the coefficient of shift working scarcely reaches 1.2 − 1.5. When an enterprise has to pay an appreciable sum for all the equipment which it has, regardless of whether or not it is working, then even one hour of idle equipment (with a capital charge according to its hire valuation) will be as unprofitable as, let us say, an idle worker who receives full wages. Payment for capital will force the enterprises to devote their energies to the more efficient utilisation of the capital which they already have, rather than to the receipt of additional fixed and circulating capital. In the better utilisation of existing productive capacity are contained immense reserves for raising the productivity of social labour and increasing the volume of output.' [15]

Linear programming and a charge (or subsidy) for labour

The study of linear programming has led some Soviet economists to the view that enterprises ought to make payments to the state for the use of scarce types of labour or receive subsidies from the state for the employment of surplus types of labour, in order to ensure the efficient allocation of labour resources.[a] Formally, this is simply another application of part (4) of the Kantorovich theorem, and is exactly analogous to the case for payment for the use of scarce natural resources and capital goods.[16] In a popular exposition[17] Kantorovich has put the matter as follows.

'Women who are no longer young are doing road repair work. This hard work requires considerable physical effort. Alongside them stands a strong man, calmly watching their work and filling out work records. Even today this is not an unusual situation. The moral aspect and the ethical aspect, so to speak, and the economic aspect here are all cause for concern.

It is well known that labour is the basic and prime source of public wealth and well being. The state's economic might and the individual family's prosperity both depend on how fully and effectively the country's labour resources are used. If, let us say, thousands of women repair the roads while thousands of healthy young men fill out forms and file papers, it is bad for both of them and harms the country as a whole. If the men took to repairing the roads, they would, of course, perform the work more effectively.

If each person were to work where he is most needed, where he could employ his efforts and talents more fully, all of us would receive far greater material benefits. And this can be achieved through a whole complex of measures. In particular, through planning and proper vocational guidance for young people, as well as the use of economic levers.

Specifically, how can we solve the important task of the rational distribution of the labour force, how can we give the labour force a stake in

(a) A tentative step along the road mapped out by Kantorovich is the Regional Employment Premium introduced in the UK as part of the Selective Employment Tax.

this? Needless to say, economic measures are needed here. To solve this problem, I think we could take the following path. It is necessary to establish a system whereby enterprises pay money for the use of labour, as they do for fixed and working capital. This payment should be introduced in regions where there is a shortage of labour. Where there is a surplus on the other hand, the enterprises should be paid a subsidy for expanding production. Naturally, the enterprises would pay for the use only of types of labour in short supply.

How would this operate in practice? Let us say that a mine or metallurgical combine is to be built. From the geological point of view, the most advantageous location for such an enterprise would be in Siberia. But already Siberia has a shortage of labour. New enterprises require chiefly young and middle aged men. Payment would have to be introduced for the use of their labour. The profit from new mines and ferrous metallurgical plants in Siberia is so great, thanks to the wealth of natural resources, that despite the payment for using the labour of these categories of workers, the enterprises will still be highly profitable. But this payment, established for a given locality, would resemble a lever regulating more rational and effective use of labour resources. Thereby labour resources in short supply in the given locality would be sent wherever they could yield the greatest effect. On the other hand, these measures would compel the enterprises to strive for greater mechanisation and automation of production or to find other possibilities to replace heavy labour.

The introduction of such payments in the East, say, or in large cities in the centre of the country would compel the enterprise managements to reduce the use of categories of labour in short supply, wherever possible. On the other hand, it would make possible a better supply of personnel to up-to-date enterprises already in existence.

Now assume that we need to build a factory whose output requires great labour expenditure. Where should it be built? Obviously where there are reserves of labour, where a surplus exists. And if in these circumstances the enterprise hires women and older men, it would receive a subsidy. This would create conditions favouring the construction of enterprises in regions where there is a manpower surplus. At the same time, this subsidy would ensure fuller use of all categories of labour and more steady demand for it.

Payments for the use of certain categories of labour could be introduced also in individual branches of the economy.

The state should not bear the losses when it introduces payments and subsidies. The money should go into a specific fund. Part of it would be used for the subsidies and part for improving the everyday living conditions in regions where there are manpower shortages, as well as for training and retaining personnel. Naturally, the payments and subsidies would in no way affect the wages of the workers and employees.'[a]

Linear programming and profit

Marxists have traditionally regarded profit under capitalism as a measure of the exploitation of the workers by the capitalists, and have ignored the liberal contention that profit is really an essential index in any economy as a guide to the efficient allocation of resources. In the actual practice of Soviet planning profit played a negligible role in guiding and evaluating the work of enterprises. In an interview with the first American workers' delegation (1927) Stalin stated that 'the extraction of profit is neither an aim nor a motive force of our socialist industry'.[18] Many Soviet economists now consider that profit is the appropriate synthetic success indicator to use for guiding and evaluating the work of a socialist enterprise or association, and they regard this conclusion as simply an application of property (4) of the multipliers which, Kantorovich proved, characterise the optimal plan.

Kantorovich has explained that property (4) can be paraphrased as follows: 'In other words, using valuations determined in this way, it turns out that in the optimal plan are used only profitable activities, and the activities which are not used in the optimal plan are less, or at any rate no more profitable, that the ones which are used'.[19] 'At each factory, or in any production process, if a method of production is used in the optimal plan the sum of expenditure must equal the total value of production (if both are evaluated at objectively determined valuations[b]) — in other words production must be justified by being profitable* ... bringing prices near to the objectively

(a) Such payments, of course, are similar to Pigou's suggested taxes and subsidies in cases of divergencies between social and private costs, and to the use of shadow prices rather than actual prices for project evaluation in developing countries. The case for them arises because of the divergence between actual wages and the shadow wages necessary for indirect centralisation.

(b) 'Objectively determined valuations' is Kantorovich's term for the multipliers which characterise the optimal plan, which are usually known in English as 'shadow prices'. They are 'objectively determined' in the sense that they result from certain mathematical operations on the original data of the problem, and are thus to be contrasted with 'subjectively determined' valuations arrived at by planning officials, which all too often represent no more than the arbitrary decision of some official.

* The reader may be surprised that in applying the system of objectively determined valuations consideration is given only to the question of the justification of production by its profitability which is equal to zero. This is firstly due to the conclusion being given for a schematised statement of the problem, and secondly because the concept of profitability is somewhat unusual, namely:

    (a) Expenditure includes the hire valuation — rent — of an enterprise; in reality it represents a net income at the disposal of the state (in practice a portion of this must remain at the disposal of the factory and is included in its income). The same applies to other deductions which appear as expenditures: rent from land (section 6), payment for the use of scarce types of labour (section 3, p. 68).

    (b) Only planned profitability is envisaged as zero. In fact owing to the over-fulfilment of the planned targets of production and the lowering of expenditure norms, the actual profit should be positive even allowing for expenditure mentioned under (a).

determined valuations will provide a much more exact agreement between the material and monetary balances — owing to the real and practical nature of these valuations — which will lead to raising the function of the rouble in economic analysis and economic decisions. The importance of economic criteria in the evaluation of the activity of factories and sectors will also be increased. The profitability of factories will become decisive in such an evaluation which must replace the numerous and partly contradictory partial indices used for the evaluation of the operations of a factory, leaving to them only an auxiliary role.'[20]

Linear programming and investment efficiency

In traditional Soviet economic thought and planning practice it is necessary to choose between the share of investment and consumption in the national income, between regions to which investment should be directed, between industries where investments can be made, and between alternative ways of producing a given output. The first three are political choices, the last a technical one to be solved by comparing the recoupment periods of the rival techniques.[21] Kantorovich has argued that the traditional methods of deciding between investment projects have led to widespread waste, and that an alternative approach is necessary. He has put forward the following propositions:

(1) The calculation of investment efficiency is only one aspect of the general problem of the efficient allocation of resources.

(2) Costs and benefits at different times should be made comparable by means of a rate of interest.

1.   Kantorovich considered an economy where production can be represented by activities which are proportional (i.e. constant returns to scale prevail) and additive (i.e. there are no externalities). Consider the jth activity which, when operated at the unit level is defined by the numbers a_{1j}, $a_{2j} \ldots a_{mj}$, where $a_{ij} > 0$ signifies that the ith commodity is an output, and $a_{ij} < 0$ signifies that the ith commodity is an input. The test of the efficiency of an activity is the sign of the expression

$$\sum_{i=1}^{m} c_i \, a_{ij} \tag{1}$$

where c_i is the shadow price of a unit of the ith commodity. For efficient activites (1) is non-negative, for inefficient activities (1) is negative.

Now extend the analysis to embrace activities which relate not just to one period but to several periods, i.e. investment activities. Each investment activity is defined by a matrix $\| a_{it} \|$ where a_{ij} is an output (if $a_{ij} > 0$) or input (if $a_{ij} < 0$) of the project in the jth year. The test of the efficiency of an investment project is the sign of the expression

$$\sum_{i,t} c_{it} \, a_{it} \tag{2}$$

where c_{it} is the shadow price of the ith good in the jth year.

Hence '... in the optimal plan there does not exist a separate problem of

44

the efficiency of investment, it is an integral part of the general problem of ensuring the maximum efficiency of the whole of social production'. [22]

2. Criterion (2) can be written slightly differently. Let

$$c_{it} = r_t c'_{it}$$

where r_t is chosen so that

$$c'_{1t} + c'_{2t} + \ldots + c'_{mt} = 1 \qquad t = 1 \ldots T$$

Define $[r_t/r_{t+1} - 1]$ as the 'normal efficiency of investment' (it is a conversion coefficient which relates the price of a set of goods in one period to the price of the same set in the following period) from period t to period $t + 1$. Criterion (2) can now be written in the equivalent form

$$\sum_t r_t \sum_i c'_{it} a_{it} \qquad (3)$$

The efficiency of an investment can now be tested by inspecting the sign either of (2) or of (3).

Assume that the relative shadow prices are constant through time.[a] Then (3) is equivalent to

$$\sum_t r_t \sum_i c'_{i1} a_{it} \qquad (4)$$

To test the efficiency of an investment project it is sufficient to calculate (4) and look at its sign. $[r_t/r_{t+1} - 1]$ is an conversion coefficient which relates the price of each good to its price in the following period, and may accordingly be defined as the rate of interest for that period.

Kantorovich explained the usefulness of a rate of interest by means of examples such as the following. [23]

It is required to build a bridge. The bridge can be either of wood or of stone. Which should be built? The wooden bridge costs 1 000 000 roubles, lasts 10 years and costs 20 000 roubles per year in repairs. The stone bridge costs 2 500 000 roubles, lasts 50 years, and costs 5 000 roubles per year in repairs. Which should be built?

If one ignores interest, one might be tempted to compare annual costs as follows. For the wooden bridge annual costs are $(1\,000\,000 + 10 \times 20\,000)/10 = 120\,000$ roubles per year. For the stone bridge annual costs are $(2\,500\,000 + 50 \times 5\,000)/50 = 55\,000$ roubles per year. It might seem obvious that the stone bridge is definitely preferable. If, however, the calculation is done using a rate of interest to make costs at different times comparable, then the picture looks different.

Assume that the rate of interest is 10 per cent and compare the cost of building a stone bridge now, or building a wooden bridge now and a stone bridge in ten years time. Costs in the first case (converting all costs to the inital moment) are, the cost of the bridge (2 500 000 roubles) and the costs

(a) It is this assumption which enables Kantorovich to derive a vector of interest rates from the optimal perspective plan. In the general case in which relative shadow prices change through time, with the optimal perspective plan are associated not a vector of interest rates but a matrix of own rates of return.

of the repairs (35 000 roubles, i.e. 50 000 roubles converted to the present at
10 per cent p.a. simple interest), making a total of 2 535 000 roubles. Costs
in the second case are the cost of the wooden bridge (1 000 000 roubles),
the costs of repairing it (140 000 roubles, i.e. 200 000 roubles discounted at
10 per cent p.a. simple) and the cost of the stone bridge in ten years
converted to the initial moment (1 250 000, i.e. 2 500 000 discounted at 10 per
cent simple). Total cost of the second variant is 2 390 000. The stone bridge,
which seemed so advantageous when interest was not taken into account,
now turns out to be inferior.

'It is appropriate to make a general observation that the enthusiasm for
gigantic solutions without any particular need from which many of our planners suffer is harmful as it deprives other more efficient investments of the
necessary means. One of the causes of such incorrect solutions was inaccurate economic calculation which failed to take account of interest
(*normal 'naya effektivnost'*).'

Conclusion

Analysis of optimal planning models has led some Soviet economists to the
view that in order to avoid the misallocation of resources the present value
criterion should be used to discriminate between investment projects.

Linear programming and devolution

The traditional Soviet view is that economic management should be based
on the principle of democratic centralism, i.e. the centralisation of basic
decisions and the decentralisation of operational functions. A major result
of the impact of linear theory on Soviet economics has been to underline
the democratic half of this formula, to emphasise that the devolution of
decision making is perfectly compatible with an optimally functioning economic system.

The underlying reason why in linear theory centralisation has no advantages is, as Koopmans has pointed out,[24] that the summation of sets and
the maximisation of a linear function are interchangeable operations. Economically, under conditions of constant returns to scale and perfect competition, splitting a process of production among many producers has no
effect on the volume of output. The classic formulation of this is that half
of the basic theorem of welfare economics which states that 'every Pareto-
optimum is a competitive equilibrium'. Volkonsky has argued that 'The
theorem of the coincidence of the equilibrium point with the national economic optimum provides a theoretical basis for a system of optimal control
which uses the independence and initiative of economic units in the taking
of economic decisions'.[25]

Not only has centralisation no positive advantage in linear theory, but
devolution of decision-making has the positive advantage that it may enable
the economy to move along an optimal path even when the centre lacks the
information necessary to determine an optimal plan on its own. In 1961
Danzig and Wolfe proved that it was possible to split some large linear

programs into subprograms corresponding to the almost independent parts, and a master programme which ties together the subprograms.[26] Almon subsequently showed that this could be interpreted as a process of central planning without complete information at the centre, in which the centre issues prices for evaluating scarce resources, the enterprises submit production proposals, and at the end of an iterative process the centre issues quantitative targets to the enterprises.[27] Although the centre lacks the information necessary to work out an optimal plan on its own, the result of this iterative process is the compilation of an optimal plan. Katsenelinboigen, Ovsienko and Faerman, after describing this algorithm, state:

'This is the mathematical side of the process of optimising a hierarchical system. Its direct significance is that on the basis of the initial data characterising the technical and human possibilities, and also of a definite kind of objective function for the system as a whole, the indicated algorithm allows the calculation of the optimal plan for the whole system to be broken up into the solution of a number of visible problems of local optimisation, relating to particular economic units.

The nature of the local optimal problems is such, however, that all the initial information, necessary for its solution, relates to the productive process of the corresponding complex. This information can be concentrated in the planning organ of the given complex. The process of local optimisation can be regarded as the independent activity of this organ. The connection of these actions with the higher level takes place only through a small number of controlling parameters (in our example shadow prices), issued from above, and in summary characteristics of the productive possibilities of the complex, issued from below. In this way here is formalised the independence of economic layers, linked in the general optimal process by the centralised optimising of the complexes at the higher level.'[28]

Conclusion

The study of linear programming has led some Soviet economists to a number of important policy conclusions strikingly at variance with the traditional teachings of Marxism—Leninism, as set out for example in *Economic problems of socialism in the USSR*, and provides a 'scientific' basis for economic reform.

In this connection it is very important to note that substantially different policy conclusions are drawn by different economists in the socialist countries from the Kantorovich theorem. The Czechslovak economist Kouba, in a paper on the vexed question of the plan and the market has quoted another Czechoslovak economist I. Rendek as having written in 1966 that the study of optimal planning models 'yields two conclusions of importance for the management system:

1) under certain conditions the market can be an instrument for achieving economic optimum. Consequently, there is precise mathematical proof

that the market is capable of operating as a leading factor in the national economy under socialism;

2) conditions can be provided under which the participants of the economic process — guided by the logic of the market — act in accordance with the optimum economic plan (without the need to apply administrative compulsion). From this angle the plan appears as a model of the futures market. It should be emphasised that this quality belongs to an optimum plan only. A non-optimum plan has to be put through by administrative methods if it is not to remain a document of little significance. Consequently, *our criticism of command plans will carry little weight until it is aimed at the root of the matter, i.e. against the absence of optimal planning.*' [29]

Among Soviet mathematical economists opinion is divided as to the significance to be attached to shadow prices, and research is going ahead to study their properties and the possibility of using them in the solution of particular planning problems. Many Soviet economists have persistently argued that Kantorovich's method for calculating optimal plans is useful, but that the idea that the shadow prices have any economic significance is incorrect and alien to Marxism.

Drawing any kind of policy conclusions from a study of the conditions for the existence of optimal solutions to linear programming problems is vulnerable to criticism on a number of grounds. First, 'second best' considerations, secondly the fact that linear programming is concerned with only one class of problems of the efficient allocation of resources (it does not deal with cases where the technology is non-additive or non-proportional), thirdly that the efficient allocation of resources is only one of the topics with which economic analysis and policy is concerned, although Robbins explicitly, and Kantorovich implicity when he extended his economic interpretation of linear programming from some problems of the organisation of production to national economic planning, both current and perspective, identified this one topic with the whole of economics.

The policy conclusions drawn by Kantorovich himself are substantially different from those drawn by Kouba and Rendek. As far as inputs are concerned, he considers that rent payments for the use of land and natural resources, quasi rent payments for the use of capital goods, and subsidies or charges for the use of particular types of labour, should be introduced into economic practice. This would facilitate indirect centralisation, prevent differences in natural or technical conditions affecting the distribution of income, and turn profit into a measure of efficiency. The role of profit as an index in the work of enterprises should be enhanced. In investment planning a rate of interest should be used to make costs and benefits at different times comparable. As far as outputs are concerned, he argues that in an economy where production targets are set by the planners, the shadow prices enable enterprises themselves to evaluate the rationality of small changes in the production programme resulting from a change in the conditions since the optimal plan was drawn up. This use of shadow prices is the one

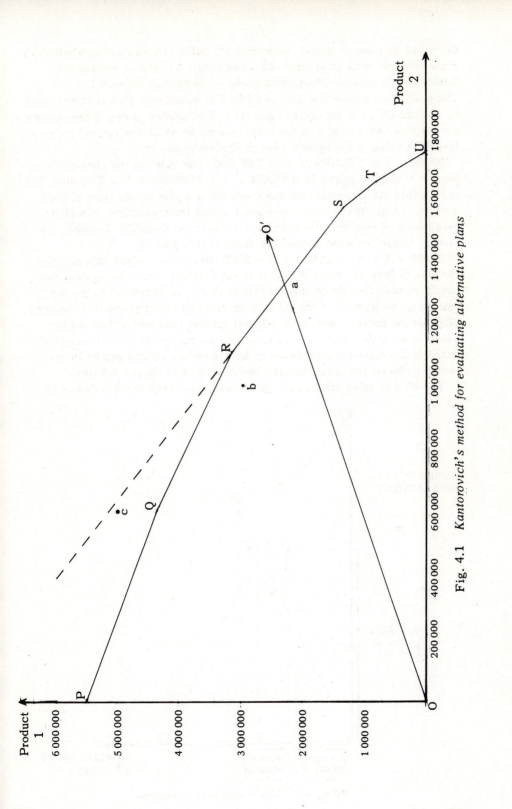

Fig. 4.1 *Kantorovich's method for evaluating alternative plans*

described on page 33 above. Kantorovich's method for evaluating alternative plans does not work in general. This can easily be seen by setting out Kantorovich's example diagrammatically, as is done in figure 4.1.

The production possibility area is OPU. The assortment plan is represented by the line 00', and the optimal plan is a. The shadow prices of the outputs are the slope of the facet of the feasible area on which the optimal point lies. The value of the optimal plan in shadow prices is $2\,500\,000 \times 1 + 1\,250\,000 \times 4 = 7\,500\,000$. The value of the alternative plan b in shadow prices is $3\,000\,000 \times 1 + 1\,000\,000 \times 4 = 7\,000\,000$. Not only is this plan feasible, but one could adopt a plan giving more of both outputs. Diagrammatically, b is a point within the production possibility area resulting from the given productive capacity. Consider, however, the plan c. Using the same method the value of this plan is $5\,000\,000 \times 1 + 4 \times 600\,000 = 7\,400\,000$. Hence the method suggests that the plan is feasible, when in fact it is not feasible. From the figure it can easily be seen that the reason for this is that c is dominated by a point that would be feasible if the entire production possibility area had the same slope as the facet on which the original optimal plan lies. (This is why Kantorovich states that the shadow prices are stable for 'small' variations in the data.) Kantorovich's ideas on how to utilise shadow prices in one particular case, the steel industry, are described in chapter 9 below.

The idea of using prices as a guide to rational decision making can be

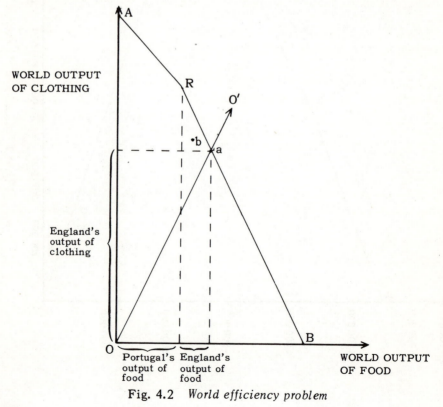

Fig. 4.2 *World efficiency problem*

regarded as a generalisation of the classical economists' idea of using comparative costs as a guide to rational decision making in the field of international trade. In a two country two commodity classical international trade model comparative costs determine the rationality of specialisation and participation in the international division of labour. An example can be set out as in figure 4.2.[30]

There are two countries, England and Portugal. Portugal's technology is such that the opportunity cost of 1 unit of clothing is 1 unit of food. (Although Ricardo's theory is formulated in terms of comparative costs it can be reformulated in terms of opportunity costs.) This determines the slope of AR. England's technology is such that the opportunity cost of 1 unit of clothing is ½ unit of food. This determines the slope of RB. Ricardo's argument, that trade can be mutually beneficial, is equivalent to the proposition that world efficiency requires Portugal to specialise in the production of food, and to obtain clothing by trade with England. England should mainly produce clothing, and obtain most of its food from Portugal by trade. (The extent of specialisation depends on demand.) Output of both products is greater than if each country produced both products in proportions determined by domestic demand. Kantorovich's argument is that, if there is a world Gosplan with an assortment plan 00', each country's optimal production plan can be calculated. If world demand and Gosplan's assortment plan are the same, then the optimal plan computed by Kantorovich coincides with the pattern of specialisation recommended by Ricardo. In addition, if the world Gosplan changes the plan from a to b, the opportunity cost ratio enables the feasibility and efficiency of the new plan to be judged. The reason for this similarity between the ideas of Ricardo and Kantorovich is that both classical international trade theory and production scheduling are examples of the same economic problem — the rational organisation of production. What distinguishes Kantorovich's analysis of the rational organisation of production from Ricardo's, is both the greater operational significance of Kantorovich's theoretical apparatus, and the fact that whereas Ricardo was a spokesman for the capitalist class, Kantorovich is concerned with raising the efficiency of socialism.

Kantorovich's variation on the theme of the allocative function of prices is the idea that in an economy where production targets are determined by planners at intervals, the shadow prices associated with the optimal plan enable the rationality of changes in the production programme to be assessed, without recomputing the plan. This idea is not valid in general and does not appear to have been applied anywhere.[a]

(a) Kantorovich's method is a special case which can be used to evaluate the feasibility and efficiency of possible alternative plans within the production possibility area, and the feasibility of possible plans above the line formed by continuing the facet on which the original optimal plan lies; provided that the original optimal plan is not on a vertex (when there is both a left hand and a right hand shadow price). It does not work for alternatives such as c. Kantorovich's theorem of the characteristics of an optimal plan is simply an n dimensional generalisation of the familiar fact that with all the points on the surface of a two dimensional concave production possibility area one can associate a straight line the slope of which can be regarded as a price ratio.

Kantorovich's theoretical derivation of the rate of interest for investment planning is non-operational, and his empirical derivation confused. There is no guarantee that the rate of interest derived in the way suggested will ensure the selection of that volume of investment which the political leaders desire. Lur'e (and Dobb) have advocated an alternative approach. Given the politically chosen share of investment in national income, the rate of interest to be used is that which enables the most efficient investment projects to be chosen and the given total of investment to be absorbed. On this line of argument the rate of interest depends partly on technology, is inversely proportional to the share of investment in national income, and can be used as a lever to regulate the share of investment in national income.

The Kantorovich concept of profit as a guide to efficiency is entirely at variance with the role that profit has traditionally played in the Soviet economy. To turn profit into a guide to efficiency would require a comprehensive reorganisation of the financial and price systems of the type described by Joan Robinson[a] and suggested in 1966 by TSEMI. Such suggestions are probably unfeasible, show a misunderstanding of why it is desirable to increase the role of profit, and the theory underlying them provides debating points for economists such as Karagedov. If current planning is abolished, and for purposes of simple reproduction the economy is based on the *khozraschet* association, then profit, a synthetic value index which sums up the work of enterprises or associations, must, in general, play a major role in guiding and evaluating their work. In chapter 8 it will be argued that it is the logic of the economic mechanism, rather than the conditions for the efficient allocation of resources, which is decisive for determining the role of this or that index in the economy.

Kantorovich does not share the confusion between quasi rents and uniform interest payments on capital. He has argued against the latter, and in favour of the former. Although it does not follow from the theory, there is in fact a good case for a more or less uniform interest rate, because it is difficult to calculate differentiated quasi rents without discouraging efficiency.

When criticising the hypertrophy of linear programming, one should not forget that the latter is very useful, both in planning, to solve problems of the rational organisation of production, and in teaching, to explain the logic, and the limitations, of the doctrine of 'the price mechanism'.[b]

(a) *On political economy and econometrics* Essays in honour of Oskar Lange (Warsaw 1964) pp 514—516.

(b) The doctrine of 'the price mechanism' is derived by defining economics to be concerned solely with the rational organisation of production, and then concentrating on the value dual rather than the planning primal. This is not very helpful if one wants to explain why cars cost more than washing machines. The production half of the basic theorem of welfare economics is derived by defining 'perfect competition' so that it is equivalent to planning. The preferences half is obtained by considering one particular type of preference for which the proposition holds.

5. A risk or a help?

'As they are not too far from prices determined by supply and demand, do not the authors use a little too much such categories as "the market" and "profit"? askes the captious reader. From all these categories the smell of the capitalist spirit is very strong. Would it not be better to avoid these categories?

No, it would not be better! When we are discussing the choice of methods for controlling our social production there exists only one choice criterion: to what extent they lead to raising its efficiency, while at the same time not threatening that which is the main, not in form but in essence, distinction between capitalism and socialism – the social ownership of the means of production and the planned development of our economy.

The market method of regulation, profit and flexible prices do not threaten this. They can be criticised only because capitalism appeared on the earth before socialism, and to the extent that these can bring advantages to a socialist economy, they must find their place in it.'

A. and N. Kobrinskii[1]

Discussing Soviet work on personal consumption, Zauberman has argued that 'close as this work is to welfare economics, it is not without a certain risk from the ideological point of view.'[2] Zauberman clearly had in mind the alleged risk to Marxism–Leninism of the exposure of Soviet economists to the basic theorem of welfare economics. The present author is of the opinion that the domain of validity of the theorem is so limited that it is no 'risk' to a socialist economy, but that it is a formulation of the 'helpful' idea that full *khozraschet* and methods for the efficient allocation of resources have a useful role to play in a socialist economy and that the maintenance of a socialist economy neither necessitates turning *khozraschet* into a formal category nor the inefficient allocation of resources.

As Koopmans has observed, 'The idea that perfect competition in some sense achieves efficiency through the maximisation of individual satisfactions runs through the whole of classical and neoclassical economic literature'.[3] After a lengthy discussion this intuitive idea was formalised in a theorem – Every competitive equilibrium is a Pareto-optimum; and every Pareto-optimum is a comparative equilibrium – which has been termed by DOSSO 'the basic theorem of welfare economics'.[4] The theorem as formulated by DOSSO is false because of the existence of counter examples both on the production and consumption sides. The standard proof of the theorem is by Debreu, and the theorem he proves is the lemma incorporating version in which the 'exceptions' are incorporated into the theorem.[a] The purpose of this chapter is to discuss some of the counter examples on the preferences side, in order to emphasis the restricted nature of the domain of validity of the theorem.

Consider the two economic units, or composite units, a and b, each of whom has to make a choice between two actions, x and y, and w and z, respectively. There are four possible social choices, xw, xz, yw, and yz.

Diagrammatically:

a's choice

		x	y
b's choice	w	xw	yw
	z	xz	yz

The problem is, will the social choice, using the market method, be rational?

Which of the four possible social choices will be made, and its rationality, depends on the preferences of a and b, on the decision rule adopted, and their knowledge, if any, of each other's preferences. A priori, various types of preferences are possible, for example: [b]

1.
$$x \, P_a \, y \, {}^{(c)}$$
$$w \, P_b \, z$$

The outcome is xw, which is Pareto-optimal. In this case, in which individual preferences are both unconcerned with, and independent of, the choices of other individuals, the market solution is socially rational. [d]

That individual preferences may be such that the interaction of atomistic individuals, each selfishly pursuing his own interest, may result in a socially rational decision, may be termed the 'Liberal paradox'.[5]

2.
$$(x \, C_a \, y) \, P_b \, (y \, C_a \, x)$$

Arrow cites as an example Americans who prefer Africans to Christians rather than pagans.[6]

(a) For a methodological discussion of how it is possible to prove theorems for which there are 'exceptions', see I. Lakatos, Proofs and refutations, *British Journal for the Philosophy of Science*, Vol. 14.

(b) The following argument assumes that a Pareto-optimum is always socially rational. The writer does not share this assumption. cf. J. Rawls, Justice as fairness, *Philosophical Review* 1958.

(c) $x \, P_a \, y$, $w \, C_b \, z$, $S_a(x,y)$; are to be read respectively, 'x is preferred to y by a', 'w is chosen by b in preference to z', 'the set of choices open to a is confined to x and y'.

(d) This is the type of preference assumed in G. Debreu, *The Theory of Value* (New York 1959), (see note 6 on p. 73). Empirical work to support this assumption is not cited.

An isolated individual cannot give effect to this type of preference.

3.
$$z \; P_b \; w$$

unless $x \; C_a \; y$

when $w \; P_b \; z$

$$(x \; C_a \; y, \; w \; C_b \; z) \; P_b \; (z \; C_b \; w)$$

Where preferences are of this type, an isolated individual, ignorant of the choices of other individuals, will make an irrational (with respect to the value judgement that individual preferences ought to count) decision. This has been called the 'Isolation paradox'.[7]

4.
a's preferences:

$yw \; P_a \; xw$	1*
$yz \; P_a \; yw$	2*
$xz \; P_a \; yz$	3*

Assume transitivity. These preferences can be represented diagrammatically:

a's choice

	x	y

b's choice	w Worst	3rd best
	z Best	2nd best

b's preferences:

$yw \; P_b \; yz$	4*
$xw \; P_b \; yw$	5*
$xz \; P_b \; xw$	6*

Assume transitivity. These preferences can be represented diagrammatically:

a's choice

		x	y
b's choice	w	2nd best	3rd best
	z	Best	Worst

What will be the outcome? Assume that the individuals move in turn, first one making a choice and then the other. Each individual is unaware of the preferences of the other.

$$S_a \; (x,y)$$

If	$x \; C_a \; y$	
then	$z \; C_b \; w$	6*
If	$y \; C_a \; x$	
then	$w \; C_b \; z$	4*

$$S_b \; (w,z)$$

If	$w \; C_b \; z$	
then	$y \; C_a \; x$	1*
If	$z \; C_b \; w$	
then	$x \; C_a \; y$	3*

Of the two possible outcomes, xz and yw, the former is, and the latter is not, Pareto-optimal. If the two individuals co-operate, rather than act in complete ignorance of each other, then the social choice will be Pareto-optimal.

The social choice adopted can be made determinate by adopting a definite decision rule. Assume that the individuals adopt the strategy of maximising sure gains (the maximin criterion).

$$S_a \, (x,y)$$

If $\qquad\qquad\qquad\qquad x \; C_a \; y$

then either $\qquad\qquad w \; C_b \; z$ or $z \; C_b \; w$

$\qquad (x \; C_a \; y, \; z \; C_b \; w) \; P_a \; (x \; C_a \; y, \; w \; C_b \; z)$ $\qquad$ Transitivity

If $\qquad\qquad\qquad\qquad y \; C_a \; x$

then either $\qquad\qquad w \; C_b \; z,$ or $z \; C_b \; w$

$\qquad (y \; C_a \; x, \; z \; C_b \; w) \; P_a \; (y \; C_a \; x, \; w \; C_b \; z)$ $\qquad\qquad$ 2*

$\qquad (y \; C_a \; x, \; w \; C_b \; z) \; P_a \; (x \; C_a \; y, \; w \; C_b \; z)$ $\qquad\qquad$ 1*

$\qquad\qquad\qquad \therefore \; y \; C_a \; x$ $\qquad\qquad\qquad$ Maximin rule

$$S_b \; (w,z)$$

If $\qquad\qquad\qquad\qquad w \; C_b \; z$

then either $\qquad\qquad x \; C_a \; y,$ or $y \; C_a \; x$

$\qquad (w \; C_b \; z, \; x \; C_a \; y) \; P_b \; (w \; C_b \; z, \; y \; C_a \; x)$ $\qquad\qquad$ 5*

If $\qquad\qquad\qquad\qquad z \; C_b \; w$

then either $\qquad\qquad x \; C_a \; y,$ or $y \; C_a \; x$

$\qquad (z \; C_b \; w, \; x \; C_a \; y) \; P_b \; (z \; C_b \; w, \; y \; C_a \; x)$ $\qquad$ Transitivity

$\qquad\qquad\qquad\qquad yw \; P_b \; yz$ $\qquad\qquad\qquad$ 4*

$\qquad\qquad\qquad \therefore \; w \; C_b \; z$

The social choice is yw. However,

$$xz \; P_a \; yw \qquad\qquad\qquad \text{3* and 2*}$$
$$xz \; P_b \; yw \qquad\qquad\qquad \text{6* and 5*}$$

i.e. the social choice is non-Pareto-optimal. This has resulted from:
(a) The fact that the individuals are unaware of each others' preferences.

56

Cooperation would be mutually beneficial, and

(b) The decision rule adopted. In the complete ignorance case, when the maximum decision rule is adopted the social choice is always irrational (i.e. non-Pareto-optimal), whereas when the initial choice is made at random the social choice is only irrational in 50 per cent of outcomes.

5.[a]

a's preferences:

$xw\ P_a\ yw$	1*
$yz\ P_a\ xw$	2*
$xz\ P_a\ yz$	3*

(5)[a]

Assume transitivity. These preferences can be represented diagrammatically:

a's choice

		x	y
		3rd best	Worst
b's choice	w		
	z	Best	2nd best

b's preferences:

$yw\ P_b\ yz$	4*
$yz\ P_b\ xw$	5*
$xw\ P_b\ xz$	6*

Assume transitivity. These preferences can be represented diagrammatically:

a's choice

		x	y
	w	3rd best	Best
b's choice			
	z	Worst	2nd best

Will the individuals make a socially rational choice?
Assume that they move in turn, first one making a choice, and then the other. Each individual is unaware of the preferences of the other.

$S_a\ (x,y)$

If	$x\ C_a\ y$	
then	$w\ C_b\ z$	6*
If	$y\ C_a\ x$	
	$w\ C_b\ z$	4*

(a) This type of preference is that postulated in the 'Prioners' Dilemma'. See Luce and Raiffa, *Games and decisions*, (New York 1958) p. 95.

57

$$S_b(w,z)$$

If	$w\ C_b\ z$	
	$x\ C_a\ y$	1*
If	$z\ C_b\ w$	
	$x\ C_a\ y$	3*

∴ The three possible outcomes are xw, yw, and zx. The former is non-Pareto-optimal (it is dominated by yz) the latter two are Pareto-optimal. When individual preferences are of type 5, and initial choices made at random, in one third of outcomes the social choice is irrational.

Consider the case in which the individuals adopt the maximin decision rule.

$$S_a\ (x,y)$$

If	$x\ C_a\ y$	
either	$w\ C_b\ z$, or $z\ C_b w$	
	$xz\ P_a\ xw$	2* and 3*

If	$y\ C_a\ x$	
either	$w\ C_b\ z$, or $z\ C_b\ w$	
	$yz\ P_a\ yw$	1* and 2*
	$xw\ P_a\ yw$	1*
∴	$x\ C_a\ y$	Maximin rule

$$S_b\ (w,z)$$

If	$w\ C_b\ z$	
then either	$x\ C_a\ y$, or $y\ C_a\ x$	
	$wy\ P_b\ wx$	4* and 5*

If	$z\ C_b\ w$	
then either	$x\ C_b\ y$, or $y\ C_a\ x$	
	$zy\ P_b\ zx$	5* and 6*
	$wx\ P_b\ zx$	6*
∴	$w\ C_b\ z$	Maximin rule

The outcome is wx

But,	$yz\ P_a\ wx$	2*
and	$yz\ P_b\ wx$	5*

i.e. the social choice is non-Pareto-optimal.

Where preferences are of type 4, co-operation results in a socially rational choice, which is stable in the sense that neither side can improve its position by making a further choice. Where preferences are of type 5, co-operation can result in a socially rational choice (yz), which, however, is unstable in the sense that either party can improve its position by a further choice, (*xz* or *wy*, respectively).

Where preferences are of this fifth type, and the maximin decision rule employed, the hidden hand will lead to non-Pareto-optimal outcomes, and Pareto-optimality requires a Rousseauvian-benevolent authority to enforce the General Will.[8] That individual preferences, and the decision rule adopted, may be of such a type that individuals' own preferences may be better fulfilled if they are compelled to make a certain choice, different from the one they would have made on their own, may be termed the 'Totalitarian paradox'.[9]

Conclusion

1. In some special cases the market is able to combine individual preferences in a socially rational way. In general, the market is not a mechanism which enables individual preferences to be combined into socially rational choices.[10]

2. The existence of numerous counterexamples demonstrates that the domain of validity of the basic theorem of welfare economics is limited. Hence this theorem is not a 'risk' to a socialist economy. Rather it is a 'help' because it directs attention to the importance of the market and of the rational organisation of production.

6. The consistency of the current plans

The problem

'If there existed the universal mind — that projected itself into the scientific fancy of Laplace; a mind that would register simultaneously all the processes of nature and of society, that could measure the dynamics of their motion, that could forecast the results of their interactions, such a mind, of course, could *a priori* draw up a faultless and exhaustive economic plan, beginning with the number of hectares of wheat and come down to the last button for a vest. In truth, the bureaucracy often conceives that just such a mind is at its disposal; that is why it so easily frees itself from the control of the market and of Soviet democracy.'

L.D. Trotsky (1932)[1]

All Soviet enterprises have a *tekhpromfinplan* which prescribes in detail their activity during the planned period. It is divided into ten sections:

1. Basic indices (summary table)
2. Plan of production and sales
3. Plan for raising the efficiency of production
4. Plan norms
5. Investment plan
6. Supply plan
7. Labour and wages plan
8. Plan for profit, costs and profitability
9. Plan for economic incentive funds
10. Financial plan.

The *tekhpromfinplan* is worked out be a process of bargaining between the enterprise and its administrative superiors during the planning year (the year preceding the planned year).[2] In the light of its own possibilities and its knowledge of the goals of the higher bodies, each enterprise sends in suggestions to its ministry. The ministry is receiving two streams of suggestions for its plan, from the enterprises and from Gosplan USSR. The suggestions from Gosplan USSR take into account inter-industry proportions and national economic requirements. On the basis of control figures supplied by Gosplan USSR (control figures are preliminary estimates, in aggregated terms, of the main items in a plan) and of the suggestions of the enterprises, the ministry works out control figures for its plan. On the basis of the control figures received from the ministry, each enterprise works out its draft *tekhpromfinplan*. The first stage of the planning process is scheduled for completion in September. The second stage in the compilation of the *tekhpromfinplan* comes with the receipt of the confirmed tasks of the enterprise, arising from the national economic plan, and consists of making the draft *tekhpromfinplan* detailed and precise. This second stage should be completed within a month of receiving the confirmed plan tasks, and in no event later than the end of the year.

It is clearly desirable that these *tekhpromfinplany* be consistent in the twofold sense that for each enterprise the planned output be feasible with the planned inputs, and that for the country as a whole the planned requirements for each commodity be no greater than the availability of that commodity. If the plans are not consistent in the first sense, then some enterprises will be unable to fulfil their plans, which may have unfortunate effects on enterprises which planned to use the good which was not produced as an input, or on final consumers for whom the good was intended. If the plans are inconsistent in the second sense, that is if for example steel-using enterprises plan to consume 130 million tons of steel and steel-producing enterprises to produce 100 million tons, then this will lead to the non-production of commodities which it had been planned to make available either as inputs to other enterprises or to final uses, and the splitting up of the economy into a priority sector whose needs are met and a non-priority sector whose needs are not met.

It is well known that 'The plans for production, labour, finance and supply are often inconsistent.'[3] The purpose of this chapter is to explain why this is so. In view of both of its intrinsic and theoretical interest, attention will be focussed on one section of the consistency problem, that of drawing up consistent supply and production plans for the commodities.

In the process of the planning of supply,[4] commodities differ according to the organ which allocates them. A convenient distinction is between centrally distributed and decentrally distributed products. The centrally distributed products include those distributed by Gosplan, Gossnab, and some of the ministries. (Of the commodities for which material balances and distribution plans are worked out by Gosplan, the balances and distribution plans for some, the so called funded commodities, have to be confirmed by the Council of Ministers.) The decentrally distributed commodities include those for which distribution plans are worked out by the territorial organs of Gossnab for all consumers in their region irrespective of their departmental status. For the purpose of the planning of supply, commodities are considered both in an aggregated and in a specified classification. The aggregated classification is used in the planning of supply. The specified classification is a detailed one which lists commodities according to their types, qualities and standards. For example, in the electro-technical industry alone 250 000 commodities are distinguished in the specified classification. It is in this specified classification that enterprises express their detailed requirements, within the limits of the quotas which they have been allocated.

The number of commodities distributed by the various organs has fluctuated markedly over the years in accordance with changes in economic policy. Table 6.1 shows the sharp drop in the number of funded commodities after Stalin's death and the approximate stability in their number in recent years.

Table 6.1   *No. of funded commodities in various years*[5]

	1953	1957	1963	1966	1968
Ferrous metals	100	66	62	65	43
Non-ferrous metals	45	26	10	11	12
Fuel and oil products	184	76	23	25	14
Chemicals and industrial resins	98	57	41	44	41
Wood materials	} 217	31	8	8	8
Cellulose-paper articles		56	11	13	4
Building materials		32	10	8	5
Agricultural raw materials	−	27	27	27	26
Industrial goods	} c. 300	37	31	27	26
Foods		32	16	16	14
Electrical energy	−	13	1	1	1
Equipment and machines	1446	439	133	132	133
Total	2390	892	373	377	327

The number of commodities for which balances and distribution plans are worked out by Gosplan has remained stable in recent years at about 2.000 (1904 in 1966, 1969 in 1968, and 1981 in 1969 − these figures including funded commodities). The total number of products for which distribution plans are worked out by Gosplan and Gossnab and formerly by SNKh USSR increased steadily in the years preceding the reform announced at the September (1965) Plenum, and has subsequently diminished somewhat. In 1957 it was about 6 thousand, in 1960 12.8 thousand, in 1962 14 thousand, and in 1966 21 thousand.

Once the balances are confirmed, the territorial supply organs and the all-union consumers receive limits, indicating the maximum quantities of the various goods which they will be allocated, and are able to allocate resources to the various applicants.

Consider a commodity distributed by Gosplan. During the planning year the consumer enterprises submit their estimated requirements (indents) to the appropriate administration (their administrative superior). The administration checks them, possibly adjusts them, adds them up, and sends them to Glavsnab (chief administration of supply) of the ministry. Glavsnab sends them to the corresponding department of Gosplan. In Gosplan they are carefully examined, and then a material balance, which is designed to ensure that requirements during the planned year will be consistent with production, is drawn up, and a production plan and a distribution plan based on it is worked out. The distribution plan is a detailed version of the requirements side of a material balance, which subdivides 'production needs' and 'capital construction' by organ (e.g. ministry).

In the distribution plan for 1968, 122 quota holders were listed (a quota holder is an organisation, such as a ministry, which has been allocated a quota of a commodity) and in addition under the heading 'other con- sumers' another 40 organisations were listed, the precise size of whose quota was determined by the glavsnabsbyty (chief administration of supply and marketing) of Gossnab USSR. Each of the quota holders listed in the distri- bution plan subdivides its quota among its subordinate organs, which sub- divides them into quotas for the enterprises. When the enterprises recieve their quotas they specify their requirements in detail (within the limits of the quota) and submit them to the supply organs. The supply orgāns, on the basis of the specified quotas of the consumer enterprises issue detailed orders (quotas) to the producer enterprises, and arrange for the attachment of consumers to producers and the allocation of orders between producers.

From the point of view of the planning of production, commodities are divided into the most important ones the plans for which are included in the State plan for the development of the national economy of the USSR, and the less important ones whose output is planned by the ministries. For example, in 1968 the nomenclature of industrial products in the state plan was 615, and the total number of centrally planned products (i.e. products planned by a central organ such as a ministry) was about 40 000. 'The starting point for the planning of the volumes of production *in physical terms* is the determin- ation of the requirements of the national economy for particular types of pro- ducts'.[6] The calculations of requirements for intermediate goods are based on the sum of the indents of consumers, which are based on norms for the utilisation of materials. The calculations of requirements for consumer goods are based on consumption norms and estimates of demand for particular goods.[7] The calculation of requirements for machines and equipment are based on the plans for *komplektirovanie*.[a] Simultaneously with calculations of requirements, calculations of productive possibilities are being undertaken. The following basic types of calculation are performed, calculations of the availability of deficit raw materials; calculations of the utilisation of deficit raw materials; calculations of productive capacities and their utilisation; calculations of the equipment required for the replacement of old equipment and the expansion of capacity; and calculations of the labour force and the possibilities of attracting additional workers.

Comparing and analysing all these calculations, the planning organs determine the maximum possible volume of output feasible with the materials and equipment available. For coordinating requirements and output the following methods are used, searching for possibilities of economising on materials and substituting less scarce materials for scarce ones; searching for the possibility of increasing production by expanding productive

(a) *Komplektirovanie* is the process of ensuring that complementary machines and equipment are available in the necessary sets and are not supplied in an indi- vidual, uncoordinated and useless way. Attached to Gossnab are a number of chief administrations for the *komplektirovanie* of particular sorts of equipment, such as *Soyuzglavneftekomplekt* for oil industry equipment, which are mainly concerned with the supply of sets of equipment to new enterprise or enter- prises which are being reconstructed.

capacities and using the existing capacity more efficiently, more rational utilisation of materials and a reduction in the output of less scarce products; importing scarce materials and equipment; and if it is impossible to increase the volume of resources, determining which are the primary needs, to be met in full, and the degree of fulfilment of the non-priority needs.

The results of all these calculations are expressed in the material balances, which are worked out for the more important products, and in the plans for production and distribution.

From the point of view of the enterprise, the planning process ends with the working out of the final version of the *tekhpromfinplan*. From the point of view of relations between producers and consumers it ends with the con- clusion of contracts between the supply organs and the producer, and the supply organs and the consumer, or directly between the consumer and the producer. From the point of view of the chief administrations of Gossnab, it ends with the working out of the final versions of the attachment plans and the production schedules. From the point of view of the ministry it ends with the splitting up of the production plan and the quotas between its enterprises. From the point of view of Gosplan USSR it ends with the working out of the final versions of the production plans, the distribution plans, the plans for inter-republican deliveries, and the plans for the delivery of output for all- Union needs (i.e. plans for the supply of resources to consumers having all- Union significance) for all of the commodities for which Gosplan is respon- sible. During the planned period it is necessary to ensure that the plan is fulfilled. After the planned period is over it is necessary to report on the extent of fulfilment to the statistical organs.

Figure 6.1 which shows the process of compiling the plan for the produc- tion and distribution of mineral fertilisers may help in giving some picture of the relationships involved.[8]

From a formal point of view, the long process of planning and counter planning, which begins with the elaboration of control figures by Gosplan USSR and the submission to the ministries by enterprises of suggestions for the plan, and ends with the working out of the final version of the plan, can be regarded as an informal iterative process designed to solve the following problem.[a] Consider a multi-commodity multi-enterprise economy where pro- duction takes place in discrete time periods. The problem of drawing up a consistent national economic plan for any period can be represented as the problem of finding numbers

---

(a) The procedure is analogous to the non-rigorous iterative way in which short term forecasts have traditionally been compiled in the UK Treasury. In both countries the apostles of formalised model building are appalled, and in both they are having considerable success in introducing new techniques.

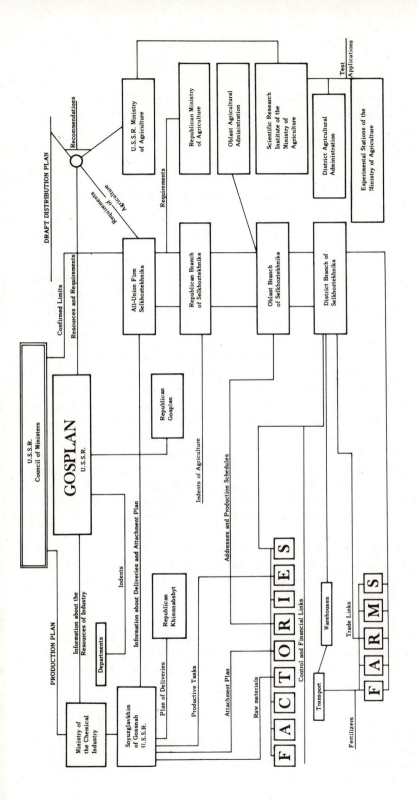

Fig. 6.1 *The process of formulating the plan for the production and distribution of mineral fertilisers for the USSR*

65

$$\begin{matrix} a_{11} \, a_{12} & \cdots & a_{1n} \\ \cdots\cdots\cdots & \cdots\cdots\cdots\cdots & \\ a_{m1} \, a_{m2} & \cdots & a_{mn} \end{matrix} \qquad \begin{matrix} m \to \infty \\ n \;=\; 60\,000^{(a)} \end{matrix}$$

where a_{ij} is the amount of the ith good produced at the jth enterprise (if $a_{ij} > 0$) or required (if $a_{ij} < 0$) in the process of production by the jth enterprise.

Subject to the conditions

$$a_j \in A_j \qquad\qquad j \;=\; 1 \ldots n \qquad\qquad (1)$$

where a_j is the vector $(a_{1j}, a_{2j}, \ldots a_{mj})$ and A_j is the set of feasible plans for the jth enterprise; and

$$\sum_{j=1}^{n} a_{ij} + b_i \geqslant 0 \qquad\qquad i \;=\; 1 \ldots m \qquad\qquad (2)$$

where b_i is the stock of the ith good at the start of the period, and b_i' is the desired stock at the end of the period. Condition (1) is that no enterprise receives an impossible plan. A plan may be impossible for technical reasons (because the planned input-output pattern is technologically not feasible) or for economic reasons (because the planned inputs cannot be made available or the planned outputs cannot be sold). If condition (1) is violated this will show itself during the planned period as a breakdown in the supply system, or as difficulties with marketing, or in the need to alter enterprise plans, or some combination of these undesirable, but frequent, phenomena. Condition (2) is that the output of each commodity is enough to meet the requirements of the system. If condition (2) is violated this will show itself during the planned period as a breakdown in the supply system, or the alteration of the plans, or as the de facto creation of non-priority sectors which have to make do as best they can, of the accumulation of unwanted stocks, or some combination of these undesirable, but frequent phenomena.

Define a 'consistent plan' as a matrix A which satisfies conditions (1) and (2). The chief difficulties in compiling a consistent plan are:

I) Collecting the necessary data. The data on requirements available to the central planners are based on the indents of the enterprises, adjusted and aggregated by the intermediate bodies. This data is not very reliable for the following reasons:

a) The indents are sent in before the enterprises know their output plans, at a time therefore when they are unable to state their requirements precisely. As a recent study has observed, 'it is impossible to base the

(b) The textbook L.Ya. Berri (ed) *Planirovanie narodnogo khozvaistva SSSR* (1968) in its chapter on the planning of supply gives a figure of 42 000 industrial enterprises and 19 000 construction sites as the number whose supply has to be planned (p. 409). A. & N. Kobrinskii give a figure of 20 000 000 as the number of commodities distinguished in the all-union industrial classification in their book *Mnogo li cheloveku nuzhno?* (1969).

determination of real requirements for material resources on the indents because the indents are based on preliminary volumes of output, which are altered to a considerable extent in the process of working out the plan,.[9]

b) The indents of the enterprises are adjusted, in an essentially arbitrary manner, by the intermediate bodies. 'Analysis of the practice of the supply of *sovnarkhoz* enterprises,[a] and also the material published in the press, indicates that the planning organs not infrequently pay little attention to the indents of the consumers ... There are three reasons for refusal to satisfy an indent:

1) insufficient resources;
2) the discovery as a result of economic analysis that the consumer has internal reserves, is exceeding the norms;
3) arbitrary reductions in the indent'.[10]

c) In view of (b) and of the disadvantages of underfulfilling the plan, enterprises are tempted to overstate their needs (and understate their productive possibilities) in reports to the centre.

d) The process of aggregating requirements, and subsequently of disaggregating the production and distribution plans, destroys some of the information on the times, places and quantities in which particular commodities are required. This is analysed in appendix 1 below.

II) Processing the necessary data. A limited number of officials, divided into numerous departments, and armed with telephones, pens and abacuses — or more sophisticated equipment — have only a limited time to solve this problem, which is very complex both because of its huge dimensions and because the variables are interrelated. When, during the course of plan calculations the output of one commodity is altered, it is necessary to alter the outputs of other commodities which are direct inputs into the process of production of the commodity whose output is to be increased, which involves increasing the output of the commodities which are indirect inputs into the process of production of the commodity whose output is to be increased, and conversely when during the course of plan calculations the output of one commodity is reduced.

A prominent Soviet economist has observed that 'every year it becomes more difficult to balance the economy, to complete a plan for its development, to control it ...
... the chief difficulty is that with the existing system of planning and control, based on manual calculations and the perception of a limited amount of information by a planner, it is difficult not only to find an optimal solution to the development of an economy, but physically impossible to balance the plan. For the compilation of such a plan for the tens of thousands of products for which the USSR state plan set targets, requires the carrying out

(a) The *sovnarkhozy* were the regional economic councils which administered industry from 1957 to 1965.

of milliards of calculations (mathematically this is a problem of solving a system of linear equations) whereas a man, equiped with a desk calculator can do 1000–2000 calculations per day. Even if the splitting up of this work were possible (which is impossible with these relationships) the whole apparatus of Gosplan could not do one-hundreth part of the necessary calculations for this group of plan indices'. [11]

The data processing problems involved in drawing up a consistent plan take the following form:

(a) The planning of production and supply for the entire economy is regarded as too large for any one organisation, and accordingly is split up among many organisations. This creates three sorts of problems:

(1) The organisations other than Gosplan USSR which allocate resources, such as the chief administrations of Gossnab, scarcely use the method of balances for securing consistency. They predominantly rely on the 'method' of planning from the achieved level. 'This leads, and must inevitably lead, to mistakes.' [12]

(2) If the various organisations concerned make incompatible assumptions, then inconsistent plans will emerge.

(3) Because the planning of production and supply is split up between numerous organisations and because de facto an enterprise is obliged to accept the instructions of all the higher bodies, it often happens that an enterprise receives conflicting or impossible plans. In particular, when the production plan and the quotas for the scarcest materials are received from Gosplan and the ministry, and the requirements for the less scarce goods are supposed to be satisfied by the local supply organs, it may well happen that the local supply organs are unable to supply those commodities which are essential for meeting the production plans.

(b) The planning of production and supply for all the commodities produced and consumed in the economy is regarded as too big a problem to be solved, and accordingly the authorities concern themselves only with the more important commodities (16 000 in 1968). This reduces the size of the problem from millions of equations to thousands of equations, but it introduces into the planning process aggregation errors, the possibility of a shortage of or the waste of an unplanned commodity, and hidden shortages. When the planning work is finished and the balances appear to be balanced, there may well be a hidden shortage of products whose output is not planned centrally but which are used as inputs into the production of centrally planned products, because the requirements for these non-centrally planned products, implicit in the output plans of the centrally planned products, are greater than their output (which is not centrally planned). As the deputy head of one of the departments of Gosplan USSR has put it: 'One of the reasons for inconsistencies is that materials which are necessary for the production of centrally planned products are themselves not completely included in the list of centrally planned products, and therefore the balancing of production and requirements in the planning organs is not completed.' [13]

(c) The process of specifying the quotas, that is, of obtaining through the supply organs or by direct contacts the precise goods needed (which are stated only in broad terms in the quotas) often gives rise to considerable difficulties. 'Under this system the production plan often does not fully correspond to the specific orders, and the latter are satisfied either not fully, or in a different assortment to that required.' [14] Five types of problem in particular arise during the process of specifying the quotas.

(1) Suppliers may not wish to supply goods of the type required. For example, when planning is in tons, metallurgical enterprises are not very keen on producing thin steel sheets, which may be useful to consumers but are costly to produce and do not contribute much to plan fulfilment. As an official of the Byelorussian supply organisation has observed: 'There are many complaints about shortages of special steels, rolled products, cold rolled sheet steel etc. At the same time there is a certain surplus of ordinary steel, thick construction and hot rolled sheet steel etc. One of the reasons for this inconsistency is the fact that the production of steel is planned in tons. Under this system of planning the metallurgical enterprises are not interested in producing thin sheet steel, because it is light in weight and labour intensive to produce.' [15] In the administrative economy, with its permanent sellers' market, producer enterprises are in a strong position and are often able to act in accordance with their own interests regardless of the effect of their actions on consumer enterprises.

(2) The producer enterprise may not be able to produce the goods required, because it lacks the necessary inputs. Months earlier, when it sent in its indent it did not know what its production plan would be. If it turns out that the orders it is now receiving differ substantially from those that it anticipated, it will be impossible to fulfil them because of the lack of the necessary inputs. [a]

(3) The producer enterprise may not be able to produce the goods required because the plan, though balanced in aggregated terms is unbalanced in disaggregated terms, that is the demand for some goods exceeds productive possibilities as a result of aggregation errors. Take tubes (of the type used in oil pipelines). In terms of tons of tubes, supply and demand may appear to be in equilibrium, but the demand for a particular sort of tube may far exceed the supply possibilities for that type of tube.

(4) A producer enterprise may find itself with insufficient orders to fulfil its production plan. This often happens as a result of enterprises stating at the end of the planning process that they do not want goods which they ordered earlier in the planning process. The following example indicates how this can happen. Take an enterprise producing a good required for investment projects, for example, cranes. It may appear to have an assured demand for cranes, based on the investment plans of its customers. The last plan to be confirmed is the investment plan. It may well happen, as a result

(a) A graphic account of this problem will be found in appendix 2 below.

of a central campaign to reduce the wasteful spreading of investment resources over numerous unfinished projects, that many of these investment
plans are rejected. The enterprises concerned then inform the crane plant
that they no longer want cranes. The crane plant, which seemed to have an
assured demand, now finds, at the beginning of the planned year, that it is
in serious danger of underfulfilling its production plan. Another reason for
enterprises not having enough orders is that quota holders may not need all
the products listed in their quota — they only applied for them so as to have
a margin in hand against a reduction in their supply requests or an increase
in their production plan, by the higher bodies.[16]

(5) The planning process is often not completed in the planning year,
so that enterprises begin the year without a final *tekhpromfinplan*.

The main technique used to ensure the efficiency of the plans is the system of norms. The main technique used to ensure the consistency of the
plans is the system of material balances.

Material balances

*The method of material balances is the basic method of planning not only
the volume of production but also the distribution of the means of production between the separate consumers, that is the planning of supply for
the national economy.*

A Soviet textbook[17]

An essential requirement for successful Government regulation of an
economy is a statistical picture of the economy arranged in a way compatible
with the instruments of regulation which the Government uses. In Britain
such a statistical picture is provided by the national accounts, which provide the information necessary for the regulation of the economy by fiscal
means, and by financial statistics which provide the information necessary
for the regulation of the economy by monetary methods. In the Soviet Union
the necessary statistical information is arranged in a series of 'balances',
the 'balance of the national economy' and its subdivisions.[(a)] The way that
the material balances fit into the system of balances is shown in the figure
6.2.[18]

A material balance shows, on the one hand the economy's resources, and
on the other hand the economy's needs, for a particular product for a
specified period of time. A material balance can be arraged schematically
as in table 6.2. The entries are reasonable self-explanatory. The material
balances differ somewhat according to whether they are for producer goods
or consumer goods, or compiled by the central organs or by a republican
organ.[19]

The method of material balances is unable to lead to the compilation of
consistent plans because the material balances are not complete, nor universal, nor do they form an integrated system, nor does technology

(a) Some of the balances record stocks, others show flows.

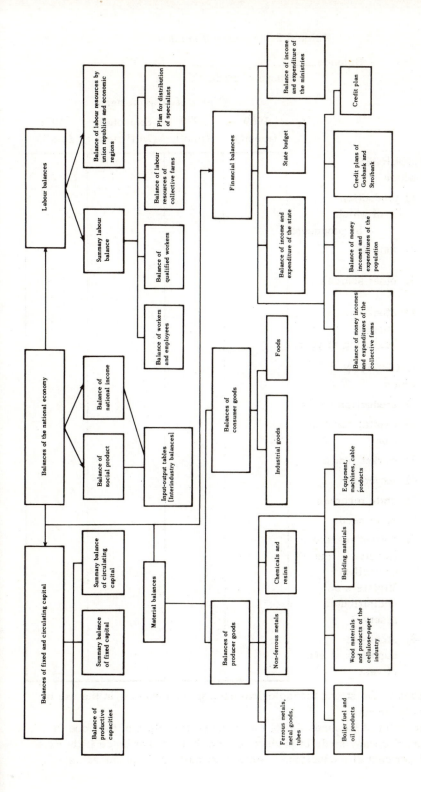

Fig. 6.2 *The system of balances of the national economy*

Table 6.2 *A material balance*

Balance _____ for 1971
(name of product)

(Units of measurement)

	1969 (report)	1970 (plan)	Expected fulfilment	1971 (draft)
I. RESOURCES of which				
1) production of which by producers				
2) imports				
3) other sources				
4) stocks at suppliers at beginning of year				
II. DISTRIBUTION of which				
1) production needs				
2) capital construction				
3) market fund				
4) exports				
5) state reserves				
6) other needs				
7) current reserve (reserve of the Council of Ministers or undistributed reserve)				
8) stocks at suppliers at end of year				

correspond to the strong technological assumptions implicit in the use of material balances.

Often material balances do not cover the entire output of the good in question. For many kinds of product material balances embrace little more than 60 per cent of production.[20] When commodity A is produced as a subsidiary product of enterprise X belonging to industry B, then X's output of A may not be known to the central planners nor to the sectoral planners responsible for the A industry.

The material balances are compiled for far fewer commodities than are produced in the economy. For most commodities balance calculations are not performed, either because they are included in a very aggregated way in balances which are calculated, or because they are altogether excluded from balance calculations.

The compilers of material balances are primarily concerned with balancing the output and requirements for a single commodity. Diagrammatically compilers of material balances are doing calculations of the type:

rather than calculations of the type:[21]

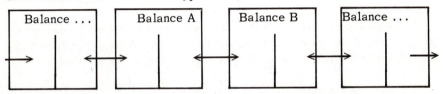

When during the course of the material balance calculations the output of one product is altered, consistency requires that the outputs of all the products that directly or indirectly are used in the production of that commodity, are altered. For example an increase in the production of cars entails an increase in the production of steel, which in turn entails an increase in the production of electricity, which in its turn ... In practice however, Efimov has explained that:

'Because of the great labour intensity of the calculation of changes in the material balances and the insufficiency of time for the completion of such work, in practice sometimes only those balances which are linked by first order relationships are changed. As regards relationships of the second order, and especially of the third and fourth order, changes in the balances are made only in those cases where the changes are conspicuous.'[22]

In other words, whereas consistency requires the evaluation of the convergent series

$$X = (I + A + A^2 + A^3 \ldots) Y$$

it often happens that X is approximated by considering the first two terms only. In view of the fact that the process of calculation is often cut short, inconsistencies are to be expected, in principle. The practical importance of this depends on the ratio of direct inputs to full inputs and the number of iterations required for consistency. TsSU, working on the 1959 input-output table for the USSR in value terms, found that usually the ratio between direct inputs and full inputs was between 1 and 2, but that much larger values occurred quite frequently, ranging up to 54.7! The number of iterations required for the estimated value of X to attain the true value of X has been estimated by Levine at between 6 and 13.

On the other hand it has been shown, using Soviet data, that in many cases two rounds of iteration were enough to bring direct input coefficients quite close to full input coefficients.[23] Furthermore, the number of iterations required is reduced by the existence of bottlenecks. The planners can arrive at a consistent plan without matrix inversion, through iteration, provided that the outputs in the excess capacity sectors are adapted to the potentials of the bottleneck sectors.[24] In addition the number of iterations required for consistency can also be reduced if the input-output matrix has certain special properties, e.g. if it can be triangulated. Soviet experience has shown that in many industries a small number of coefficients account for a large proportion of the inputs, which reduces the number of feedback effects which it is necessary to take into account when making alterations to projected inputs during the plan calculations.[25]

The method of material balances assumes that the process production can be represented by a matrix of fixed coefficients (the norms). For each commodity requirements are assumed to be represented by the relation

$$x_i = \sum_{j=1}^{n} a_{ij} x_j + y_i \qquad\qquad i = 1 \dots n$$

where x_i is the output of the ith product,

a_{ij} is the norm of requirements of the ith product per unit of output of the jth product, and

y_i is the requirements of the ith product for final demand.

This is a very strong assumption, which rules out substitutability, non-proportional inputs, learning by doing and non-constant returns to scale, and there is no reason to suppose that it is in general true. Hence one would not expect the material balance calculations to produce accurate results.

The norms used in the calculations are generally averages weighted in favour of the more efficient producers. This creates two problems. First, for efficient producers the norms may be too soft and provide no incentive to efficiency, and conversely, for inefficient producers they may be impossible. Secondly, when during the process of plan calculations the relative outputs of plants with different input-output relationships is altered, this alters the actual mean input-output relationship. If the planners continue to use a given norm, then inconsistencies will result. (This is an example of an aggregation error.)

Input-output

'The calculation of material balances for separate products, in the course of which numerous alterations are made, is insufficient for maintaining interindustry proportions, for reflecting in the plans all the connections and relations between production and consumption. The theory of planning has worked out a method which allows these connections to be taken into account more fully and more precisely, the input-output table in physical and value terms. Its utilisation allows us simultaneously to solve a number of problems, to plan the volumes of output and the distribution of production by industries, to determine the material inputs into production and the utilisation of the national income.'

V.F. Kotov (deputy head of a
department of Gosplan USSR)[26]

An input-output table is a way of arranging the national accounts which focuses attention on the productive relationships between industries. In Soviet statistical practice an input-output table is regarded 'as an organic part of the balance of the national economy, as its further development, and above all as the development and disaggregation of the balance of the production, consumption and accumulation of the national income.'[27]

The concept of an economy as a circular flow of commodities goes back to Quesnay's *Tableau Economique*. The first set of national accounts providing data on productive relationships between industries was that compiled by the USSR Central Statistical Administration in the 1920s.[28] Leontief, aware of the Soviet work,[29] subsequently developed, in the United States, a mathematical model which provides a convenient way of arranging, and a useful way of analysing and extrapolating, statistics on inter-industry relations. Since the government's instruction to TsSU and Gosplan of November 1959 on the compilation of input-output tables, a great deal of effort has been devoted in the USSR to the compilation of input-output tables. Accounting flow input-output tables for the USSR in value, physical and labour terms for 1959 and 1966 have been compiled by TsSU. TsSU has also compiled an accounting capital stock matrix for 1966. Planning input-output tables in value terms for 1962 and 1970 have been compiled by Gosplan's Research Institute, which is currently working on planning input-output tables for 1975 and 1980. Planning input-output tables in physical terms were worked out by Gosplan's Chief Computing Centre for 1962, 1963–65, and 1970. Research organisations have compiled a large number of regional input-output tables, a field in which TSEMI has been active. The Institute of Economics and the Organisation of Industrial Production has done some work for Gosplan on dynamic input-output models. Soviet work on input-output is summarised in appendix 4.

Soviet specialists consider that the introduction of the input-output method into planning practice should take place neither by the sudden supersession of the traditional methods by the new methods,[30] nor by the creation within the planning apparatus of special departments for economic-mathematical methods divorced from the planning mainstream, but that input-output should be gradually introduced into the work of the planning organs. (In actual practice what has tended to happen has been the creation within the planning organs of special departments for the introduction of economic-mathematical methods divorced from the planning mainstream.) [31]

The construction of input-output tables gives rise to numerous problems. 'The most complicated and labour intensive part of the work on an accounting input-output table is to obtain and process the necessary statistical information.' [32] As the statistical information which the enterprises send to TsSU is inadequate, the necessary additional information is obtained by sample surveys. [33] The existing data on the production and consumption of agricultural products produced on their private plots by collective farmers and others, are not very reliable.

Economic activity takes place in enterprises, which are grouped into administrative units (firms in capitalist countries, associations or economic ministries in the USSR). As input-output is concerned with data about technological relationships to be used in planning, it is desirable that data be collected about the enterprises, and not about the administrative units into which they are grouped. [34] Where an enterprise produces, in addition to its main product, subsidiary products, it is desirable that the subsidiary output, and the inputs necessary to produce it, be transferred to the appropriate industry. [35] (The proportion of 'foreign' outputs depends on the detail of the classification.) In this way it is possible to arrive at a 'commodity–commodity' table. Call the method of classification which does not take into account the fact that enterprises may produce more than one commodity, the 'industry–industry' classification. The difference between the two can be very great as table 6.3 which refers to Lithuania in 1961 clearly shows.

Many Soviet economists consider that unlike input-output tables constructed on an industry-industry basis, which reflect only the trading relationships between enterprises, input-output tables constructed on a commodity-commodity basis reflect the technological relationships of the process of production.

Either those inputs which come to the enterprise from outside, or all inputs regardless of whether they come to the enterprise from outside or from an earlier stage in the process of production within the enterprise itself, can be considered as inputs. [In Soviet statistical practice the former is known as the 'gross output' (*valovaya produktsiya*) method, the latter as the 'gross turnover' (*volovoi oborot*) method.] Input coefficients calculated from statistics gathered using the former method are determined not only by technology but also by the extent of vertical integration, and therefore the latter method is preferable for planning.

In general it is desirable that statistics for input-output purposes be collected from enterprises and not from groups of enterprises, that they allocate subsidiary activities correctly, and that the gross turnover method is used. These points are more important in the USSR than they would be in say, the U.K., because Soviet enterprises are less specialised. All Soviet input-output tables are based on data collected from enterprises and are 'commodity-commodity' tables rather than 'industry-industry' tables. In some cases the gross output method is used, in others the gross turnover method. The latter is favoured by most economists in this field, and by TSEMI, the former by TsSU.

Table 6.3 *The relationship between a 'commodity-commodity' and 'industry-industry' calculation of the outputs of particular industries with a 239 industry classification*[36]

(1)	(2) Volume of production of the industry's product produced in enterprises belonging to the industry itself	(3) Volume of production of 'foreign' products produced by enterprises belonging to the industry as % of column (2)	(4) Volume of production of the given industry produced by enterprises belonging to other industries as % of column (2)
Wine making	100	0.5	139.9
Non-alcoholic drinks	100	–	128.0
Yeast	100	1.9	92.4
Medical instruments and equipment	100	331.2	90.4
Concentrated feeds	100	–	87.0
Equipment for the building materials trade	100	202.3	81.0
Electricity and thermal power generation	100	1.3	66.7
Tractors and Agricultural machinery	100	40.6	64.0
Constructional engineering	100	72.8	48.2

The question of which prices to use in value input-output tables has been much debated in the Soviet Union.[37] TsSU uses the prices actually paid by consumers. TSEMI prefers producer prices (i.e. costs plus profit and turnover tax but excluding trade and transport expenses). The use of prices to aggregate commodities introduces into calculations utilising the tables the possibility of aggregation errors.

Another problem concerns the units to be used in physical input-output tables. In the input-output model it is assumed that each industry produces only one product, and that every product is uniform, and therefore it is possible to sum the rows in physical units. In all the input-output tables which it is feasible to construct, however, each industry produces a physically heterogeneous collection of goods. In Soviet practice, output is measured not only in natural physical units, but also in conventional physical units, and money. Conventional physical units (e.g. the measurement of various fuels in tons of coal equivalent) are used where it is clear that natural physical units do not reflect consumers' valuations. As a Soviet expert in this field puts it: 'Physical measures (weight, volume, area and so on) often cannot reflect quantitatively the consumers'value of goods.[38] ... The establishment of conventional units for the measurement of output, which convert physical measures to volumes of consumers' value has a progressive significance. Such indices are widely used in the input-output table.'[39] Where the output of an industry is very heterogeneous, e.g. the engineering industries, and the furniture industry, output is measured in money, using constant prices. The use of physical input-output tables composed of 'commodities' aggregated in this way, introduces into the calculations the possibility of aggregation errors.[a]

The input-output model assumes that all the outputs are proportional to inputs. In fact in many industries this is not so, as a number of writers have pointed out.[40] In some of the regional input-output tables attempts have been made to isolate the non-proportional inputs.[41]

The input-output model assumes that each output is produced by only one technique. In fact many goods are produced by several techniques, e.g. electricity from coal, oil or uranium. Similarly the input structures of the extractive and agricultural industries vary according to the location of the activity. This can be allowed for by setting each technique in a column of its own.

The compilation of planning input-output tables raises a number of further problems, how to estimate future technology, future personal consumption, future capital investments, and future exports and imports. The task of projecting the technical coefficients is made much easier by the fact that the vast majority of them are either zero or of negligible importance. 'Calculations by the Economic Research Institute of the State Economic Council showed that in the accounting input-output table 10–15 per cent of the coefficients in each industry embraced 90–95 per cent of all the inputs.'[42] Gosplan's Economic Research Institute analysed the coefficients of the 83 × 83 all-Union table to find out by what percentage it was necessary to alter the input coefficients of each industry in order to produce a one per cent change in the output of that industry. It turned out that 86 per cent of the non-zero coefficients had to be altered by more than 100 per cent to produce such a 1 per cent change in the output of the industry concerned.[43] A method has been developed to distinguish between the less important and the more important coefficients.[44]

When Gosplan's research institute worked out the planning input-output

(a) In accordance with normal Soviet practice, the top left hand quadrant of Soviet input-output tables usually only embraces 'material production' and excludes 'non-productive' branches of the economy. (It has been argued, however, that 'all work in a socialist economy is productive, that there are no unproductive classes or social groups.' A reviewer commented approvingly on this argument, adding that 'from the point of view of optimal planning the division of labour into productive and simply socially useful is senseless. All kinds of labour, satisfying a social need, i.e. making a definite contribution to the criterion of optimality, receive shadow prices corresponding to the quantity of their contribution.' *Ekonomika i matematicheskie metody* vol. 2, No. 5, p. 797.)

table for 1970 as part of the work on the 1966–70 five year plan,[a] the less important coefficients were largely taken from the 1959 accounting table, or extrapolated from it. The more important coefficients were projected by the 'method of technical-economic forecasting', by which is meant the following procedure. First, about 200 industrial research institutes and design organisations, on the basis of their estimates of the development of their industry, produced estimates of the chief input coefficients. Subsequently, these initial estimates were made more precise on the basis of detailed studies of technical progress and the structure of production. The forecast input coefficients were based on estimates of 15 000 norms in physical terms, which were then aggregated. The number and importance of the forecast input-output coefficients are set out in table 6.4.

Experience has shown that the big problem in projecting the technical coefficients is not in estimating technical progress in the production of goods already in production, but in estimating changes in the structure of production, i.e. the 'birth' of new products and the 'death' of old ones.[b]

The structure of personal consumption was determined mainly by extrapolation, when working out the planning input-output tables for 1970. The limited attention paid to income elasticities of demand was defended partly on the ground of the unsatisfactory nature of the household budget data, and partly on the revealing ground that in general productive possibilities, rather than demand, determines the volume of sales.[46] The forecasts for social consumption are usually based on plan norms, for example the number of hospital beds required per thousand inhabitants.

Accurate estimation of future capital investment is particularly important in a country where gross capital formation amounts to 35 per cent of the national income.[47] When the planning input-output tables were worked out in connection with the 1966–70 five year plan, the volume of investment required to support various alternative growth paths was in general calculated according to the formula:

$$K = \frac{\{[X_1 - X_0 (1 + k_u + k_r)]c_n + X_0 k_r c_r\} (\beta + n_1) + \bar{f}_0 (b + \rho + n_0)}{1 - d_{pr}}$$

(a) The work done by Gosplan's research institute in working out a planning input-output table for 1970 was similar in many respects to the work done by the Cambridge Growth Project in working out planning social accounts for the UK for 1970. In both cases the aim of the work was to produce a range of possibilities between which an informed political choice could be made, and in both, personal consumption, investment, government expenditure, and the input-output coefficients for 1970 were estimated, and used to calculate variants of the outputs of the main industries of the economy in 1970. Interesting features of the Soviet work were the reliance on estimates by specialist institutes, rather than on extrapolation, for estimates of the planning input-output coefficients; and the large number of industries distinguished in the Soviet planning input-output table (130).

(b) Information supplied at interview in Latvian Institute of Economics, Riga.

Table 6.4 *Some features of the matrix of direct input coefficients in the planning input-output table for 1970* [45]

Industry	No. of sub-industries	No. of direct input coefficients		% of material inputs embraced by the forecast coefficients
		Total	Calculated by the method of technical-economic forecasting	
Metallurgy	7	422	92	97
Fuel	7	385	60	96
Electrical	1	59	7	95
Engineering & metal working	39	2477	692	69
Chemicals	11	668	198	84
Wood & wood processing	5	318	106	94
Building materials	14	579	577	100
Light industry	12	488	60	92
Food industry	14	678	168	93
Agriculture & forestry	3	110	64	96
Building	5	256	238	97
Other branches of material production	7	287	58	35
Total	125	6727	2320	88

where K is the volume of investment in the industry being considered,

X_1 is the volume of output of the industry planned for the final year of the planned period,

X_0 is the volume of output of the industry in the base year,

k_u is a coefficient which characterises the increase in output which is possible by improving the utilisation of existing capital,

k_r is a coefficient which characterises the increase in output from the expansion and reconstruction of existing enterprises,

c_n is a coefficient of the capital intensity of new building,

c_r is a coefficient of the capital intensity of the expansion and reconstruction of existing enterprises,

β is a coefficient which characterises the relationship of the full increase in capital to the average annual increase in the planned period,

$\bar{f_0}$ is the volume of capital in the base year,

b is a coefficient characterising the depreciation of fixed capital in the planned period,

n_0 is the norm of unfinished construction at the beginning of the planned period,

n_1 is the norm of unfinished construction at the end of the planned period,

ρ is the norm of investment in maintaining capacity, and

d_{pr} is the share of investment which does not increase the value of fixed capital.

All the norms used in determining the requirements of each industry for investment, were worked out by the industrial scientific research and design institutes in accordance with the methodology worked out by Gosplan's research institute.

Economic planning is a hierarchical, or multi-level process. At the top the time path of a few summary indices, e.g. national income, is decided, at the bottom the expansion plans of every enterprise. The calculations made at every stage can be summarised in a model, which indicates the assumptions made, the data required, and the steps in the process. The strategy of development can be analysed with the help of an extremely aggregated growth model. A classic case is the Feldman model, which brings out clearly (on the assumptions made) the advantages of concentrating on heavy industry. More recently, Mikhalevsky has attempted to use a number of tools borrowed from Western economic thought (e.g. production functions) to explain past Soviet economic growth and lay the foundation for planning the macro-economic indices.[48] Input-output is a tool to be used at a lower level of the planning hierarchy, to plan the relationships between the various industries. It forms a link between planning the basic national economic indices and the plans for separate industries and regions.[49] A Soviet economist has suggested that input-output fits into planning as illustrated in Fig. 6.3.[50]

Although input-output tables have been compiled in the Soviet Union for a decade, their integration into the planning process has proceeded slowly. The integration of input-output into the planning process gives rise to numerous problems:

1. The results of input-output calculations may be irrelevant to planning because the indices of the plan and those of the input-output table are non-comparable.[a] For example:

(a) The input-output tables themselves may be non-comparable because different methods are used in their compilation. The all-Union tables compiled by TsSU are in consumer prices. The input-output tables for the Baltic republics, compiled under the aegis of TSEMI, are in producer prices. The compilers of the 1959 all-Union value and physical tables used different methods of calculating inputs. In the value table, only those inputs were calculated which came from outside the enterprise concerned, whereas in the physical table all inputs, including those produced within the enterprise itself, were included.

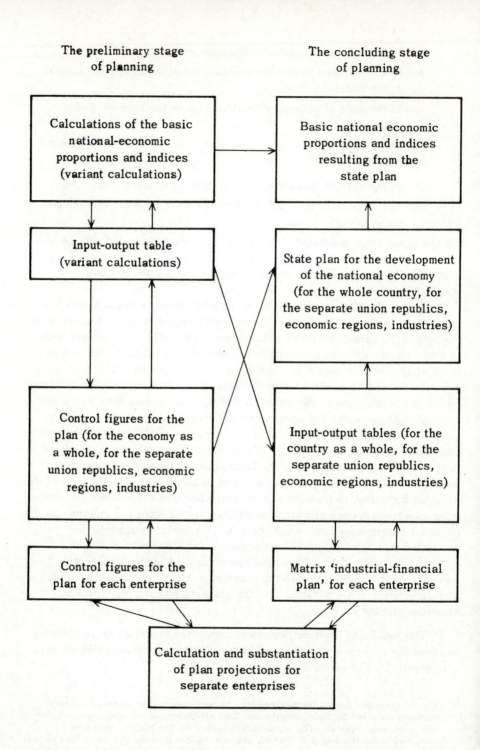

The preliminary stage
of planning

The concluding stage
of planning

Calculations of the basic
national-economic
proportions and indices
(variant calculations)

Basic national economic
proportions and indices
resulting from the
state plan

Input-output table
(variant calculations)

State plan for the development
of the national economy
(for the whole country, for
the separate union republics,
economic regions, industries)

Control figures for the
plan (for the economy as
a whole, for the separate
union republics, economic
regions, industries)

Input-output tables (for the
country as a whole, for the
separate union republics,
economic regions, industries)

Control figures for the
plan for each enterprise

Matrix 'industrial-financial
plan' for each enterprise

Calculation and substantiation
of plan projections for
separate enterprises

Fig. 6.3 *The suggested use of input-output in planning*

a) Input-output tables include all the output of particular products. Plan calculations ignore the small industrial enterprises, run by state farms, building trade and transport organisations, and collective farms and consumer cooperatives.

b) The product classification of the plan, and of the input-output table may be different. When comparing the 1959 all-Union physical input-output table with the basic indices of the seven year plan, it was found that only 77 products were comparable, 80 products in the input-output table were not in the plan nomenclature, and 33 products in the plan nomenclature were not in the input-output nomenclature.[a]

c) Plans and input-output tables are calculated in different prices. (Enterprise wholesale prices + turnover tax = producer prices (industry wholesale prices). Producer prices + trade and transport costs = final consumer prices.)

'In plan calculations output is calculated in enterprise wholesale prices, and social product in industrial wholesale prices. The method of compiling planning input-output tables used at the present time such that in them products are reckoned in those prices at which were calculated the accounting input-output table. Because the first, and last, accounting input-output table was worked out by the Central Statistical Administration in final consumer prices of 1959, all the planning input-output tables are calculated in those prices. In this way, as a result of using different prices, 'output' in the input-output calculations exceeds 'output' in the plan calculations by the extent of the turnover tax and the trade-transport mark up.

Consequently, the volume of output of an industry for the planned year arrived at by the input-output calculations must be translated from final consumer prices of 1959 to producer prices of 1959, and finally, to enterprise wholesale prices of that year, the prices of which are accepted as comparable to those of the planned period (up to 1966 comparable prices for the measurement of the gross output of industry are the enterprise wholesale prices of July 1955). Such a three stage re-estimation of the volume of output can scarcely avoid lowering the reliability of the estimates.'[51]

(a) Up till now TsSU used an industrial classification for checking the fulfilment of the plan different from that used by Gosplan in planning the economy. In planning gross and sold output 54 branches and subbranches of industry were distinguished, and for investment more than 150. TsSU gathered data on the fulfilment of the plan on the basis of a classification into 240 branches and subbranches. 'All this has created considerable difficulties in working out plans and in the analysis of the most important economic indices.' (*Ekonomicheskaya Gazeta* 1968 No. 46, p. 14.)

The new *Metodicheskie ukazaniya k sostavleniyu gosudarstvennogo plana razvitiya narodnogo khozyaistva SSSR* (1969) contains a unified industrial classification worked out by Gosplan together with TsSU. This classification *ought* to be used by all the organisations concerned with the planning and control of, or research into, the economy. There are still unresolved problems with this classification. (*Planovoye khozyaistvo* 1969 No. 6, p. 22.)

d) Soviet input-output tables are based on a 'commodity-commodity' classification, whereas plans are drawn up for industries, where by 'industry' is meant a totality of enterprises, and for enterprises. (This is a more serious difficulty in the Soviet Union than it would be in Britain because Soviet industry is less specialised.) Gosplan's Research Institute has worked out a way of arranging the inter-industry flows to allow for this.[52]

e) In planning a group of industries (sewn goods, footwear, woollens, cotton materials, wool scouring, artificial leather, celluloid materials) have their gross outputs calculated differently from all other industries, certain items (raw materials, basic already processed materials and profits) being excluded.

f) There are also other differences between input-output indices and those used in planning practice.[53] 'At the present time to liquidate fully the inconsistencies between the indices of the planning input-output table and the national economic plan, which have been mentioned, is extraordinarily difficult in connection with the lack of the necessary accounting and planning information.'[54]

2. A major difficulty in reconciling input-output with the traditional system of planning by material balances, let alone superseding the latter by the former, is that the latter are worked out for many more products than the former. 'At the present time,' wrote Shvirkov in 1963,

'the USSR Council of Ministers approves in the annual plan for the development of the national economy the volume of production in physical terms of more than 600 types of industrial output. Moreover, about 400 indices which are subdivisions of these 600 products are confirmed in addition. Thus Gosplan USSR must calculate the volume of production of more than 1000 products for submission to the Council of Ministers of the USSR. Naturally, the volume of production of these products must be co-ordinated. Such balancing can most effectively be carried out with the help of an input-output table.'[56]

Pursuing this line of thought would require an input-output table of order 1000 × 1000. Shvirkov suggests 800 × 800 on the ground that this is the upper limit possible with existing computer technology. This approach seems unsatisfactory. Such tables would be difficult to compile and invert. In addition it would leave open the relationship between Gosplan's input-output table and the many thousands of commodities distributed by the supply organs.

3. There has been a tendency in input-output calculations to use 'progressive coefficients', regardless of the production possibilities for 'progressive' goods in short supply, resulting in impossibly high outputs of some goods in the input-output calculations. For example, comparison of necessary output levels as calculated using the physical input-output tables, and using the traditional methods, in 1962 and subsequent years, generally showed close agreement. When there were divergencies, this generally showed, not the inadequacy of traditional methods, but the folly of

using input coefficients for mineral fertilisers into agriculture, or aluminium into cables, which reflected a desirable, but unfeasible, input structure.[56] This problem arises from the fact that in the input-output model technology is fixed and output levels flexible, whereas in planning practice technology is flexible and output levels constrained by resource availability.

4. In order that enterprise plans be consistent with the national or regional input-output tables it is desirable that the enterprise plans be drawn up in matrix form using the same statistical conventions as the input-output tables.[57]

5. There is a shortage of economists competent in this field. (This is of diminishing importance with the rapid growth of higher eduction in economic cybernetics.)

6. The most important practical obstacle to the use of physical input-output tables in planning is that the ones so far compiled fail to account for a large proportion of the output of important products. For example in the plan table for 1963, one third of electricity went to 'other productive uses'.[58]

7. The input-output model assumes that constant returns to scale prevail throughout the economy. In fact, however, increasing returns to scale are normal in manufacturing, diminishing returns in extractive industry, and agricultural production is heavily dependent on 'chance inputs' (e.g. rain, wind and sunshine). Consequently it is not normally possible to rely on an input-output coefficient when the output under consideration is substantially different from the output for which the coefficient was calculated.

Input-output tables are a valuable source of information about the structure of an economy. They give a vivid picture of inter-industry flows, the commodity composition of imports and exports, and the commodity structure of accumulation and consumption; and indicate the main proportions of the economy.[a] For example, analysis of the 1959 all-Union table provided the deputy head of the department for forecasting the development of agriculture of the research institute of Gosplan USSR with the material for a vigorous critique of the inadequate support which agriculture is receiving from industry.[59] Similarly, analysis of the 1961 input-output table for Lithuania, for example, showed that only a very small proportion of Lithuanian industrial production flowed into Lithuanian agriculture. Since Lithuania is mainly an agricultural republic, it was decided that this was unsatisfactory, and that the proportion ought to be increased.[b] The all-Union tables have provided data for an analysis of the efficiency of production, and for price formation.

Because an input-output table can be represented by a simple mathematcal model, and because of the assumption of constant coefficients, an input-output table can be utilised for variant calculations.

(a) For example that in 1959 the 'rate of surplus product' (m/v) in the Soviet Union was 88%. See Eidelman op. cit. p. 276.

(b) Information supplied at interview in Gosplan Lithuania, Vilna.

$$X = (I - A)^{-1}Y$$

assuming that A is given, we can calculate X for varying values of Y. Variant calculations were not undertaken with material balances because of their great labour intensity. Variant calculations have a useful role to play in perspective planning, because they enable the planners to experiment with numerous alternative growth paths and pick the best. The first major use of variant calculations in Soviet national economic planning was in connection with the compilation of the 1966–70 five year plan. Gosplan's research institute analysed the result of various possible shares of accumulation in the national income for 1966–70. It became clear that stepping up the share of accumulation in the national income would increase the rate of growth of the national income, but that this would have very little effect on the rate of growth of consumption (because almost all of the increased output would be producer goods). The results of the calculations are set out in tables 6.5 and 6.6.

Table 6.5   *Structure of the national income for 1970 (in %)*

Components of the national income	Variants				
	I	II	III	IV	V
Consumption	75.2	73.8	72.4	71.0	69.6
Accumulation	24.8	26.2	27.6	29.0	30.4
of which industrial fixed capital	9.0	10.5	12.0	13.5	15.0

Table 6.6   *Average growth rates for 1966–70 (in %)* [60]

	Variants				
	I	II	III	IV	V
National income	5.6	6.1	6.6	7.1	7.5
Consumption	6.7	6.8	6.9	7.0	7.0
Accumulation	2.5	4.1	5.7	7.25	8.7

A sharp increase in the share of accumulation in the national income in the five year plan 1966–70 would lead to a sharp fall in the share of consumption in the national income, and only a small increase in the rate of increase of consumption (within a five year plan period). What is very sensitive to the share of accumulation in the national income is the output of the capital goods industries, as tables 6.7 and 6.8 show.

Table 6.7   *Output of steel on various assumptions*

	Variants				
	I	II	III	IV	V
Production of steel in 1970 (millions of tons)	109	115	121	128	136

Table 6.8   *Average growth rates of selected industries for 1966-70*

	Variants				
	I	II	III	IV	V
Engineering and metal working	7.1	8.2	9.3	10.4	11.4
Light industry	6.3	6.6	6.8	7.0	7.2
Food industry	7.1	7.3	7.4	7.5	7.6

The Director of Gosplan's research institute has observed that: 'As a result of this research it was concluded that an increase in the share of accumulation, speeding up the growth rate of the economy as a whole, does not provide a marked increase in the growth rate of consumption. This conclusion, clearly, has an important scientific and practical significance.' [61]

One important difference between planning by material balances and planning by input-output is that the former is concerned with gross production and gross consumption of commodities, and focuses attention on supply bottlenecks, whereas the latter starts from final consumption, and focuses attention on the net output available for final consumption. As an official of Gosplan Lithuania has observed 'The plan for production in a republic should provide a definite level of personal and social consumption, deliveries to other regions, accumulation and increase in stocks, and start not from targets for gross output but from final product. But frequently this requirement is not satisfied, because of difficulties with the calculations, and the working out of the economic plan for the republic begins with the establishment of the gross outputs of industry, and agriculture, the volume of investments, deliveries etc. Only multi-variant calculations on the basis of an input-output table, done on a computer with varying levels of final product, make it possible to work out a plan in a strictly logical order — from requirements to production.' [62] Moreover, as Dadayan has observed: 'The production and consumption of coal and steel are significant not in themselves, but only to the extent that they provide for the production of products intended for final consumption ... Society does not become one iota richer if the industrial apparatus devours not 300 but 500 million tons of coal or 90 and not 50 million tons of steel.' [63]

Above it was argued that the use of material balances is unable to lead to the compilation of consistent plans because the material balances are not complete, nor universal, nor do they form an integrated system, nor does technology correspond to the strong assumptions implicit in the use of material balances. Input-output tables are complete, that is they do include all the output of particular industries. This however raises a number of problems, which were discussed above, concerning the comparability of the indices of an input-ouput table and the national economic plan. In particular, the indices of an input-output table, which refer to the outputs of 'pure' industries violate the important plan principle of *adresnost'*,[a] and have to

(a) The principle of *adresnost'* is that there should be no plan targets which are the responsibility of no-one in particular. To each plan target there should correspond an organisation (address) responsible for implementing it.

be recalculated to fit the plan industries, which is not difficult but which does not enhance the reliability of the results. Unlike material balances, input-output does form an integrated system. This fact enables the full implications of possible output changes to be worked out, and numerous plan variants to be experimented with. As in the case with material balances the technological assumptions of input-output — fixed coefficients — do not accord with reality, ruling out such phenomena as alternative techniques of production, non-proportional inputs, learning by doing and non-constant returns to scale. In fact the technological assumptions of input-output are more restrictive than those of material balances, because in planning practice the norms of the material balances are flexible. Considered as a technique for drawing up consistent plans,[64] the most important defect of an input-output table is that it is not universal. The number of industries in the largest input-output table — 600 — is much smaller than the number of products for which material balances are regularly drawn up, and is so small as to be scarcely relevant to the problem of drawing up consistent plans for 20 000 000 commodities.

Summary

Input-output is a useful addition to the techniques at the disposal of the planners, which provides useful data on the relationship between industries and the relationship between the macro-economic indices and the physical structure of production, and which enables variant calculations to be made in perspective planning, and which is useful for working out control figures in current planning. It is not, however, a technique which enables the consistency problem to be solved.

Conclusion

'In general, with the existing nomenclature of balances it is impracticable to take account of all the direct and indirect links in the economy. As a result of this the balancing of all the links in the production of the social product is in practice not achieved, which leads to the violation of the proportional development of the economy.'

N.E. Kobrinskii and A.M. Matlin[65]

'It is suggested that the development of mathematical methods of planning will enable the troubles of the planning of supply to be overcome. Deviations from normal economic activity, including non-productive costs, which result from breakdowns in supply, can be completely liquidated, however, only by raising *khozraschet* to the required level, when *khozraschet* will create between enterprises healthy productive relations, when the responsibility of personnel, and of enterprises will be raised.'

E.O. Kaitsa[66]

It has not been possible to ensure that the plans for all the many thousands of administratively allocated commodities are consistent, using material balances or input-output or a combination of these techniques. The fact that the economy is run on the basis of inconsistent plans has a number of deleterious effects:

(1) It leads to inattention to non-priority sectors, such as personal consumption. As inconsistencies come to light, and shortages are revealed, priority sectors receive what they need and non-priority sectors have to accept what they are given.[a]

(2) It leads to repeated alterations to the plans. As inconsistencies come to light, plans have to be altered to deal with them.

(3) It leads to difficulties with supply, which result in the idleness of men and machines,[b] (according to one estimate 25% of all working time is lost through difficulties with the supply system).[67] It also results in cost increases (resulting for example from the cost of sending *tolkachi* or expediters to find materials, the cost of sending telegrams, the additional cost incurred in the procurement and use of unsatisfactory substitute materials, and the use of commodities obtained from the auxiliary enterprises of collective farms, or from local industry, which may be substantially more costly than the same commodities produced by large scale industry). In addition, it results in difficulties in meeting the requirements of customers (because the necessary materials are not available).

(4) It leads to difficulties with marketing. Enterprises may find that there is no demand for the products that they have been instructed to produce.

(5) It contributes to the unresponsiveness of output to demand. Take commodities whose output is not balanced by the central planners, such as shoe polish or spares for machinery. Unless resources are left for the production of these goods, and an economic mechanism is available which will ensure that the resources are used in accordance with the needs of customers, then these useful commodities will not be produced in the required types and quantities.

(a) A recent article has explained how this works out in the case of tubes (of the type used in oil pipelines). 'In accordance with the quotas which they have received the consumers send in orders for the necessary assortment. It now turns out that the planned output of some kinds of tube is less than requirements and that some kinds of tube were almost excluded from the plan. There arises a shortage. In order somehow to make ends meet it is necessary to divide the industries of the national economy into priority and secondary. Willy nilly the secondary industries have to adapt their needs to the existing situation, and take not those tubes which they need but those tubes which they are given.' (Osada, Spivakovsky and Nizhegorodov, *Pravda* 6 March 1969, p. 2.).

(b) Urban unemployment and unused capacity resulting from lack of aggregate demand, are important sources of idleness of men and machines in market economies, which do not arise in the administrative economy.

(6) It is one of the factors explaining the length of time taken to build new plants – a notorious feature of Soviet investment planning.[a]

(7) It is one of the factors hindering the development of agriculture. Machinery and equipment is allocated to the collective and state farms in a way which does not ensure their most efficient use, and the opportunity for the agricultural enterprises to determine the output patterns of the plants producing machinery and materials for agriculture is limited.[68]

(8) It is one of the factors explaining the low level of specialisation in production. Enterprises, and ministries, fearing that they will be unable to secure through the supply system the components that they need, produce their own at higher cost, and the development of low cost component enterprises is hindered.

(9) It is one of the factors explaining the existence of shortages, both of consumer goods and of producer goods, which is such a characteristic feature of the Soviet economy. Take large suitcases. Equilibrium in the large suitcase market ought to be maintained by balancing. But in fact this cannot be done, and in an environment characterised by suppressed inflation and the determination of the production plans of consumer goods factories by planners rather than in accordance with the needs of the retail trade, large suitcases become a scarce good (*deficitnyi tovar*). (If the planners do notice the shortage they are likely to over-react, and large suitcases will become a surplus commodity, like the reduction gears of appendix 2.)

(10) It leads to the irrational distribution of stocks. Under conditions of strict rationing, and the practice of reducing quotas allocated in the future if current quotas are under-utilised, enterprises have a strong incentive to hoard materials. Stocks accumulate at those enterprises which are relatively good at exaggerating their real requirements, and production is hampered by shortages of materials at those enterprises which play the game according to the official procedure.

It is generally recognised that the existing system of working out and implementing the plans for the administrative allocation of resources is unsatisfactory. At the present time there are five main directions, not mutually exclusive, in which an improvement in the situation is being sought, the enlargement of stocks, the decentralisation of the planning of supply, an improvement in planning techniques, a greater emphasis on direct contacts within the supply system, and the gradual transition from the planning of supply to wholesale trade.

(a) 'Big difficulties arise in investment as a result of the incomplete balancing in the plan of the requirements of the construction sites and the quotas allocated to them, in particular for equipment, ferrous metals, cable production etc. Often when allocating these materials to the construction sites it turns out that the quotas which they have received do not correspond to the specifications which they have requested, which leads to the overexpenditure of materials, the irrational utilisation of labour, to redoing already completed work, and as a consequence, to the dragging out of construction periods.'
V. P. Krasovsky, *Problemy ekonomiki kapital'nykh vlozhenii* (1967) p. 60.

If there were adequate stocks at consumers, then many of the adverse consequences of the inadequacies of the supply system would be eliminated. In that case, the failure of necessary goods to arrive would not cause a plant to come to a halt, or result in dearer materials being substituted or necessitate obtaining materials from another enterprise on an informal basis, as happens now. It would simply be dealt with by running down stocks. This would be an example of what in the literature on systems is called decoupling by means of a buffer.[69] It is not a new idea. Forty years ago, in his famous *Notes of an economist* Bukharin pointed out the difficulty of constructing buildings with bricks that had not yet been produced, and the need for reserves,[70] but his views were rejected at that time on the ground that one should plan to 'widen' a bottleneck, not 'on' the bottleneck. The desirability of an increase in stocks has been argued by Probst,[71] Smekhov[72] and Krylov,[73] considerable attention was paid to the question of stocks at the January 1968 conference on problems of improving material-technical supply at the Scientific Research Institute of the Economics and Organisation of Supply, and the importance of adequate reserves for the improvement of the supply system was recognised in the decree of the Council of Ministers of 28th April 1969 entitled 'On measures for the further improvement of the material-technical supply system of the national economy'.[a] [74]

An important feature of the reform has been the decentralisation of the planning of supply which has resulted from the increased importance of the territorial supply organs. The purpose of this is to bring resource allocation more into line with real requirements and possibilities. The increased role of the local supply organs (the territorial administrations of Gossnab) is shown in table 6.9.

Table 6.9   *No. of products allocated by various organs*[75]

Year	Total nomenclature	Gosplan USSR	SNKh USSR	Gossnab	Chief administrations of Gossnab	Territorial administrations of Gossnab	Ministries
1966	21 665	1 904	1 221	–	18 530	–	–
1967	15 297	2 253	–	20	11 942	–	1 081
1968	16 312	1 969	–	103	3 198	9 228	1 814

There are a number of important organisations to whom this decentralisation of the planning of supply has not been applied. The enterprises of the Ministries of energy and electric power stations, defence, the gas industry, and transport construction, Mosgorispolkom (i.e. Moscow city council), Lengorispolkom (i.e. Leningrad city council) and a number of other

(a) The traditional view of the authorities was that large stocks were a sign of waste, and efforts were devoted to maintaining stocks at a low level and if possible reducing them. Low stocks, or stocks irrationally distributed, ensure that breakdowns in the supply system have the maximum effect in disrupting production, and the changed attitude of the authorities is an important development.

organisations send in their specified quotas not to the territorial supply organs but to their own ministry or to the central supply organs.

In some circles it is considered that the way to overcome the problems of the supply system is to improve planning by widening the detail of the plan and making extensive use of computers and mathematical methods.

'The supporters of the existing system of supply of socialist enterprises generally explain its character by reference to the supposed interests of centralised planning and the shortages of separate types of products. Moreover, they are inclined to see the reason for all these short-comings in the supply of means of production and materials to the factories, mines, construction sites, collective farms and state farms, and of food products and consumption goods to the population, in the inadequate detail of national economic planning.

Economists supporting this point of view believe that if, for example, how much a collective or state farm should receive, not just in the way of tractors and combines, lorries and mineral fertilisers, but also pitchforks, spades, string for packing tomatoes and shavings for packing eggs, were determined in a centralised way, or at any rate by an order from the higher organs, then, in the opinion of these planning officials, the material needs of every enterprise would be fully met. If, on the other hand, these collective and state farms received plans for the sale to the state not only of grain and meat, milk and potatoes, but also beans, bristles, parsley and celery, then the supply of food products to the population, and raw materials to industry, would be guaranteed.

Such a description of the position of the supporters of unlimited central-isation may seem like an exaggeration. This is not so, however. The proof of this is the fact that at the present time many economists and planning officials place great hopes on the creation with the help of com-puters of a single automated system for the management of the national economy. With the help of an all embracing all union classification of indices for the management and planning of production it is proposed to take account of the needs of every enterprise for all requirements and determine down to the last detail the production programme of every enterprise, beginning with turbines and ending with fishhooks.'[76]

In the Ministry of Building and Road Engineering, and in the Ministry of Oil Refining, the requirements for material resources are now worked out directly by the Ministry without reliance on the unreliable indents.[77] The Soyuzglavsnabsbyty (i.e. the chief administration of supply and marketing of Gossnab) are charged with the efficient distribution of orders between plants, and Soyuzglavmetal is using linear programming to work out optimal production schedules and attachment plans, and Soyuzglavkhim (in collab-oration with TSEMI) is applying the transport problem of linear programming to the task of minimising the cost of linking up producers and consumers for a number of chemical products (more than 50 in 1967 and more than 100 in 1969).[78] Methods of iterative aggregation have been suggested with the help of which one could go from consistent plans for a highly aggregated group of commodities to consistent plans for all the commodities.[79] The process of planning is itself now planned, by means of network planning (e.g. the critical path method).

The idea that the use of mathematical methods will be sufficient to overcome the problems of current planning is most implausible, and while it has some support among the officials of the central economic organs has no support among research workers in the field of the application of mathematical methods to current planning. Three research workers in the field of the application of linear programming to oil refining (this is a classical field for the application of linear programming and useful results were achieved in the United States already in the 1950s) have described their work on the current planning of five oil refineries in the Ukraine. The optimal plan diverged substantially from the actual plan. This did not show that the optimal planners are able to bring about substantial savings, but simply that with the present price system a plan that minimises costs is not necessarily optimal from the national economic point of view. What these calculations showed, was not that mathematical methods can save current planning, but that the price system requires further improvement. The researchers, general conclusion about the significance of optimising models for current planning is that they

'do not resolve the important, perhaps the most important, problem – how to interest the direct producers, that is the enterprises, in the maximum display of their reserves, in the most efficient utilisation of their own resources, so that they produce more, better and cheaper.

The economic reform envisages the expansion of direct contacts between suppliers and consumers. In this case Gosplan and the Ministry should switch over from current planning to perspective questions, to determining the directions of technical policy in the industry. The role of the central organs in current regulation should be reduced to the planning of state reserves, the satisfaction of non-economic needs and export-import operations. The purpose of the models of current planning should also be altered – they will probably be used not for the establishment of directive output indices for producers and the establishment of quota limits for consumers, but for the discovery of bottlenecks in the balance of production and consumption, in order that the state reserves be manoeuvred in the best way. The role of the optimisation models in the calculation of indices of indirect regulation and *khozraschet*, in particular objectively determined valuations, will also be increased.'[80]

Great efforts have been devoted in recent years to building up long term contacts within the supply system between producers and consumers. The point of this is to develop long term coordination of the plans of complementary enterprises. In 1967–68 Gossnab linked up on a long term basis more than 5.5 thousand consumer enterprises and 1.5 thousand producer enterprises.[81]

A number of economists consider that the conclusion to be drawn from the impossibility of drawing up a consistent plan for the national economy and the harmful effects that this has on the economy is to abolish current planning and move over to wholesale trade in producer goods.[a] For example Matlin realises that it is impossible to draw up consistent plans for all commodities, and concludes that what is required is to utilise flexible prices, supply and demand and the market mechanism.[82] A number of steps in this direction have been taken.

(a) Even before the reform, trade between enterprises was de facto quite important. The need for it arose as a result of the inadequacy of the planning process.
   For a description see chapter 3 section 2 (Poluchenia materialov iz sluchainykh istochnikov) of E.O. Kaitsa op. cit.

Appendix 1 Aggregation as a cause of inconsistent plans

One can distinguish three main sources of error in planning arising from the aggregation of heterogenous goods into artificial homogenous goods. First, the process of aggregating requirements for many goods into requirements for the aggregate good and of disaggregating the plan for the aggregate good into plans for the heterogenous goods required, may destroy knowledge of the relative quantities in which the goods are required, thus destroying some of the information necessary for the construction of an optimal plan. Second, enterprises instructed to maximise, or materially interested in maximising, the output of the artificial aggregate product may distort the product mix away from that desired by consumers. Third, the planners may compile inconsistent plans because the method of aggregation which they use is inconsistent.[a]

First, if consumers require a_1 units of good 1, a_2 units of good 2...a_n units of good n, and if the planners aggregate these requirements by means of multipliers $b_1, \ldots b_n$, and then plan an ouput of c $(\equiv \sum_{i=1}^{n} a_i b_i)$ units of 'good q', they are setting producers the task of finding an n component y vector, such that $y.b = c$. There is an infinite number of such vectors, of which a is only one, so that in general consumers will not receive the output pattern required.

The two goods case, with variable coefficients in consumption, can be represented diagrammatically, as in figure A1.1. Consider the two goods a_1 and a_2, say coke and oil, with planners multipliers 1 and ½, so that consumers' requirements for one ton of coke and two of oil are aggregated into a requirement for $1 \times 1 + 2 \times \frac{1}{2}$ tons of coal equivalent; and so on for larger requirements.

The output produced by the consumers of coke and oil depends on their consumption of these products. If they receive any of the combinations of a_1 and a_2 represented by the curve $P''P''$ they will produce an output P''; and similarly for $P'P'$ and PP. $P'' > P' > P$. In order to produce output P', consumers' minimum requirements (in terms of q) are for 6 units of a_2 and 2 units of a_1. The planners aggregate these requirements into a requirement

---

(a) A survey of the theory of aggregation, with bibliography, will be found in H.A.J. Green, *Aggregation in economic analysis* (1967). For a Soviet discussion of the conditions for consistent aggregation in the input-output model, see N.V. Dyumin and Yu. S. Arkhangelski, Agregirovanie v mezhotraslevom balanse, *Ekonomika i matematichskie metody* vol. 2, 1966.

Aggregation is said to be consistent when the use of information more detailed than that contained in the aggregates would make no difference to the results of the calculations.

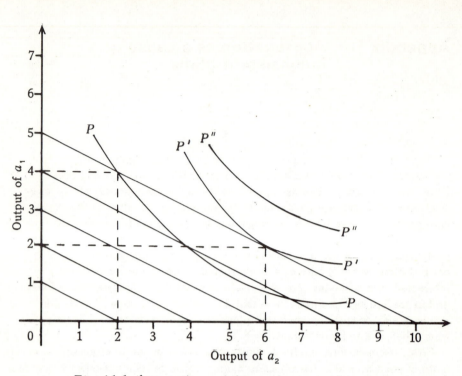

Fig. A1.1 *Aggregation and the requirements of consumers*

for $6 \times \frac{1}{2} + 2 \times 1 = 5$ units of q. Any point on the line $(0,5)$ $(10,0)$ satisfies this plan. Suppose producers produce 4 units of a_1 and 2 units of a_2: supply $(4 \times 1 + 2 \times \frac{1}{2} = 5)$ equals demand $(6 \times \frac{1}{2} + 2 \times 1 = 5)$. On paper, in terms of q, the plan is consistent. In fact, however, consumers are faced with a shortage of a_2 $(6 - 2 = 4)$ and a surplus of a_1 $(4 - 2 = 2)$, so that consumers find that their output plans and supply plans are inconsistent (or that output plans are inconsistent with input availabilities), and production, at P, is below the planned level.

A necessary condition for aggregation not to lead to inconsistency is that the planners' multipliers coincide with the consumers' rates of substitution. It is for this reason that in the compilation of physical input-output tables in the Soviet Union, where it is clear that crude physical measures such as weight, volume or area do not reflect relative consumers' valuations, adjustments are made to bring the physical measures into line with relative consumers' valuations.[1][a] The greater the divergence between the planners' multipliers and the consumers' rates of substitution the greater is the inconsistency of the plan. This provides a criterion for aggregation: aggregate

(a) The desirability of measuring the consumption of fuels in the United Kingdom using as conversion factors for the different fuels their marginal rates of transformation in production or their marginal rates of substitution in consumption, rather than coal equivalent tons, is argued in R. Turvey and A.R. Nobay, On measuring energy consumption, *Economic Journal* vol. LXXV (1965).

close substitutes and do not aggregate across gaps in the chain of substitution.

In industries with only one product, for example the electricity supply industry, the process of aggregation and disaggregation does not cause inconsistent plans. The problem arises in industries where output is very heterogenous, as in the textile industry. Where decentralisation is advocated as a way of eliminating errors caused by disaggregation, this provides a criterion for deciding in which industries to decentralise, decentralise in industries of the textile type, and do not decentralise in industries of the electricity type.[2]

Secondly, where enterprises are instructed to maximise, or are materially interested in maximising, the output of q, they are likely to distort the product mix away from that desired by consumers. Let consumers' requirements be $a_1 \ldots a_n$, planners' multipliers be $b_2 \ldots b_n$, and planning be in terms of q. The instruction to maximise q is tantamount to an instruction to find a vector $(d_1 \ldots d_n)$ such that

$$b.d. \rightarrow \text{max} \tag{1}$$

Consumers' requirements will not be met unless

$$d_i \geqslant a_i \quad (i = 1 \ldots n) \tag{2}$$

In general the output programme which satisfies (1) will not satisfy (2).

The two goods case, with varying coefficients in production and consumption, can be represented diagrammatically as in Figure A1.2.

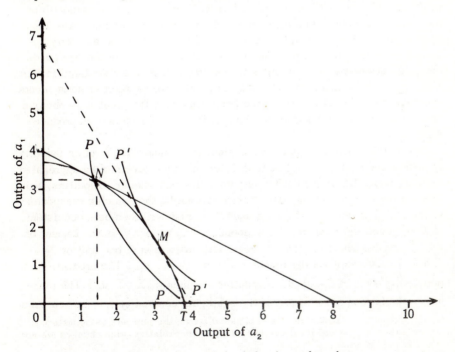

Fig. A1.2 *Aggregation and the behaviour of producers*

The production possibility area is OTT. Output of q is maximised, given the planners' multipliers 1 and $\frac{1}{2}$, at the point N where output is $3\frac{1}{4}$ of a_1 and $1\frac{1}{2}$ units of a , i.e. 4 units of q. Consumers' requirements are such that for any combination of supplies of a_1 and a_2 represented by the curve $P'P'$ they are able to produce P' units of output, and similarly for PP. $P' > P$. Given the production possibility area OTT and the isoproduct curves $P'P'$ and PP, the optimal output plan is point M, which enables producers to produce the highest possible output as measured by consumers.

Unless the planners' multipliers coincide with the marginal rate of substitution of the two goods in consumption and the marginal rate of transformation in production, at the optimal point, the use of planners' multipliers to aggregate goods will result in an irrational output. Production of the rational output requires a market in which the price ratio $6\frac{3}{4} : 3\frac{3}{4}$ rules, or that the planners calculate this price ratio and set it to the enterprises as a parameter, or that the planners' multipliers coincide with this ratio.

Third, when planning is in aggregated terms, either or both of the following assumptions are implicit in the plan: (1) the relative outputs of the two products which make up the aggregated industry will remain unchanged; (2) the input structures of the products which make up the aggregate industry are the same.[a]

Consider, for example, the case of the car and lorry industries, planned as the single 'motor-vehicle' industry. Suppose that the planners plan an increase in the output of motor vehicles, that increase in output to be wholly accounted for by an increase in the output of cars. Assume that the input structures of cars and lorries are different. Then if the planners calculate the input needs of the enlarged motor vehicle industry using norms or input coefficients which are weighted averages of those of the car and lorry industries, the weights being the current relative outputs of the two goods, the calculations will not accord with reality. If plans are calculated in this way, they will be inconsistent — the car plants will be short of some inputs and have a surplus of others. In the two goods case the problem is obvious and the planners may be able to allow for it; but some industries produce many products.

During the process of plan compilation, the planned output of an industry is often altered. It may well be that different output levels of an aggregated industry imply different relative outputs of its component commodities, and that the output level eventually chosen will not be that which corresponds to the norms or input coefficients used. The plan will then be inconsistent.

More generally, consider the n goods, $x_1 \ldots x_n$. $x(k)_i$ is the amount of the ith good produced in the kth year. The production of one unit of $x_i (i = 1 \ldots n)$ requires the inputs $a_{i1} + a_{i2} + \ldots a_{im}$. The production of one unit of each of the goods x_i requires the inputs $\sum\limits_{i=1}^{n} \sum\limits_{j=1}^{m} a_{ij}$. The planners calculations are in terms of the aggregate commodity q. q is measured

(a) It is assumed that planning is in physical terms, the planners using material balances or physical input-output tables, so that relative price changes are not a source of errors.

in such a way that one unit of x_i is equal to $1/n$ units of q. Assume that in year 1 one unit of each of the goods x_i is produced, so that output of q is one, and input requirements are $\sum_{i=1}^{n} \sum_{j=1}^{m} a_{ij}$. Assume that in year 2 an output increase of 10% is planned. According to the planners' calculations, the input requirements of the enlarged q industry are $110/100 \sum_{i=1}^{n} \sum_{j=1}^{m} a_{ij}$. This calculation will be correct only if either or both of the following conditions hold:

(a) $\qquad a_{ij} = a_{pj} \qquad\qquad\qquad i,p = 1\ldots n$

$$j = 1\ldots m$$

The economic meaning of this requirement is that the goods have identical input requirements. This provides a criterion for consistent aggregation: do not aggregate commodities with different input requirements. It also provides a criterion for aggregating goods in order to minimise errors: aggregate goods with similar input requirements, and do not aggregate goods with dissimilar input requirements.

(b) $\qquad\qquad x(1)_i/x(1)_j = x(2)_i/x(2)_j$

The economic meaning of this condition is that the goods are produced in the same proportions in the two years. (Examples of goods whose relative outputs remain unchanged at different aggregate output levels are goods produced at different stages of a vertical process of production.) This provides a criterion for consistent aggregation: aggregate goods only if the ratio of their outputs is the same in the planned period and the base period. It also provides a criterion for minimising errors caused by inconsistent aggregation: aggregate only those commodities whose relative outputs will remain more or less unchanged during the planned period.

This suggests that errors caused by inconsistent aggregation are likely to be greater the longer is the interval between the planned period and the period to which the norms of input coefficients refer, because of the discrepancy between the output patterns in the two years. This suggests the importance of continuous up-dating of the norms used in material balance calculations, or the input coefficients used in input-output calculations.

During the process of plan compilation not only commodities but also enterprises are aggregated. The sources of error in aggregating enterprises are analogous to those in aggregating commodities.

First, the process of aggregating requirements for commodities at particular places into requirements for commodities, and then disaggregating the plan for commodities into plans for the delivery of commodities to particular places, may destroy knowledge as to where the commodities are needed. This is a problem in data processing which becomes very difficult as the number of enterprises grows very large. One of the reasons why Soviet industrial production is concentrated in large enterprises and small enterprises discouraged, is to deal with this problem.[a]

Second, enterprises instructed to produce commodities (or materially interested in producing commodities), as opposed to the delivery of commodities to particular places, may ignore the needs of consumers.

Third, planners may compile inconsistent plans because the method of aggregating enterprises used is inconsistent. When planning is in terms of aggregating enterprises, either or both of the following hidden assumptions are implicit in the plan:

(1) the input structures of the enterprises are the same;

(2) the relative outputs of the enterprises will remain unchanged.

Consider for example two coalfields planned as 'the coal industry'. If the planners calculate the input requirements of the coal industry using norms of input coefficients which are weighted averages of those of the two coalfields, then unless either or both of the hidden assumptions are satisfied, inconsistent plans will be drawn up. When there are only two enterprises with very different input structures allowance can be made for this; but some extractive industries have many fields, and in addition there are other industries with many enterprises and varying input structures.

During the process of plan compilation, time too, is aggregated. Planning is in terms of units of time, say a quarter. A producing enterprise can fulfil its plan by producing output in say the tenth week of the quarter, although the consuming enterprise may need it in the third week of the quarter — information which was destroyed by the planners during the process of aggregation and disaggregation.

(a) The size distribution of British and Soviet industrial enterprises is very different. Whereas 92.3 per cent of all industrial enterprise in Britain employ 100 workers or less, in the Soviet Union only 29.8 per cent of enterprises fall into this category. The Soviet Union, with an industrial labour force almost three times of Britain, has only about one fifth as many industrial enterprises.
Ya Kvasha, Kontsentratsiya proizvodstva i melkaya promyshlennost', *Voprosy Ekonomiki* 1967 No. 5.

Appendix 2   The case for wholesale trade

The following is a complete translation of an article in *Izvestiya* 29
September 1964.

A letter and a commentary

Another speed

I found out accidentally everything that is stated in this letter. The
sovnarkhoz included me in one of the commissions for checking the composition of incomplete output at Leningrad factories. We were at the
Kotlyakov factory. We came across facts here which even a stranger could
not fail to notice. The whole place was filled up with reduction gears
(these are the main product of the factory).

What is going on? Quite recently, only three years ago, there was a shortage of reduction gears in the country. Tens of thousands of factories
produced a few reduction gears of various types. As a result they were dear
and of poor quality. It was decided to set up several big specialised
factories.

At the Kotlyakov factory a sheme was worked out to raise the capacity of
the plant to 125 000 reduction gears a year. The construction of new shops,
the ordering of special lathes, and the introduction of production lines, was
begun. Building continues.

Now, however, there is serious doubt as to whether it is worthwhile continuing with the work. It has suddenly turned out that reduction gears are not
necessary. Nobody wants them. By the end of the first half of the year three
million roubles worth of them had piled up in warehouses. The factory ran
into debt with the bank and was transferred to a special credit regime. To
produce another product on the special production lines for the reduction
gears is impossible.

G. Bakhareva
Head of the economic laboratory of the
Nevsky factory named after V.I. Lenin.

V. Rumyantsev, the director of the Kotlyakov factory, read the letter
attentively, without haste. He fell silent, and then he said:

'Evidently comrade Bakhareva has done her work well. Everything in the
letter is correct. Until quite recently we made 8 000 reduction gears a year,
in the current year we could make more than 40 000, and next year 75 000.
Three years ago this was a very scarce product and we were criticised for
the fact that we were only producing a small quantity; now the annual plan

(38 000) is below capacity. By February it was clear that even for this plan there would not be enough orders. During the year the plan was reduced to 32 000. We have been provided with a market for 26 000. What will happen in the fourth quarter?'

In a word the director confirms the startling fact. What happened? In spite of everything one would think that the Kotlyakov factory was not expanded for nothing. It is difficult to believe that the country does not need its 32 000 reduction gears. Nobody in *Soyuzglavtyazhmash* could explain clearly to me what had happened. This is scarcely surprising. This organ, on which the fate of factories depends, in practice decides nothing and has not got a staff to study economic prospects. It is clear what has happened. Not all the small ('for oneself') reduction gear works were closed which should have been closed with the opening of the big factories. The *sovnarkhozy* preserved them for reasons of over insurance. Specialists, acquainted with the industry, name in particular the Gorokhovetsky, Nikolsky and Pavshinsky factories, which are producing even now small quantities of reduction gears in addition to their main product. This production could easily be transferred to the Kotlyakov factory, or to the Izhevsky factory, which also specialises in them. Furthermore, the factories of several industrial state committees in Kharkov, Rostov and in Leningrad itself will produce this year small quantities of the *very same* reduction gears as the Kotlyakov factory. They will produce them knowing that at the specialised factories they are both cheaper and better. This is a model of an irresponsible, departmental, approach to state business. This approach has greatly increased the difficulties with which the Kotlyakov factory is faced.

In life we are now meeting with other cases very similar to the case of the reduction gears. In recent months one has come to hear more and more the unfamiliar words 'difficulties with the *marketing* of output'.

Perhaps these are just personally observed chance happenings? Letters to the editor, however, serve as an infallible barometer. Several months ago the articles 'Orders and refusals' and 'The factory and the bank' were published in *Izvestiya*. In the second article there was a discussion of only one of the consequences of the trouble. This was a case where a purchaser returned a machine which had been ordered a year earlier. The reason was the usual one, no money available. Since this is the truth, the local branch of the bank agrees and does not pay the account. The innocent supplier suffers. This is simply one of the consequences of disorganised marketing. and in itself a big problem. We received dozens of letters in response to the article 'The factory and the bank'. In them were hundreds of facts, refusals to accept goods, non-payment for goods, mysterious debts for heaven knows what.

The cause of all this is quite simple. Imagine that you are the director of, say, a crane factory. Not later than the first of July of every year you indent for sets of goods for the manufacture of cranes in the following year. Your orders include reduction gears. How many of them you will need and of what type, it is impossible to know precisely. Somewhere or other your future customers are only just indenting for your cranes. This means that you guess your needs on the basis of last year's experience with some allowance made for growth. Your made up indent goes on its way.

The indent goes to the *sovnarkhoz* of the economic region, then to the republican organ, then it arrives at the union supply-marketing (*snabsbyt*) *glavk*, in this case *Soyuzglavtyazhmash*. There all the orders are added up. The total number of reduction gears requested in the whole country, is calculated. Then the same staircase is traversed from top to bottom. After several months it is known at the factory how many reduction gears have been requested.

During this time things have not stood still at your factory. You have received the indents of your customers, and you discover that they want quite different cranes, and in different quantities, than what you had assumed. You immediately reorganise your intended production programme and rack your brains to find out where you can get the necessary sets of goods (the ones you ordered are now inappropriate).

As we go further into things there are more troubles. The last plan to be confirmed is the investment plan. Your customers discover that they can buy only about half the number of cranes that they ordered. With the rest you may do what you like. You then write to Leningrad 'half the reduction gears that were ordered are unnecessary'. There they also begin to rescind some orders. This is a picture of events, deliberately stripped of irrelevant details. In actuality, thousands of circumstances which either alleviate or aggrevate the difficulties, intervene.

What ought we to do? Once the argument reaches this point one often hears people say, it is necessary to raise responsibility, it is essential to increase discipline, something or other should be strengthened, something or other should be intensified, and so on.

Various administrative measures are suggested, such as altering the period for sending in indents. It is said, for example, that the production plan should be compiled before the supply plan. This, however, is similar to the argument about which came first, the chicken or the egg. What for the consumer is a supply plan, is for the supplier a production plan. Simultaneous coordination is required.

Evidently a radical solution is required. Let us look at things in a wider context. If we abstract from details, a gratifying event which we long awaited has taken place. The period when all the goods in the economy were scarce, has ended. The time when there was not enough of everything has ended. The method of planning which was suitable for permanent shortages, however, still remains. This method, first, envisaged the centralised distribution of all, or nearly all, resources, which in current conditions is impossible and unnecessary. Secondly, it ignored the factor of marketing, because in the years of the first five year plan marketing was much easier than production.

Bearing in mind these circumstances, it is not difficult to see in what direction it is necessary to search for a solution. Many economic officials consider that it is necessary, for example, to develop direct contacts between enterprises, which N.S. Khruschev has called 'the most convenient and profitable' form of supply and sales. It is suggested to place them at the basis of planning the output and sales of commodities so that factories do not have to go up and down a long staircase of higher organs which do not decide anything. We have come across, in particular, one interesting confirmation of the practicability of this path.

Last year, together with the well known economist M. Kobrina, an old manager of the school of Sergo Ordzhonikidze, we were at the Moscow factory *Krasnaya Presnya* which makes founding machines. It was already November. Comrade Sergeev, the Director of the factory, placed on the table a long list, dozens of repudiations. For a good third of the output there was nowhere to send it. When he turned to 'his' *snabsbyt* they lifted their hands in dismay and said 'we have no orders for your machines'.

Then the factory sent letters to three hundred possible purchasers (at the factory the addresses of possible purchasers are well known). They were sent in the belief that there would be answers.

In the spring we telephoned Krasnaya Presnya. Sergeev did not immediately remember: 'Oh, those? They were all sold.'

But that is not all. At Krasnaya Presnya it was foreseen that the character of demand might alter, and then it would not be so easy for things to come right in the end without a reliable sales plan. This was foreseen and new customers were looked for. This was not done as it would have been done in Gosplan by a man.intermittently looking after founding machines.

People living in Moscow and concerned with founding machines could find out that at the Voskresensk chemical combine there was dissatisfaction with their equipment for mixing and grinding the ingredients for mineral fertilisers. Having found out, they could act in this way. At their expense, they brought to Voskresensk and set up one of their machines (runners) accompanying it with their engineers, and proved that it mixes fertiliser ingredients much better than the screw conveyors working there. The Voskresensk people asked that there should be sent to the line with runners a mill also, and the designers at Kranaya Presnya took on this job as well.

This is a second advantage of direct contacts, allowing those concerned to do engineering work themselves, to push there where it is most needed in the interest of the national economy, without pressure from above.

Should this accidental experience become a norm? If some offices are superfluous, for the state this can only be beneficial. Under this system the union planning organs would retain the key positions in determining the directions of development of this or that industry, and coordinating the actions of the enterprises in accordance with the tasks of technical progress and the requirements of the country. Under this system the union planning organs would enter the picture when the supplier and the customer were unable to agree among themselves.

Maybe someone can suggest a better way. What is important is the principle, that the methods of planning should keep in touch with the changing situation.

We began with reduction gears. One of the various kinds of gears is the familiar car gear box. When a car sets out, you use the first speed, This is inevitable, otherwise the motor would not begin. It is, however, also inevitable, that when the car has picked up momentum, you use another speed.

O. Latsis

Appendix 3   The use of input-output in regional economic planning

The construction of accounting regional input-output tables was one of the first fruits of the (revived) Soviet interest in the use of mathematical methods in planning the economy. Work on regional input-output tables was begun by the Laboratory for Economic — Mathematical Methods (which subsequently grew into the Central Economic-Mathematical Institute) of the Academy of Sciences of the USSR under the leadership of the late Academician Nemchinov, with the compilation, in 1959, of an accounting input-output table for the Mordovian ASSR for 1958. Soviet work in this field is summarised in appendix 4.

Most of the problems of drawing up regional input-output tables are similar to those arising in the compilation of national tables. In this appendix we will not duplicate the discussion of chapter 6 but will consider points relevant only to the regional tables.

When projecting technology the compilers of the Estonian tables considered, for some industries, various coefficient vectors, embodying various methods of production. For the construction industry linear programming was used to choose the optimal plan.[1] Fifteen variants of final consumption were experimented with when working out the Estonian input-output table for 1970.[2] In one variant of the Estonian calculations food product consumption norms suggested by the Laboratory for the study and planning of nutrition of the Academy of Sciences of the USSR, and non-food product consumption norms recommended by the Scientific Research Institute of trade and social nutrition, corrected for Estonian conditions, were used.

One variant of personal consumption for Estonia for 1970 was based on income elasticity calculations. The population was divided into two groups, rural and urban and the data of a 1963 family budget survey was used to calculate linear consumption function for all the consumer goods specified in the input-output table for these two groups.

The base year used in these calculations may have been unrepresentative. To overcome this problem, in the Estonian calculations a control year — 1963 — was used to check the representativeness of the base year — 1961.[3]

All the calculations were carried out in 1961 or 1963 prices. Future price changes were not allowed for.

Working out the 1970 input-output table for Latvia, it was found that starting from final demand and the projected technical coefficients sometimes led to impossibly large volumes of output of particular products. Accordingly another approach was tried, starting from given volumes of output and structure of final product, and balancing the table by adjusting imports and exports. Latvia's imports and exports for 1970 are determined by Gosplan USSR, for broad commodity groups, but within these groups much adjustment is possible.

Developments

On the basis of the planning flow input-output table for 1970, the capital stock matrix for 1960 and a dynamic model which incorporates different time lags in different industries proposed by Ennuste, flow and capital stock matrices for Estonia for each of the years in the period 1970–1980, distinguishing thirty industries and six variants, have been calculated.

Already, in constructing the 1970 input-output table for Estonia, optimising techniques were used. The ultimate goal to which all this work is tending is the construction of planning, dynamic (including capital stock matrices), optimal (taking into account choice of technique) input-output tables. (The criterion of optimality being the maximisation of the trade surplus of the republic).[a] Plans based on these tables could be implemented by the appropriate adjustment of centrally fixed prices, which profit maximising enterprises would take as parameters.

Analysis of Tables

Some interesting calculations have been performed in triangulating the input-output matrices for the Baltic republics.[4] The input coefficients of the three accounting Baltic tables have been compared using the formula of Chenery and Clark and Watanbee.[5]

The use of regional input-output tables in regional planning

Up till now regional input-output tables have largely remained a field for experimental calculations and scientific research, and have not been incorporated into planning practice.

An exception is the Lithuanian republic, where the planning input-output table for 1970 was used when drafting the five year plan for 1966–70, to check the consistency of the projected national income with the projected industry outputs.[6]

As a result of the experiments already carried out, workers in this field feel that input-output tables can now be introduced into practice. On February 14th and 15th 1966 an expanded Plenum of the Academy of Science's Scientific Council on the problem 'The use of mathematics and computing technology in economic research and planning' was held to

(a) 'The theory of optimal planning (for example the theory of competitive equilibrium as formulated by Arrow–Debreu or as modified by D. Gale, and also the works of L. Kantorovich, A. Lur'e and others) proves, that a sub-system, (such as a region) works optimally in the interest of the national economy as a whole, when it maximises the difference between its income and expenditure (i.e. an active trade balance), if the flows (exports and imports) are valued in prices which establish equilibrium between supply and demand for the system as a whole.' Yu. Ennuste, *Izvestiya Akademii Nauk Estonskoi SSR: obshchestvennye nauki* 1969, No. 2, p. 144.

discuss regional input-output tables. A deputy director of TSEMI expressed the view that 'Now after having carried out a number of experimental calculations, the main problem is the practical introduction of planning input-output tables into the work of the planning organs.'[5]

TSEMI's guide to the construction of regional input-output tables states that :

'An input-output table can, in principle, be included in the existing system of planning both at the preliminary stage of working out the plan, and also at the concluding stage of balancing and co-ordinating the plan indices. At the preliminary stage of planning it must be used as an instrument to work out the control figures (at the level of the country as a whole or at the stage of a separate economic region). At the concluding stage it can serve for the achievement of full consistency of the plan indices of all products and for the co-ordination of the plan s of enterprises with the regional and national plans.'[8]

For purposes of regional planning the Soviet Union has a central organ, the Council for the Study of Productive Forces (SOPS) attached to Gosplan USSR, and local organs, the planning commisions of the sixteen big economic regions. (The USSR, excluding Moldavia which is not included in any big economic region, is divided into eighteen big economic regions. Two big economic regions – Byelorussia and Kazakhstan – do not have planning commissions, because it is unnecessary to have in one and the same region both a republican Gosplan and the planning commission of a big economic region.) Input-output tables have not yet been drawn up and incorporated into the regular planning procedures of the big economic regions.

Most of the difficulties which arise in attempting to use regional input-output tables in regional planning are similar to those which arise in connection with national tables, and the discussion of chapter 6 will not be duplicated here, where we will consider additional difficulties which arise only with regional tables.

It is easier to compile input-output tables for regions which are Union republics than for regions which are not, because more statistical material is available for the former. A book [9] one of whose authors is the Chairman of the West Siberian planning commission, stated that :

'Scientific workers of the Council for the study of productive forces attached to Gosplan USSR have worked out a methodology for the compilation of an input-output table for an economic region,[a] *but because of lack of essential statistical information*, to work out a planning according to this methodology is impossible for the time being.' [10]

All the regional input-output tables so far compiled have been for political units, in particular Union republics, and not for big economic regions. (The accounting input-output tables for the three Baltic republics have been consolidated to form an input-output table for the Baltic

(a) The reference is to the first (mimeo) edition of L.E. Mints, V.V. Kossov and E.F. Baranov (eds) *Mezhotraslevoi balans ekonomicheskogo raiona* (1967).

economic region.[11]) The reasons for this are not only that more statistical data are available for Union republics than for big economic regions, but also that local economists are available to compile the tables (every Union republic has an academy of sciences with an Institute of Economics.)

The only region where input-output has been used in planning practice — Lithuania — is likewise a Union republic and not a big economic region. The reason is that Lithuania possessed both a planning input-output table and a Gosplan.

In order for accounting input-output tables to be used in planning the development of the big economic regions, it is necessary that they be compiled and that the regional planning commissions have the authority of the Union Republican Gosplans.

Further, the need for input-output in planning the big economic regions is not immediately apparent. The planning commissions of the big economic regions are largely concerned with such problems as the labour supply of the region, the development of local deposits of raw materials and the siting of new enterprises, the solution of which would not be helped very much by regional input-output tables.

Conclusion

1) In the field of regional input-output tables, it would seem, Soviet economists are ahead of those in other countries.

2) Up till now the work done has only had a scientific-experimental character, and had not been widely introduced in practice. As two leading authorities in this field put it:

'This is not the first year in which input-output tables have been worked out in the Soviet Union, and by now considerable experience in their con-struction has accumulated. Unfortunately, it is impossible to say this about their utilization in practical work, which is explained by the diffi-culties connected with the inclusion of the input-output method in the traditional system of planning.' [12]

3) There exist a number of problems in the compilation of accounting input-output tables, planning input-output tables and the utilisation of plan-ning regional tables in regional planning.

When an economic region has a series of accounting input-output tables, stretching over a number of years, it is possible to compare these, in order to check the representativeness of the most recent tables, and to find out the trends at work, and so assist in projecting the structure of final demands and the input coefficients.

Dutch experience has shown, however, that in making forecasts of inter-mediate demand with the help of an input-output table it is more important to use an up to date input-output table than to have access to a mass of out of date data. [13]

The fact that the planning input-output tables for the Baltic republics were based on accounting tables referring to a period nine years earlier,

Area	Date	Units of Measurement	Accounting or Planning	No. of Industries	No. of positions 2nd quadrant	No. of positions 3rd quadrant
USSR	1959	Consumer prices	Accounting	83	n.a.	n.a.
USSR	1966	Consumer prices	Accounting	110	n.a.	n.a.
USSR	1962	Consumer prices	Planning	83	n.a.	n.a.
USSR	1970	Consumer prices	Planning	130	n.a.	n.a.
USSR	1959	Physical	Accounting	157	n.a.	n.a.
USSR	1966	Physical	Accounting	237	n.a.	n.a.
USSR	1962	Physical	Planning	346	n.a.	n.a.
USSR	1963	Physical	Planning	435	n.a.	n.a.
USSR	1964	Physical	Planning	n.a.	n.a.	n.a.
USSR	1965	Physical	Planning	n.a.	n.a.	n.a.
USSR	1970	Physical	Planning	600	n.a.	n.a.
USSR	1959	Man years	Accounting	83	n.a.	n.a.
USSR	1966	Man years	Accounting	86	n.a.	n.a.
USSR	1966	Consumer prices	Accounting	86	Capital stock matrix	–
Armenia	1963	Consumer prices	Accounting	91	n.a.	n.a.
Byelorussia	1962	Consumer prices	Accounting	500	n.a.	n.a.
Latvia	1961	Producer prices	Accounting	239	13[6]	10[7]
Lithuania	1961	Producer prices	Accounting	239	13[6]	10[7]
Lithuania	1962	Producer prices	Accounting	180	n.a.	n.a.
Estonia	1961	Producer prices	Accounting	239	13[6]	10[7]
Kaliningrad oblast	1960	n.a.	Accounting	15	n.a.	n.a.
Karelia	1961	n.a.	Accounting	75	n.a.	n.a.
Mordovia	1958	Consumer prices	Accounting	14	n.a.	n.a.
Mordovia	1959	Consumer prices	Accounting	86	11[10]	8[7]
Tartaria	1959	Consumer prices	Accounting	165[11]	6[12]	7[7]
Tartaria	1960	Consumer prices	Accounting	150	n.a.	n.a.
Tartaria	1961	n.a.	Accounting	56	n.a.	n.a.
Tartaria	1962	n.a.	Accounting	56	n.a.	n.a.
Tartaria	1963	n.a.	Accounting	56	n.a.	n.a.
RSFSR	1966	Consumer prices	Accounting	109[13]	n.a.	n.a.
Georgia	1964	n.a.	Planning	119[14]	n.a.	n.a.
Latvia	1970	Producer prices	Planning	150	n.a.	n.a.
Lithuania	1970	Producer prices	Planning	150	n.a.	n.a.
Estonia	1970	Producer prices	Planning	150	n.a.	n.a.
Estonia	1961	Producer prices	Accounting	150	Capital stock matrix	–
Estonia	1970	Producer prices	Planning	150	Capital stock matrix	–
Chemical Industry	1960	n.a.	Accounting	n.a.	–	–
Chemical Industry	1962	n.a.	Planning	n.a.	–	–

n.a.	= not available
–	= not applicable
SRI Gosplan	= Gosplan's Scientific Research Institute

Compiled in the USSR

Method of calculating inputs	Compiled by	Method of calculating region's imports and exports	Were non-proportional inputs isolated?	Were alternative techniques distinguished	Date of publication
Gross output	TsSU	–	No	No	1961[1]
Gross output	TsSU	–	No	No	1968[2]
n.a.	SRI Gosplan	–	No	No	Unpublished
n.a.	SRI Gosplan	–	No	No	Unpublished
Gross turnover	TsSU	–	n.a.	n.a.	Unpublished
Gross turnover	TsSU	–	n.a.	n.a.	Unpublished
Gross turnover	CCC Gosplan	–	n.a.	n.a.	Unpublished
Gross turnover	CCC Gosplan	–	n.a.	n.a.	Unpublished
Gross turnover	CCC Gosplan	–	n.a.	n.a.	Unpublished
Gross turnover	CCC Gosplan	–	n.a.	n.a.	Unpublished
Gross turnover	CCC Gosplan	–	n.a.	n.a.	Unpublished
n.a.	TsSU	–	No	No	1962[3]
n.a.	TsSU	–	No	No	1969[4]
n.a.	TsSU	–	No	No	1969[5]
Gross ouput	TsSU Armenia	n.a.	n.a.	n.a.	Unpublished
n.a.	n.a.	Balance	n.a.	No	Unpublished
Gross turnover	TSEMI	Direct	No	Yes	Unpublished
Gross turnover	TSEMI	Direct	No	Yes	Unpublished
Gross turnover	TSEMI	Balance	No	No	Unpublished
Gross turnover	TSEMI	Direct	No	Yes	Unpublished
n.a.	n.a.	Mixed	n.a.	No	Unpublished
n.a.	n.a.	Balance	n.a.	No	Unpublished
n.a.	TSEMI[a]	Balance	n.a.	No	1962[9]
Gross turnover	TSEMI[a]	Mixed	Yes	Yes	Unpublished
Gross turnover	Tatar sovnarkhoz	Mixed	Yes	Yes	Unpublished
Gross turnover	Tatar sovnarkhoz	Mixed	n.a.	No	Unpublished
Gross turnover	Tatar sovnarkhoz	Balance	n.a.	No	Unpublished
Gross turnover	Tatar sovnarkhoz	Balance	n.a.	No	Unpublished
Gross turnover	Tatar sovnarkhoz	Balance	n.a.	No	Unpublished
Gross output	TsSU	n.a.	No	No	Unpublished
n.a.	SRI Gosplan Georgia	n.a.	No	No	Unpublished
Gross turnover	TSEMI	n.a.	n.a.	n.a.	Unpublished
Gross turnover	TSEMI	n.a.	n.a.	n.a.	Unpublished
Gross turnover	TSEMI	n.a.	n.a.	n.a.	Unpublished
–	Institute of economics, Estonia	–	–	–	Unpublished
–		–	–	–	Unpublished
–	SRI Chemical industry	–	–	–	Unpublished
–		–	–	–	Unpublished

SRI Chemical industry = Scientific Research Institute for technical-economic research in the chemical industry

CCC Gosplan = Gosplan's Chief Computing Centre

seriously reduced the practical value of the exercise.

4) Many Soviet economists consider that the use of input-output can substantially increase the efficiency of planning. They regard it, however, not as an isolated tool, but as an integral part of a comprehensive system of optimal planning.

7. Some problems of current planning

'The optimisation of the national economy means above all the optimisation of the economic relations. Therefore optimal planning requires not only the use of mathematical methods and electronic computing technology, but also the improvement of the forms of socialist productive relations, including legal forms. The choice of these forms lies beyond the boundaries of mathematical programming, but no doubt mathematical approaches to their optimisation will be found in the not too distant future. Such possibilities have already been noted, and the search for, and utilisation of, them is prompted by the requirements of practice.

In particular, the correct combination of the interests of the controlling and the controlled levels of production is one of the most important tasks of an optimally controlled economy. It is quite possible (and even highly probable!) that the liquidation of the striving of the lower levels to hide their productive possibilities, the orientation of the interests of the masses to the search for new, better variants of production and many other consequences of such a combination, at the present time conceals bigger reserves for the growth of the socialist economy, than the use of mathematical programming with the preservation of the former relations between the controlling and the controlled levels of the economy.'

V.V. Novozhilov[1]

An integral feature of the administrative economy is the determination by the planners of obligatory values of a large number of variables in the *tekhpromfinplan* of every enterprise. It is now being argued by a number of Soviet economists that this process is wasteful and that the planners ought to confine themselves to higher level goals, such as the perspective development of the national economy, and abandon the practice of setting numerous obligatory values of the *tekhpromfinplan* of every enterprise. As two Soviet economists, one of whom is a leading figure in the field of economic cybernetics, have argued in a book entitled *Economic-mathematical models in planning*, 'it is extremely important to underline that planning, as the social regulation of the proportions of production, has two substantially different aspects. First, the determination of the perspective development of the national economy (starting from the goals of future development) and the determination of the means of their achievement – the economic macroproportions. Secondly, the regulation of current production, the current physical microproportions, which are defined within the limits of the annual plans or the plans worked out for still shorter periods.

The realisation of the perspective plans is based on the utilisation of such highly efficient methods of influencing the economy as investment policy; credit, financial and foreign currency policy; wages policy and so on. With the help of the indicated methods the big socio-economic tasks are efficiently resolved in our country, scientific-technical and economic growth are assured.

However, as is clear from the preceding discussion,[a] the basic work of the planning organs now, lies in the field of the current regulation of the proportions, solving problems which are different in principle and using other methods. The successes of planning in this field are more or less modest.'[2] Similarly, a Hungarian economist justifying the decision of his government to abolish the system of setting compulsory indices to enterprises has written that 'These indicators were, in some way or other, derived from the national economic plan but were mostly, by nature of things, only indirectly related to the latter. They restricted the scope of decision of enterprise leaders, restricted their chances of, and their inclination to initiative, their ambitions and sense of responsibility. The indicators did not, and in fact could not reckon with the local endowments and requirements of the enterprises, and, therefore did not help and sometimes even hindered the choice of the most favourable, economically most efficient solutions, i.e. the most rational utilisation of resources.'[3] Some of the ways in which current planning hinders the most rational utilisation of resources are as follows.

Slack plans

A notorious feature of the administrative economy is the tendency by enterprises to strive for a slack plan. The fact that in a socialist economy, which is supposed to have eliminated the contradiction between the productive forces and the productive relations which Marxists consider to be the reason for the inevitable downfall of capitalism, enterprises should seek to conceal their productive possibilities has long been regarded as undesirable by many Soviet economists,[4] and a major feature of the reform was a new incentive system designed to motivate enterprises to aim at taut plans. The reasons why enterprises strive to secure a slack plan when the economic mechanism is of the administrative type, seem to be as follows.

First, slack plans are an insurance against undesirable consequences of the 'administrative uncertainty' which characterises the Soviet economy.[b]

(a) 'The preceding discussion' is a brief description of the traditional system of planning by material balances, which, the authors consider, can not even lead to consistent plans, let alone optimal ones.

(b) Absence of the uncertainty which supposedly characterises capitalism is sometimes adduced as a major advantage of socialist planning, at any rate of investment. (See M. Dobb, *Welfare economics and the economics of socialism* (Cambridge 1969) passim especially pp. 122—123, and M. Nuti, Investment reforms in Czechoslovakia, *Soviet Studies* January 1970 p. 370.) Those who argue this way never pause to consider whether the uncertainty generated by the market mechanism is greater than or less than the uncertainty generated by the administrative economy. Indeed, they write as if they were unaware of the uncertainty generated by the administrative economy, which is in fact one of its most characteristic features.

114

There is uncertainty about the value of the plan for the following year, resulting from the absence of firm plans for a number of years ahead and the practice of planning from the achieved level. Uncertainty about the value of the plan for the following year is a major disincentive to adopt a taut plan as such a plan may merely result in the receipt of a more difficult plan in the following year. There is uncertainty about the final value of the plan for the 'planned' period, resulting from the instability of the plans. When a *Pravda* correspondent enquired of the chief accountant of an enterprise working under the *new* system why enterprises were still adopting slack plans, he was shown by way of reply a letter from Rosglavkhlopkoprom of the Ministry of light industry of the RSFSR received on 27th December raising the annual profits plan (of the year about to end) by 275 thousand roubles.[5] The instability of the operational 'plans' is an obstacle to the adoption of taut plans. Another type of uncertainty is uncertainty about the timely arrival of inputs resulting from the way that the supply system operates. A slack plan provides the enterprise with a buffer to absorb any increase in the plan or breakdown in supply during the planned period.

Secondly, the incentive system adopted may stimulate enterprises to aim at slack plans. It is convenient to distinguish between three types of incentive system, incentives related to plan fulfilment and over fulfilment, incentives for taut plans, and incentives for actual high results.[a] The first system is the one traditionally employed in the Soviet Union, the second was introduced in Czechoslovakia and Poland at the end of the 1950's and the beginning of the 1960's and the third is customary under managerial capitalism.

The system of incentives for plan fulfilment and overfulfilment can be written

$$B = a + b(Q_a - Q_p) \qquad \text{When } Q_a \geqslant Q_p.$$
$$B = 0 \qquad \text{When } Q_a < Q_p$$

$a, b > 0$

where B is the value of the bonus,

Q_p is the planned value of the bonus forming index, and

Q_a is the actual value of the bonus forming index.

This system is a strong disincentive for a risk averting enterprise to adopt a taut plan (because there is a risk that it may be underfulfilled which would lead to the total forfeiture of bonus payments), and would be a strong incentive to secure a high $(Q_a - Q_p)$, which can be achieved both by achieving a high value of the bonus forming index (achieving a high Q_a) and by securing a slack plan (obtaining a low Q_p) or by some combination of these strategies, were the values of a, b and Q_p in period $t + 1$ independent of the value of Q_a in period t. Generally Q_p in period $t + 1$ is related to Q_a in period t.

(a) This three fold distinction is Veselkov's. See F.S. Veselkov, *Stimuly vysokikh planovykh zadanii* (1968) p.3.

(This is known as 'planning from the achieved level'.) This provides a powerful disincentive for aiming at a high $(Q_a - Q_p)$ because such a result will simply make life more difficult in the following plan period.

It is important to realise that not only material but also moral incentives are related to plan fulfilment and overfulfilment. Bazarova has pointed out that in cases of plan underfulfilment 'the moral consequences are far from being unimportant. The enterprise which has not fulfilled its plan is responsible to the ministry or chief administration, to the regional (or district) committee of the party, to those shops and workers who did fulfil their obligations.'[6] For a Soviet manager, the attitude of his administrative superiors and controllers towards him is of great importance. This creates a situation in which a *Pravda* journalist gave as a reason for the failure of the reform to lead to the adoption of taut plans: 'It is no secret that the following idea is still firmly established in the consciousness of many managers: 110% means honour, a banner, a bonus and a place in the presidium, but 99% means scowls, reproaches and a stern talk in the district committee.'[7]

The system of incentives for taut plans can be written

$$B = aQ_p + ka(Q_a - Q_p)$$
$$a, k > 0$$

The first term provides an incentive to adopt a high plan. The higher the value of the bonus forming index, the higher the bonus. If $Q_a > Q_p$ $k < 1$. This condition ensures that an increase in the plan of e produces a greater bonus than overfulfilment of the plan by e, and hence provides a disincentive for the enterprise to conceal its possibilities and aim at a low plan when the plan is being drawn up and an incentive for it to aim at the highest possible plan, a so called 'taut' (*napryazhennyi*) plan.[a] Once the plan has been adopted there is still an incentive to overfulfil it (because $k > 0$), (although there is also an incentive, because $k < 1$, if any additional productive possibilities are discovered in the planned period not to take advantage of them but to incorporate them in the plan for the following period).

If $Q_a < Q_p$ $k > 1$

This condition ensures that underfulfilment of the plan by e reduces the bonus by more than the same reduction in the plan, and hence provides enterprises with a disincentive to adopt high plans which they are subsequently unable to fulfil, and provides them with a disincentive to underfulfil the plan.

(a) 'In the economic literature there is still not a sufficiently well founded answer to the question, what is a taut plan.' (V.K. Poltorygin, Napryazhennyi plan predpriyatiya i khozyaistvennaya reforma, in M.Z. Bor and V.K. Poltorygin (eds) *Planirovanie i khozyaistvennaya reforma* (1969) p. 41.) A taut plan is often identified with an efficient plan. As both Ames and Poltorygin have pointed out, however, if the enterprise has a U shaped cost curve there is a difference between the least cost output and the maximum output. (E. Ames, *Soviet economic processes* (Homewood Illinois 1965) p. 54; V.K. Poltorygin op cit.) Is a taut plan for the production of goods which are not needed 'efficient'?

116

Ceteris paribus, this type of incentive scheme is an incentive to adopt taut plans and a disincentive to underfulfil them.

The system of incentives for high results actually achieved can be written

$$B = aQ_a$$

This is the system normal under managerial capitalism (e.g. when executives receive bonuses tied to the level of the firm's profits). Ceteris paribus, this type of bonus system is an incentive to achieve a high value of the bonus forming index.

These formulae can easily be extended to the case where the bonus is related to several bonus forming indices, or to cases where non-proportional incentive schemes are used.

Prior to the reform the incentives used were of the first type, and had the negative effects one would expect, and this was an important reason for the reform, a major feature of which was a switch from incentive systems of the first type to incentive systems of the second type.

The process of formulating an enterprise plan can be regarded as a game between the authorities (e.g. the *glavk*) who do not know the productive possibilities of the enterprise, and the enterprise, which is interested in obtaining a slack plan. It is therefore scarcely surprising that the plans are often slack or impossible (impossible plans can arise if the *glavk* makes excessive corrections to the plan suggestions of the enterprise on the ground that the enterprise is aiming at a slack plan) both resulting in waste.

Criteria

The national economy is a complex hierarchical system whose objective is to maximise national economic welfare. At each level of the hierarchy it is necessary to adopt an appropriate criterion to guide decision makers to optimal solutions. Because maximisation of national economic welfare is too vague a criterion some more precise criterion must be adopted as a proxy for it.[a] The criteria used in the Soviet Union often stimulate waste. The central planners, concerned with maximising output, often ignore the cost of the output and its usefulness. Although the Soviet Union has caught up with the United States in the production of a number of important intermediate goods, they are often produced less efficiently, and the volume of final products derived from them is often lower, than in the United States.[8] In some of the experiments which preceded the reform it was found that instructing clothing factories to produce according to the requirements of shops led to a fall in the growth rate. But this did not signify that the experiments were a failure. It simply resulted from the fact that when given a choice the shops ordered a wider assortment of clothes than the planners would have ordered,

(a) The importance of choosing the right criterion in planning has been emphasised by C.J. Hitch and R.N. McKean. See their book *The economics of defence in the nuclear age* (Cambridge Mass. 1960) pp. 158—181.

as a result of which production runs were shorter and 'output' (measured in constant prices rather than in units measuring consumer satisfaction) lower.[9] The Ministries are primarily concerned with plan fulfilment and hence sometimes ignore proposals which would raise national economic efficiency but might jeopardise a Ministry's plan, such as the construction of specialised enterprises to provide low cost components for enterprises belonging to several ministries.[10] The enterprises are primarily concerned with securing a low plan for the production of goods with which they are familiar, and have little incentive to pay attention to the needs of customers, or innovate or make the most efficient use of the resources which they have.

The enterprise plan specifies the value of a large number of target variables. This may well be a source of waste. If there are targets for the use of inputs this may encourage their wasteful use. If gross output is a target variable then costs may be unnecessarily high or the assortment pattern undesirable.

A characteristic of enterprise operations is storming, that is a tremendous burst of effort towards the end of the planned period in order to fulfil the plan. This may well have adverse affects on quality.

The introduction of a new technology, to produce an old product in a more efficient way, or to produce a new product, tends to have an immediate adverse effect on plan fulfilment. Innovation is discouraged by a system that places so much stress on quarterly plan fulfilment (and where prices are unrelated to the usefulness of commodities).

Incentives for the efficient use of inputs are weak. For example, if the labour force were to be reduced, the wages fund would be reduced correspondingly, and this increase in efficiency by the enterprise would have brought no benefits to the enterprise.

It is precisely because of the long experience of unsatisfactory criteria for guiding and evaluating the work of enterprises that the idea of using profit as a synthetic success indicator gained ground in the Soviet Union in the early 1960s.

Instability of the plans

A characteristic feature of enterprise plans which has a serious adverse effect on the work of enterprises, is their instability.[11] The operational (quarterly and annual) plans of enterprises are often altered repeatedly during the course of the 'planned' period, and sometimes even retrospectively. The main reason for this is the fact, the reasons for which were explained in chapter 6, that the plans received by the enterprises are always inconsistent. As these inconsistencies come to light during the planned period, it is necessary to alter the plan to allow the economy to function. A typical example of an inconsistency leading to the alteration of a plan is the impossibility of fulfilling a plan because of the lack of a necessary input. It often happens that plans have to be altered because of inconsistencies between the current and perspective plans, for example the current plan assumed that there would be available as an input the products produced by a plant that has not yet been completed. The alterations in the plans made by the planners to correct imbalances in the plans may well create the need for futher alterations.

The above alterations in the plans result from the fact that the methods used in compiling them are such that the plans are always arithmetically inconsistent and alterations to them inevitable. There is, however, another cause of alterations in the plans, the fact that when the plans were drawn up insufficient account was taken of the possibilities for expanding output which then existed. The alterations in the plans for agricultural output which followed the September (1953) and the March (1965) Plena were a result of the failure of the CC prior to these plena to pursue policies which would lead to the efficient allocation of resources. Similarly, it often happens that designs (e.g. for equipment or for entire enterprises) are altered after they have been adopted as a result of a decision to adopt a superior technology which existed at the time the design was adopted and which should have been adopted in the first place.

There is also a third cause of alterations to the plans, namely changes in the situation (e.g. in technology, the weather or consumer tastes) after the plan is compiled. This type of alteration in the plan is not at all reprehensible (if the plan were left unchanged despite changes in the situation that would be reprehensible).

Clearly one way of minimising the need for changes in the plans would be for enterprises to have substantial reserves of inputs. This was referred to in the conclusion to chapter 6 as one of the ways of reducing the harmful effects on the economy of the inconsistency of the plans.

The instability of the enterprise operating plans is an integral feature of the administrative economy (because a method for solving the consistency problem does not exist, combined with the tendency to run the economy with a considerable degree of planners' tension) has an adverse effect on the work of enterprises, and is one of the reasons why enterprises try to receive slack plans.

Rationing of producer goods

The material inputs which enterprises need for production are not simply purchased from producers as they would be in a market economy but are allocated to consumer enterprises by the state supply organs. In effect this is a rationing system for producer goods. This system hinders the efficient working of enterprises and encourages enterprises to make socially wasteful decisions.

The efficient working of enterprises is hindered by the permanent shortage of almost all commodities which is associated with the supply system.[a] The supply system is such that goods often arrive late, resulting in the idleness of men and machines, and when they do arrive are of unsatisfactory quality. The difficulties to which the supply system gives rise are felt particularly harshly by the non-priority sectors of the economy. (A recent court case provides a vivid example of the problems which the supply system creates for the non-priority sectors of the economy. A state farm needed wood to build cow sheds and pig stys. Wood is one of the commodities that is centrally allocated, but unfortunately the farm received through the supply system only 10 per cent of the wood that it needed. Without cow sheds and pig stys the animals are scarcely likely to survive the winter. The deputy director of the farm for building obtained the necessary wood by reaching an agreement to buy the wood from a local quarry which was about to burn the trees on some land in order to clear it before starting quarrying. The deputy director of the farm and the director of the quarry were subsequently arrested, tried and found guilty. In his speech the prosecutor dismissed the defence that this example of enterprise initiative and direct contacts was in the interests of the state. 'This was done, in the interpretation of the defendants, in the interest of the state, although it seems to me that the state would have gained more if the quarry kept to its business and the farm to its, to produce agricultural products, in particular in view of the fact that wood is supplied to it in a centralised way.'[b]). Hence the administrative economy, which works satisfactorily (from the point of view of the leaders' objectives) when there is a large non-priority sector of the economy (such as agriculture and personal consumption) which feel the brunt of shortages and waste, becomes less satisfactory when as a result of policy changes it is no longer possible to regard personal consumption as a residual, and formerly residual areas of the economy such as agriculture and housing construction come to be regarded as priority sectors in addition to

(a) To a considerable extent, it is not the shortages that create the need for the supply system, but the supply system that creates the shortages.

Devons has observed that in the British aircraft industry in World War II 'a real but quite small shortage was soon inflated into a desperate and enormous scarcity. For as soon as the users found out that there was a shortage, they would conceal any stocks that they already possessed and would put in exaggerated demands for further supplies, in order to ensure that they got the maximum share of the limited supplies available. This applied not only to the manufacturers using the component, but also to the squadrons both at home and overseas. And this paper shortage would not be deflated until the users were so flooded with supplies that they felt confident that they could get what they wanted without building up their own private hoards. And then the inflated demand would collapse overnight.' E. Devons, *Planning in practice* (1950) p. 79.

(a) The trial was reported in *Literaturnaya Gazeta* 1969 No. 27 p. 10. The defendants were also guilty of other crimes, for example, because spare parts, though theoretically supplied through the supply system were in practice unobtainable, the farm bought some stolen parts on the black market. In addition it was necessary to fake some documents for all these expenditures to appear as legitimate transactions in the books of the farm.

the already existing priority sectors (defence, space, industrial investment).

In order to insulate themselves from the fallible supply system, enterprises often produce their own inputs, raising the cost of production by not benefiting from economies of scale, and ministries try to become self-sufficient rather than rely on the fallible supply system.

Prices

The traditional pricing system was such that prices were not suitable as a guide to efficient resource allocation, partly because some goods and services were not priced at all, and partly because the prices of those commodities that were priced were not such as to lead enterprises to make socially rational decisions.[12]

Capital goods were free to the enterprise. Hence the enterprise had no incentive to sell superfluous equipment nor did it have an incentive to ensure that its applications for capital goods were economically justified. For example in 1965 a state farm on the virgin lands sent in an application for 10 tractors, although it already had 40 'unemployed' tractors.[a]

There was no payment for the use of natural resources. Hence there was no incentive to economise on their use. At the present time more than twice as much water is used in the production of a ton of steel than is envisaged by the technical norms. Though free to the steel plants this water has a cost to society.[13]

The so-called 'prices of economic events'[b] were poorly developed. By these are meant the prices of goods or services used or delivered under special circumstances, e.g. high prices of electric power during peak hours, higher interest rates for overdue credit payments, penalties for delayed unloading of railway carriages. The permanent sellers' market, combined with the absence of competition and the lack of fines for the late delivery of goods, placed customers in a weak position.

A substantial part of industrial production is priced according to an individual cost plus formula. This provides no incentive for the efficient use of inputs. It may even create a situation where the demand curve for

(a) G.S. Lisichkin, *Plan i rynok* (1966) p. 60.
This is analogous to the fact that in United States defence contracting there is a tendency by firms to hoard

'engineers, technicians, skilled production workers, and administrative personnel not required on current contracts but useful for winning and executing future contracts ... Performing work "in house" which could be done more efficiently by specialist vendors is another means ... of building up new capabilities for future business. Engaging in technical tasks and buying equipment essentially unrelated to an ungoing development effort also enhances an organisation's ability to compete in new fields for profitable future contracts.'

(F.M. Scherer, *The weapons acquisitions process: Economic incentives* (Boston 1964) p. 183). Such phenomena arise whenever the accounting cost of an activity is less than the user cost of not doing it.

(b) The phrase is Zielinski's. See, On the theory of success indicators, *Economics of planning* 1967, No. 1.

inputs slopes up to the right.[a]

Industry wholesale prices do not reflect the relative usefulness of goods to customers, and this facilitates waste, as the following example illustrates.

An enterprise in Tambov was making an obsolete, though adequate, machine for vulcanising tyres. This gave it a 1968 sales plan of 8 600 000 roubles. It was proposed that in 1969 it should switch over to a new automatic line which vulcanises at much greater speed and with considerable economy of labour. Prices, however, are such that sales in 1969 would be only 5 000 000 roubles if the new machine were produced.

'Isn't national economic efficiency taken into account in determining the the prices of new produces?'

'The price of new chemical equipment depends primarily on its weight.'[14] Hence it is not in the interest of the plant to produce the new machinery. This would reduce its sales and thus its incentive funds. This difficulty in adapting output to requirements arises from the combination of the existing price system, the absence of competition, the permanent sellers' market, and the fact that enterprises are judged not by the extent to which they satisfy demand but by the extent to which they fulfil the plan. If the planners had available to them sufficient information and time then there would be no problem: the planners would simply instruct the enterprises to make socially rational decisions. The planners, however, do not have available sufficient information and time to make socially rational decisions throughout the economy. The advocates of an optimally functioning economic system consider that whereas instructions from the planners, and prices determined by administrators at lengthy intervals, are unable to bring about rational decision making throughout the economy (because the planners lack the necessary time and information required to issue the necessary instructions, and administratively determined prices reflect the situation at some more or less distant date in the past) this function could be performed by prices determined by agreement between producers and customers (within limits determined by the planners).

Personal consumption

An important negative aspect of the administrative economy is inattention to

---

(a) Attention has been drawn to the importance of individual cost plus prices and their adverse effects on efficiency, by Zielinski. See his article, On the theory of success indicators, *Economics of Planning* 1967 No. 1 pp. 14–15. Cf V.V. Sitnin, *Problemy pribyli i khozyaistvennogo rascheta v promyshlennosti* (1969) pp. 152–158, N.V. Garetovsky, *Finansy i kredit v usloviyakh khozyaistvennoi reformy* (1969) pp. 153–155, and I.K. Salimzhanov, B.A. Neroslavskaya and Ye.P. Rychin, *Tseny na tovary kul'turno-bytovogo i khozyaistvennogo naznacheniya* (1969) pp. 23–24.

'Individual cost plus prices' is an analytical term. In Soviet practice such prices are known variously as settlement prices or temporary prices.

Wakar and Zielinski have referred to the process by which planning drives out cheap inputs and replaces them by more expensive ones, as 'Gresham's Law in reverse'. See their article in *American Economic Review* March 1963.

private consumption. Aspects of the inattention to private consumption in the USSR are the restricted assortment of consumer goods and services available (e.g. the inadequate arrangements for maintenance of the housing stock), the poor quality of many of the goods that are available (e.g. the poor quality of many of the potatoes and apples), the intermittent supply of consumer goods (it often happens that basic goods such as eggs are simply unavailable for several days), and the poor supply of consumer goods in provincial towns and villages.

Queues and shortages are characteristic features of the administrative economy. It often happens that a particular commodity is unavailable in a particular place, or can only be obtained by queuing, because the commodity has been priced below the equilibrium price (and the activities of the trade and production organs are determined not by consumer demand as expressed in the market but by administrative considerations). This gives rise to irritation among fustrated purchasers and those who have to stand in queues, and to black marketeering. An important theme in the writings of Novozhilov was the argument that shortages and queues are not inevitable, that by suitable use of the price mechanism they can be overcome. In 1926 he published an article in which he criticised the idea being propagated at that time by politicians and newspapers that the Soviet Union was suffering from a 'goods famine', argued that it was actually suffering from a suppressed inflation and that the way to deal with the problem was to raise prices.[15] In his famous 1959 paper he reverted to this theme and explained that the underpricing of goods leads to expenditure of 'time and effort on the search for scarce goods and standing in queues. At the same time unproductive and even criminal actions (speculation in scarce goods, under the counter sales by assistants of the scarce goods etc.) become the source of unjustified enrichment'.[16] Novozhilov's repeated variations on the theme of the price mechanism as the most efficient way of allocating scarce goods between consumers have been repeatedly rejected by the authorities on the ground that the way to overcome shortages is not to raise prices but to expand output. Commenting on Fedorenko's 1968 book a deputy chairman of Gosplan USSR explained once more that 'It is very easy it turns out, to overcome a shortage of this or that product − it is sufficient to raise their prices ... [However] the raising of prices consciously places limits on the possibilities of satisfying the needs of the members of society instead of devoting all our efforts to their satisfaction by means of growth (increasing investment) and raising labour productivity.'[17] Hence in 1970 we read, for example, about a shortage of crockery in the biggest department store in the country, and about how in the town of Bryansk there are long queues in factory canteens because plates are a scarce good.[18]

In the administrative economy the production of consumer goods does not respond quickly to changes in demand. For example, in the period 1962−65 above the norm stocks in the retail network were never less than two milliard roubles (about one per cent of the national income). Table 7.1 shows how the stocks of some goods continued to rise as demand fell.

Table 7.1   *Sales and stocks: 1965 as percentages of 1960* [19]

Commodity	Sales	Stocks in retail network
Cotton fabrics	78.7	227.9
Woollen fabrics	81.6	130.0
Iron beds	76.2	128.5
Sewing machines	48.4	226.0

The result of planning from the achieved level, combined with inflexible prices and plans for output rather than sales, was that when demand for some goods was saturated, instead of producing different desired commodities, the unwanted goods were produced as before and piled up in warehouses. Simultaneously there were other goods the output of which increased at a slower rate than the demand for them. In 1965 the demand for leather footwear increased by 11 per cent over 1964 and stocks fell by 13.5 per cent; the demand for furniture increased by 10.3 per cent and stocks fell by 15.7 per cent. A similar situation existed with respect to ready made clothes. In other words, supply diverged sharply from demand. For those goods for which demand was falling supply continued to increase and unwanted goods accummulated. For those goods for which demand was increasing fast supply expanded less fast.

A major feature of the reform was a change in the method of determining the production plans of many enterprises producing consumer goods. Whereas formerly these plans were determined by the higher administrative bodies, under the reform they are determined by agreement between producer enterprises and the retail trade. In many cases this has led to major changes in the assortment pattern, as table 7.2 illustrates.

Table 7.2   *Alterations in the production plan of the Beloomutski Clothing Factory (Moscow Region)* [20]

Production
(thousands of articles)

Article	According to plan drawn up in the traditional way	According to plan drawn up on the basis of direct contacts	Output according to new plan as % of output according to old plan
Winter clothes for school children	66.6	116.8	175.4
Half length winter coats for school children	20.0	13.2	66.0
Spring coats for school children	53.3	98.9	185.5
Childrens raincoats	61.7	20.9	33.9
Coats for nursery school children	18.6	4.4	23.7
Winter coats for pre school children	41.3	15.5	37.5

The striking divergence between the assortment pattern based on instructions from the planners, and that based on orders from the retail trade corroborates the observation of two Poles: 'The adaption of production to needs can be made only by the market buyer — and ultimately by the consumer — but never by the central planner who fixes the prices of goods by himself and without reference to the market and who judges an enterprise by its execution of central directive indices ...'[21]

Bureaucratisation

In 1937 Lange argued that 'the real danger of socialism is that of a bureaucratisation of economic life, and not the impossibility of coping with the problem of allocation of resources.'[22] The experience of the Soviet Union and other socialist countries corroborates the argument that the bureaucratisation of economic life is a serious danger under socialism, and a major reason for the transition from the administrative economy in Yugoslavia and Hungary, the abortive transition in Czechoslovakia, and the discussion of economic reform in the USSR has been to reduce the bureaucratic elements in economic life.[23]

Whereas in a market economy decisions are made by managers in response to economic signals, in an administrative economy they are made by officials in accordance with official procedure.[24] The programme of the optimal planners to reduce the bureaucratisation of economic life is twofold. First many of the decisions currently being made by the planners in an arbitrary, voluntaristic, way, should be made by the use of objective, scientific methods. The optimal planners have devoted great efforts to developing objective, rational, methods for decision making, for example in the field of the optimal development and location of industries.

Secondly, whereas at the present time many decisions by enterprise management require the approval of some higher official,[25] the optimal planners propose that such decisions should be made by enterprise management in response to economic criteria.

Conclusion

'This study discusses many unfavourable aspects of our economic mechanism. But we must not forget that planning has made it possible to ensure full employment and the rapid increase in the quantity of production which has been described above. Hence, improvements in administering the economy must be brought about in such a way as to ensure that any changes will develop further these advantageous aspects of our economic mechanism rather than endangering them.'

J. Kornai[26]

In conclusion it may be noted:

(1) It is important not to contrast the situation actually existing now with an idealised situation that might exist. If enterprises were simply instructed to maximise profits, and given a free hand, the experience of capitalist

125

firms suggests that they might well operate within the efficiency frontier.

(2) Although the administrative economy clearly has costs, it is important when contemplating possible reforms to offset possible gains in efficiency against possible adverse effects on major policy objectives (such as the ability of the state to determine the main directions of development, price stability, the level of employment, the distribution of income, and regional policy).

(3) Where decentralization is advocated because the enterprises have better knowledge than the planners of their own possibilities, it is important to bear in mind the general planning rule that 'Because centralization restricts lower-level actions, it should be justified only on the grounds that the restrictions lead to better overall behaviour of the organisation. This is true only when significant interactions exist between lower level units. If a sub-unit interacts very weakly with other parts of the organisation, it is desirable to assign the sub-unit only loose goals consistent with those of the organisation as a whole (a "suitable" return on investment, say). In this way, the sub-unit is free to exploit its own detailed knowledge of its operations and environment.'[27] In other words, centralize where, and only where, this is necessary in order to internalise what would appear as externalities at some lower level.[28]

(4) The elements of the economic system are closely linked together, and this must be borne in mind when introducing reforms. The price system, the supply system, the incentive system, the criteria used, and the degree of centralization are inseparably interconnected. For example, to give the enterprise more autonomy in determining its assortment pattern, given the existing price system, is scarcely likely to increase efficiency.

The Hungarian economist Kornai long ago observed that 'One cannot exchange a cog in an integrated, functioning machine for another one of quite a different type. The latter may be new, but it will obstruct the working of the machine nevertheless ... A solution can only be found by taking a comprehensive view of both centralization and decentralization and by renouncing the idea of piecemeal tinkering with the economic mechanism in the course of efforts to change it ... The reforms we need are of a kind which will improve all the major methods and institutions of our economic mechanism in a systematic, parallel and harmonious manner. In other words, the job of transforming the system of plan index numbers should be matched by an overhaul of the system of incentives and of prices, as well as of the functioning of the monetary and credit systems etc.

It is not necessary that all these changes should be brought about all at once in every sphere; this would probably create too much of an upheaval. It is possible to carry out the reforms that are needed in a number of stages. What is essential is that the changes brought about in various spheres should complement one another in an organic manner. They should constitute parts of a thoroughly thought out, centrally coordinated series of reforms based on a unified conception.'[29]

126

The theory of the optimally functioning economy is being developed precisely to serve as the 'unified conception' which could form the theoretical basis of a 'thoroughly thought out, centrally coordinated series of reforms.'.

Appendix   The optimal value of an enterprise output plan–a suggestion for behavioural research

Considerable work has been done recently in working out a comparative statics theory of the Soviet enterprise[1] analogous to the comparative statics theory of the profit maximising firm,[2] in which the distinguishing feature of the Soviet enterprise is taken to be that it is an output maximiser rather than a profit maximiser. The most obvious difference between a Soviet enterprise and a capitalist firm is not that one is an output maximiser and one a profit maximiser, but that one has a plan to fulfil and the other does not. To ascertain the effect of the plan on the efficiency of the enterprises, and to determine the optimal value of the plan, are important planning problems.

In the British Ministry of Aircraft Production in World War II officials argued about the relative desirability of setting aircraft firms 'target' and 'realistic' programs. The main argument in favour of the target or carrot principle was that firms would exert their maximum effort only if asked to do a little more than the firm could really be expected to achieve. The main argument for realistic planning was the waste and lack of balance in the production of aircraft components and materials when planning was of the target type. Although the argument for realistic planning was soon generally accepted, production was usually 10–15% below programme, and no aircraft programme was ever achieved 100% for more than a single month.[3]

Hofstede[4] analysing the effect of budgets on the cost behaviour of capitalist firms, summed up his results in the diagram which follows. It is assumed that without a budget costs will be at the level N. The diagram shows the effect on costs of various budgets ranging from very loose to very tight. In case 1 the budget is very loose. The budgetee is aware of this and sets his aspiration level somewhat better. The result will be equal to the aspiration level. The introduction of a budget has resulted in a deterioration in the cost situation. In case 2 the budget coincides with N. Aspiration level and result coincide with the budget. In this case the budget does not influence behaviour. In case 3 the budget is below N. The budgetee adopts his aspiration level to the budget. The result shows that the budget has a positive influence in reducing costs. In case 4 the budget has become still tighter. Although the budgetee aspires to do better the result is not as good as the aspiration level. In case 5 the budget is very tight. The budgetee sees it as 'almost impossible' and sets a less ambitious aspiration level than in case 4. In case 6 the budget is so tight that the budgetee sees it as

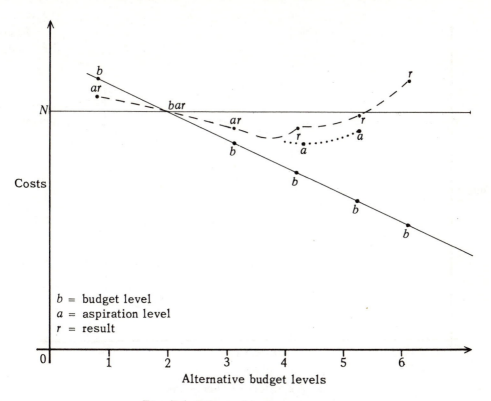

Fig. 7.1 *Effect of budget on costs*

impossible and stops trying. He sets no aspiring level and his negative attitude about the impossible budget may make the actual result worse than would have been the case without the budget.

Clearly of the 6 possible budgets two (1 and 6) make the situation worse than it would otherwise have been, one (2) has no effect, and the optimal budget is between 3 and 4. The problem is complicated when we look at budget levels over time. Case 4 can scarcely remain the budget for repeated periods because if the budget is normally not attained it will cease to control costs.

Suppose that the output plan has a similar effect on the output of Soviet enterprises. Then we have the situation shown in figure 7.2. The optimal plan is P_0. The plan is underfulfilled, but output is maximised. The fact that Soviet enterprise plans are normally overfulfilled, suggests that they may be the left of a, that is, that they may be having an adverse effect on output.

The suggestion put forward in this appendix can be expressed as follows. Normally economists assume that the output of an enterprise is a function of its material inputs:

$$Q = f(x \ \ldots x_n)$$

But in fact one of the arguments of the production function may be the

129

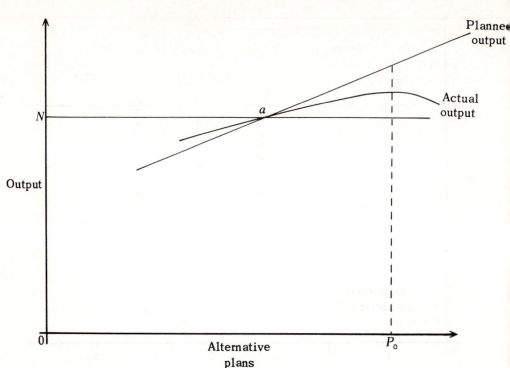

Fig. 7.2 *Effect of plan on output*

enterprise plan via its effect on the behaviour of enterprise management :

$$Q = f(x_1 \ldots x_n, P)$$

and one of the necessary conditions for a maximum is

$$\frac{\partial Q}{\partial P} = 0$$

i.e. the marginal product of the plan equals zero.

Conclusion

It would be desirable to conduct empirical research on the influence of the plan on enterprise behaviour in order to develop rules for determining the optimal value of the enterprise plan.[5]

130

8. Can the optimal planners help improve the economic mechanism?

Kantorovich and Gorstko have argued that:

'The practical value of the conception of optimal planning, the proof of the fact that this method is not purely theoretical, is confirmed by the fact that a number of its conclusions (payment for capital, the significance of profit as an index and others) coincided with the suggestions of practical men, organisers of production, progressive economists and technicians, put forward in the process of preparing the economic reform.

Experience has clearly demonstrated the progressive nature of the new system of management, which facilitates the development of the creative initiative of collectives and stimulates the enterprises to search for internal reserves.' [1]

A central feature of the 'new system of management' is the system of enterprise incentive funds.[a] The purpose of this chapter is to describe and evaluate the system of enterprise funds introduced as part of the reform in order to consider whether it really is true that 'experience has clearly demonstrated the progressive nature of the new system of management' and hence the validity of the conclusion of the optimal planners (the derivation of which was explained in chapter IV above) of 'the significance of profit as an index'.

There are three (major) enterprise incentive funds, the material incentive fund or MIF, the socio-cultural and housing fund or SCF, and the production development fund or PDF. The MIF is a source of cash bonuses; the SCF is a source of finance for equipment for canteens and kindergartens, passes to rest homes and sanatoria, and the building and repair of housing and children's holiday camps; and the PDF is a source of finance for the modernisation and expansion of plant and equipment. The planning of the incentive funds of an enterprise is only part of the financial planning of an enterprise which in turn is only a part of enterprise planning which includes in addition technical, supply, labour and marketing planning.

(a) The existence of a source of finance to be utilised for material incentives is not an innovation introduced into the Soviet economy by the reform. During NEP the trusts had a fund for improving the life of the workers, which according to a statute of 1928 was equal to 10 per cent of the net profit of a trust, and which was used mainly for financing housing. There was a separate system of incentives for managerial personnel. In 1936 the various incentive funds were combined into the director's fund, which was formed from 4 per cent of the planned profit and 50 per cent of the above plan profit. In 1955 the director's fund was replaced by the enterprise fund.

In general the MIF is planned as follows:

$$MIF_p = [a\Delta S_p + bP_p] \frac{WF}{100} \tag{1}$$

where MIF_p is the planned material incentive fund,

ΔS_p is the planned percentage increase in sales in the planned year compared to the previous year,

P_p is the planned level of profitability,

WF is the wages fund, and

a and b are norms fixed by the ministry.

For example, let $a = 0.5$, $b = 0.3$, $\Delta S_p = 10$, and $P_p = 15$. Then $MIF_p = 9.5$ per cent of the wages fund. [a] Profitability is defined as follows:

$$P = \frac{PR}{K_f + K_c} \tag{2}$$

where PR is profit, K_f is fixed capital, and

K_c is circulating capital.

This definition of profitability is an innovation introduced into the Soviet economy by the reform. Prior to the reform profitability was defined as the ratio of profit to costs, i.e. material and wage costs.

The 'Methodological instructions on the transfer of enterprises, associations and branches of industry to the new system of planning and economic incentives' approved by the Interdepartmental commission attached to Gosplan USSR on 2nd December 1966, stated that fixed capital is to be valued at cost (without allowance for depreciation). The purpose of this was to put 'old' and 'new' enterprises on an equal footing, i.e. to avoid penalising 'new' enterprises and thus hindering technical progress. That part of fixed capital on which it is not necessary to pay interest to the state is also excluded from the capital stock for the purpose of calculating profitability.

The value of circulating capital for the purpose of working out planned profitability is the total value of circulating capital.according to the norms for circulating capital. The value of circulating capital for the purpose of working out actual profitability is actual circulating capital less loans from

(a) Formula (1) and the similar formulae (5) and (6) for the formation of the other funds, give a misleading idea of how the funds were formed in the transitional period prior to the establishment of stable norms (1966–69). In actual fact, when enterprises transferred to the new system it was not the incentive funds which were derived from the norms, but the norms which were derived from the incentive funds. The MIF_p was calculated by adding up the anticipated bonuses for the engineering-technical personnel and employees, the payments from the enterprise fund, and the enterprise's share of the additional profit included in the plan as part of the transition to the new system. Given MIF_p, ΔS_p and P_p, and the proportion of the MIF_p derived from each of the fund forming indices, a and b were calculated.

Gosbank to finance stocks and less the value of stocks which have not yet been paid for by the enterprise.

In some cases the increase in planned sales is replaced as a fund forming index by the increase in planned profits so that the formula for planning the MIF is

$$\text{MIF}_p = [a\Delta PR_p + bP_p] \frac{WF}{100} \tag{3}$$

where ΔPR_p is the planned percentage increase in profits in the planned year compared to the previous year. Moreover, in industries such as ship-building (which has a long production cycle) and coal mining (some mines have a declining output), in unprofitable and planned loss enterprises, and in some non-industrial sectors of the economy, formulae other than (1) or (3) are employed. There are similar exceptions to the general formulae described below for the formation of the other funds. As from 1970 (1) has been modified so as to encourage increases in labour productivity. This is explained in detail below.

(1) is a simplification, the full formula is:

$$\text{MIF}_p = \left([a\Delta S_p + bP_p] \frac{WF}{100} + cQ_p \right)\left(1 + dN_p \right) \tag{4}$$

where c and d are norms,

Q$_p$ is the planned addition to profits from an increase in prices authorised as a result of an improvement in the quality of production, and

N$_p$ is the planned proportion of new products in the total output of the enterprise.

cQ$_p$ is normally a relatively small sum, and although the decree of the Central Committee and Council of Minister of October 4th 1965 envisaged that the last term in (4) would be significant, the rules governing it have not yet been worked out properly and it was not included in the Methodo-logical instructions of December 2nd 1966. Hence it is not very inaccurate to consider the simpler formula (1) as the operative one, prior to the application of the new rules formulated in the regulation on stable norms issued in 1969, which is explained below.

For accounting purposes the bonuses paid to the workers out of the wages fund are included in the MIF, although they are planned as part of the wages fund.

The purpose of (1) is clear, to provide the enterprise with an incentive to increase its planned sales (which is regarded as a proxy for the volume of consumer satisfaction resulting from the work of the enterprise) and its planned profitability (which is regarded as a measure of the efficiency with which the enterprise is operating). The reason for relating the size of the incentive funds to the wages fund rather than, say, to total profits directly, is to reduce the dispersion of per capita incentive payments between enterprises resulting from the dispersion of profitability rates and profits per capita, between enterprises.

V.F. Kotov, deputy head of the department of finance and costs of Gosplan USSR, has suggested that to value fixed capital at historic cost without allowance for depreciation, is mistaken, and that it would be better to value fixed capital at cost less depreciation. In view of the fact that when machinery goes into batch or mass production its price is reduced, and the fact that the prices of machines are periodically altered, it would be desirable to use comparable prices in the valuation of fixed capital. How to do this 'remains a methodologically unsolved question'.

Kotov has also suggested that to allow bank loans to be deducted from the total of circulating capital when working out actual profitability, is undesirable. If an enterprise has above the norm stocks these will normally be financed by loans from Gosbank. Hence above the norm stocks do not reduce the enterprise's profitability (except by the low interest payments on bank loans), although (when these additional stocks do not result from a cause beyond the control of the enterprise) they are an inefficiency which, Kotov argues, ought to be reflected in the enterprise's actual profitability figure.[2]

The planned socio-cultural and housing fund is calculated as follows:

$$SCF_p = [f\Delta S_p + gP_p] \frac{WF}{100} \tag{5}$$

where f and g are norms fixed by the ministry.

The purpose of (5) is to provide the enterprise with finance for socio-cultural and housing purposes, and with an additional incentive to raise its sales and profitability.

The planned production development fund is calculated as follows:

$$PDF_p = hD_p + E_p + [i\Delta S_p + jP_p] \frac{K_f}{100} \tag{6}$$

where D_p is planned depreciation,

E_p is the income which it is planned to realise by the sale of superfluous equipment, and

h, i and j are norms fixed by the ministry (h is normally between 0.15 and 0.45 and its model value is 0.40).

The entire capital stock of the USSR is to be revalued as of 1st January 1971 (with the exception of agriculture where the capital stock is to be revalued as of 1st January 1972) and simultaneously the depreciation norms, i.e. the norms which relate the depreciation fund to the capital stock, will be reviewed.

The purpose of the *PDF* is to provide the enterprise with a source of finance for the modernisation and expansion of production, and with an additional incentive to raise its sales and profitability.

The actual size of the enterprise incentive funds depends both on the planned size of the funds and on the degree of plan fulfilment. The actual *MIF* is calculated as follows:

134

$$MIF_a = [a\Delta S_p + ka(\Delta S_a - \Delta S_p) + bP_p + kb(P_a - P_p)]\frac{WF}{100} \qquad (7)^{(a)}$$

where the subscript a denotes the actual (as opposed to the planned) value of a variable.

If the plan is fulfilled 100 per cent, then (7) reduces to (1). When $\Delta S_a > \Delta S_p$ and $P_a > P_p$, i.e. when the plan is overfulfilled, $k \leq 0.7$. The purpose of this is to provide enterprises with an incentive to adopt a high plan. If the plan is overfulfilled then the enterprise receives additional payments into its MIF, but these payments are at least 30 per cent less than they would have been if the additional output and profitability had been included in the plan. When the plan is underfulfilled, $k \geq 1.3$. The point of this is to prevent an enterprise acquiring large incentive funds by adopting a high plan which remains underfulfilled, and to provide the enterprise with a disincentive to underfulfill the plan.

(7) is a simplification. The MIF_a may be reduced also if the plan for the more important items of output is underfulfilled. In addition, as from 1969 the procedure was introduced of placing part of the MIF in reserve (for use in future years or transferred to the SCF) if the rate of increase of average wages exceeds the rate of increase of labour productivity. At the end of 1969 an official of the State Committee on Labour and Wages noted [3] that 'the question is now being discussed' of differentiating the norms which relate the proportion of the MIF placed in reserve to the excess of the increase in average wages over labour productivity, according to the circumstances of particular enterprises.[b] There is a rule that

$$MIF_a \geq 40 \text{ per cent } MIF_p \qquad (8)$$

The actual socio-cultural and housing fund is calculated analogously:

$$SCF_a = [f\Delta S_p + kf(\Delta S_a - \Delta S_p) + gP_p + kg(P_a - P_p)]\frac{WF}{100} \qquad (9)$$

The actual production development fund is calculated analogously:

$$PDF_a = hD_a + E_a + [i\Delta S_p + ki(\Delta S_a - \Delta S_p) + jP_p + kj(P_a - P_p)]\frac{K_f}{100} \qquad (10)$$

(a) 'The existing procedure for calculating the incentive funds is very complicated. As a result there are many mistakes in calculating the incentive funds especially in cases of overfulfilment or underfulfilment of the plan. Analysis of the calculations at several administrations showed considerable mistakes in the calculation of the incentive funds leading both to their increase and decrease.'

K.V. Shelyutto and Chertok E.A. *Ekonomicheskaya reforma i mestnoi promyshlennosti* (1969) p. 57.

(b) One aspect of the reform has been the introduction of fines for contract violation, i.e. for failing to deliver the goods specified at the time specified. These do not seem to have been very effective. It has been suggested that their effectiveness would be increased if they were paid not out of the profit of an enterprise, but out of its MIF.

135

Payments into the enterprise incentive funds are made quarterly in arrears on the basis of the quarterly plan fulfillment data (advances into the funds may be made in the first and second months of the quarter) out of the enterprise's profits (and depreciation).

Out of its gross profits (sales revenue less material and labour costs and depreciation) an enterprise pays the state interest on its capital, rent or fixed payments, and interest on bank loans. The net profit remaining is the figure for profit used in calculating profitability. Out of this net profit the enterprise incentive funds are formed (except for that part of the *PDF* which comes from depreciation or the sale of superfluous equipment). The residual profit is paid to the state. (Interest on capital, and rent or fixed payments, are innovations introduced into the Soviet economy by the reform.)

The distribution of profit is shown in table 8.1.

Table 8.1   *Utilisation of the profit of industrial enterprises working under the new Conditions of Planning and Incentives in 1968 (in percentages)*

Profit received — total		<u>100</u>
Of which:		
Paid into the state budget		67
paid prior to the transfer to the new system	9	
interest on capital	17	
rent and fixed payments	5	
residual profit	36	
Remaining at the disposition of the enterprise		33
Of which:		
paid into the enterprise incentive funds and other funds	14	
used for financing investment	10	
other uses	9	

Source: *Narodnoe Khozyaistvo SSR v 1968 g* (1969) p. 772.

During the period of transition to the new system the size of the *MIF* and *SCF* relative to the wages fund showed a wide dispersion, even within a single industry, as table 8.2 shows.

Table 8.2   *Enterprise incentive funds in non-ferrous metallurgy*
according to the plan for 1966 as a percentage of the
Planned Wages Fund [4]

	Moscow hard alloy kombinat	Ust-kamenogorsk kombinat	Norilsk mining-metallurgical kombinat
MIF	11.82	7.47	3.19
SCF	4.02	1.88	0.97

In 1967 it was decided [5] that, in general, the following relations should hold:

$$MIF_p \leq 10 \text{ per cent } WF \qquad (11)$$

$$SCF_p \leq 4 \text{ per cent } WF$$

Similarly during the transitional period the size of the *PDF* relative to the capital stock showed a wide dispersion. For 580 enterprises transferred to the new system in 1966 the *PDF* was on average 2 per cent of the total fixed capital of the enterprise and about 4 per cent of the active part of the fixed capital. For 25 per cent of the enterprises it was 5 per cent or more, and for 10 per cent of the enterprises it was less than 1 per cent, of the active part of fixed capital. [a] In 1967 it was estimated that when the whole of industry had transferred to the new system the *PDF* for industry as a whole would amount to 5.5–6 per cent of the active part of fixed capital and 1/5 of all investment in industry.

During the transition to the new system (1966–69) the *MIF* and *SCF* depended mainly on profitability rather than on the increase in sales (or profits). For example, in 1967 about 70 per cent of the *MIF* was derived from profitability, and only about 30 per cent from the increase in sales. It has been decided that this is unsatisfactory. In the regulation on stable norms adopted in 1969 it is stated that the proportion of the incentive funds derived from incremental sales should be not less than 40 per cent for industry as a whole, and in the production of consumer goods and services not less than 60 per cent. (One reason for the tendency to relate the enterprise incentive funds predominantly to profitability rather than to the increase in sales (or profits) is that the former is often more stable than the latter, i.e. it often fluctuates less from year to year.) The *PDF* depends mainly on the depreciation payments, as table 8.3 makes clear. 5 306 million roubles was just under 2 per cent of the value of gross industrial production.

'Some enterprises, and sometimes ministries as well, are arguing that the *PDF*, formed on the basis of the existing norms, will not be utilised rationally, because the enterprises do not need such large *PDF*s. At the same time there are enterprises and ministries which argue that the *PDF* formed

---

(a) By the 'active part of fixed capital' is meant machines and equipment as opposed to buildings. It is appropriate to compare the *PDF* with the active part of fixed capital because the *PDF* is largely devoted to replacing and improving the machinery and equipment available to the enterprise.

Table 8.3 *Formation of Enterprise Incentive Funds for Industrial Enterprises Working in the new Conditions in 1968 (millions of roubles)*[6]

	Total paid in	Paid out of profit	Paid out of deprec- iation	Receipts from sale of equipment	Other sources
Total	5 306	4 038	1 027	164	77
of which					
MIF	2 581	2 526	–	–	55
SCF	852	837	–	–	15
PDF	1 873	675	1 027	164	7

on the basis of the norms is insufficient for maintaining and modernising the capital stock. Hence there arises the need to solve the problem of the optimal value of the *PDF*. This question is becoming steadily more urgent.'[7] Soviet planners are likely to deal with this problem partly by adjusting the norms in the light of experience of which enterprises need their *PDF*s and which enterprises do not, and partly by means of the centralised incentive funds.[a] (In a questionnaire answered by 241 directors of enterprises in Siberia and the Far East in 1969, 74 per cent of the respondents thought that the size of the *PDF* was inadequate.[8])

The rules for paying bonuses out of the *MIF* are worked out by each enterprise in accordance with its own conditions, on the basis of the model regulation decreed by the State Committee on Labour and Wages and the Presidium of the All-Union Central Council of Trade Unions on 4th February 1967. Five types of premia are paid out of the *MIF*, current premia according to the factory premium system, once and for all premia for excellent work, grants to needy personnel, bonuses based on annual results, and premia for intra-enterprise socialist competition. Different rules govern the payment of premia to workers, engineering-technical personnel and employees, and managerial personnel.[b]

The creation of the enterprise incentive funds has had two kinds of

(a) In May 1968 the Interdepartmental Commission decided that in trusts, associations, kombinats and administrations which have gone over to commercial methods, up to 10 per cent of the *MIF* and up to 50 per cent of the *PDF* may be centralised, that is they are paid out of the profit of the enterprises and used by the higher organisation. The centralised *MIF* is used both for premia to enterprise personnel for activities that have a positive significance for the organisation as a whole, and for premia to officials of the higher organisation. The centralised *PDF* is used in the interest of the organisation as a whole.

(b) In the Soviet Union industrial personnel are divided into three categories, 'workers', i.e. manual workers, 'employees', i.e. white collar workers such as clerks in the accounts department, and 'engineering-technical personnel', i.e. engineering and technical personnel with a higher or secondary technical education.

138

effects, distributive and allocative.

The main distributive effect has been to improve the incomes of employees and engineering-technical personnel relative to workers. In enterprises which transferred to the new system in 1966, the average pay of employees was 10.3 per cent higher, of engineering-technical personnel 8.2 per cent higher, and of workers only 4.1 per cent higher than in 1965. It is officially considered that this is a desirable reaction to excessive equalising tendencies in 1959–65. In that period the average monthly wage of workers rose by 15.7 roubles and of engineering-technical personnel by 10.5 roubles.[9] In some branches of industry foremen were receiving lower wages than the men they were supervising. In addition the *MIF* has been used in the struggle against labour turnover and indiscipline by rewarding long service workers and workers with good attendance records.

The new system is considered to have had a number of positive allocative effects. It has led to widespread selling, or giving way, of superfluous equipment. (This increases both the *PDF* and, ceteris paribus, profitability.) In addition the reform has had a positive effect on a number of indices which are conventionally regarded as measures of efficiency. The head of Gosplan's department for the introduction of the new system has cited table 8.4, which refers to 580 enterprises transferred to the new system in 1966, to illustrate the positive effect of the reform on efficiency.[10]

Table 8.4   *The effect of the reform on efficiency*

Index	Year			
	1964	1965	1966	1967
Sales per rouble of capital	1.42	1.43	1.57	1.65
of which				
sales per rouble of fixed capital	1.83	1.86	1.91	2.02
Profit per rouble of fixed capital	0.24	0.25	0.32	0.36
Sales per rouble of centralised investment	18.85	20.78	22.59	25.41
Wages per rouble of sales	0.143	0.142	0.133	0.129
Percentage of increase in output resulting from increase in labour productivity	59	67	72.5	74.1

The new system has given rise to a number of problems, both distributive and allocative. 'The main question in utilising the *MIF* at the enterprises is the provision of premia for the workers.'[11] In the enterprises which transferred to the new system in 1966 the average addition to the wages of the workers paid out of the *MIF* was less than 1.2 roubles per month (about 1 per cent of their wages).[a]   In 1967 the situation altered somewhat, as table 8.5 indicates.

Table 8.5   *Bonuses paid out of profits for 4th quarter of 1967* [12]

	All persons employed	Workers	Engineering-technical personnel	Employees
Average monthly bonuses (excluding bonuses paid out of the wages fund) in roubles	8.1	3.7	36.0	20.6
as percentage of average wages	7.0	3.3	21·8	20.2

Unlike the engineering-technical personnel the workers receive premia not only out of the *MIF* but also out of the wages fund. (In 1966 bonuses paid to the workers out of the wages fund were 9 per cent of the wages fund for industry as a whole.) 'This, however, does not eliminate the question of ways of increasing the premia of workers, of further raising their interest in the work of the enterprise.' [13]

On the allocative side the new system has encountered a large number of problems.

1) The enterprise incentive funds are formed in the way outlined above and paid out of profits (except for that part of the *PDF* which is paid out of the depreciation fund and by receipts from the sale of equipment). It is perfectly possible, and has happened in some cases, that actual enterprise incentive funds, calculated in accordance with the above rules, exceed the profits out of which they are supposed to be paid.

2) Ceteris paribus, the larger the wages fund the larger the *MIF* and *SCF*. This provides an enterprise seeking to maximise its incentive funds with an incentive for the wasteful use of labour. This has been recognised by the authorities, and measures to deal with it have been taken. A direct incentive to reduce the labour force has been provided by the Central Committee decree recommending the experience of the Shchekino kombinat to party committees throughout the country. This means that whereas formerly if an enterprise increased its efficiency and reduced its labour force its wages fund was reduced correspondingly and it received no benefit, now its wages fund will remain at the old level and the remaining personnel will share the saving. In addition the Interdepartmental Commission attached to Gosplan USSR has decided that when calculating the enterprise incentive funds for 1970 no account will be taken of increases in the wages fund for 1970 over 1969 for existing enterprises, and the norms will be related to the 1969 wages

(a) This is scarcely surprising in view of the de facto way in which the *MIF* was formed during the transitional period. See footnote(a) p. 132 above.

fund. Furthermore, the regulation on stable norms adopted by the Interdepartmental Commission in 1969 incorporates incentives for increasing labour productivity (this regulation is discussed further below).

3) In the Soviet Union almost all producer goods are rationed, and enterprises work in accordance with instructions from above. Hence enterprises with substantial PDFs and SCFs have difficulty in obtaining the necessary investment goods and in finding organisations to do building work for them. For example, in the first half of 1967 only 49 per cent of the PDF was used, and the situation was no better with respect to the SCF. It is officially considered that this was only a teething trouble. An official of Gosplan USSR has explained that 'A decision has been taken about putting the utilisation of the MIF and SCF in order. The task is two sided: the higher organisations must provide material resources; productive capacities; building, installation and design organisations, for these purposes; and the enterprises and ministries must submit in good time calculations of the size of these funds and their requirements for material resources. Beginning with the elaboration of the plan for 1968 such calculations and the planned provision of the resources required by the funds is becoming a system.' [14] Academician Fedorenko, the Director of TSEMI, has suggested that the way to deal with this situation is by the expansion of wholesale trade in producer goods. [15]

4) Implicit in the rules governing the formation of the incentive funds a criterion for discriminating between investment projects which may produce undesirable results. Consider an enterprise with a profitability of 5 per cent contemplating whether or not to go ahead with an investment with an estimated profitability of 10 per cent. If it goes ahead with it its incentive funds will benefit, although the investment may be socially irrational. The converse applies to high profitability enterprises.

5) The use of profitability as an index for measuring the efficiency of enterprises sometimes hampers technical progress. Immediate profitability is sometimes reduced both by the output of new products and by the introduction of new equipment. There are two reasons for this. First, 'profit' as measured by Soviet accountants differs substantially from 'profit' as defined by economists, and in particular takes no account of the increase in the present value of future earnings associated with, a reduction in the share of output accounted for by commodities with only a limited future life, and an enlargement of productive capacity. This is simply a special case of the well known fact that 'profit' as measured by accountants and 'profit' as defined by economists differ substantially, and that the former cannot be relied upon as a guide to efficient resource allocation. [16] Secondly, Soviet prices reflect the cost of goods rather than their usefulness, and hence prices are not an incentive for technical progress and are often a brake upon it. [a]

(a) Considerable attention has been paid in recent years to working out methods of price formation for new industrial commodities that will stimulate, rather than hamper, technical progress.

The authorities recognise the need to improve the incentives for technical progress, and work on incorporating incentives for technical progress into the new system is under way. An official of Gosplan USSR has outlined what appears to be a scheme for adding to the two existing fund forming indices (or perhaps correcting them by) indices which are conventionally regarded as representing the technical level of production, such as the capital/labour ratio, labour productivity, and the capital intensity of output. There already exist special incentives for technical progress.

One way to reduce the braking effect of the high costs associated with the bringing into production of a new product on technical progress would be to finance them by bank loans, to be repaid out of future profits when costs have fallen, rather than charging them against the current profit and loss account.[a]

6) The bonuses paid out of the *MIF* have replaced only two of the existing premia systems, the premia for engineering-technical personnel based on the results of the enterprise, and the payments out of the enterprise fund. There still exist in industry 10 inter-industry premia systems, for the creation and introduction of new technology, for beginning the production of new products, for export deliveries, for the production of consumer goods from waste, for the collection of scrap metal, for saving electricity ... , and 19 industrial premia systems, for mastering the design capacity in the chemical industry, for the production and delivery of energy equipment in engineering and so on. 'This undoubtedly reduces the effectiveness of the premia paid out of the *MIF*, because first, at many enterprises the premia paid according to the special regulations is a considerable proportion of the incomes of the recipients and sometimes even exceeds the payments out of the *MIF*, and secondly, contradictions arise between the conditions for paying premia according to the various systems and some people have extensive possibilities for various kinds of manoeuvres to receive premia, often to the detriment

(a) This suggestion has been made by Selyunin, who ascribes the idea to Vaag. See Selyunin's article in *Sotsialisticheskaya industriya* 13 March 1970. In addition there is a special fund to finance the introduction of new technology.

of the overall results of the enterprises.'[a] N.K. Baibakov, Chairman of
Gosplan USSR, suggested, in his speech at the May 1968 conferences on the
reform, dealing with this problem by gradually merging the various incentive
funds into a single *MIF* embracing both the existing *MIF* and the special
incentive funds.

7) The norms relating the fund forming indices [profitability and incremental sales (or profit)] to the wages fund are often unstable, that is they tend
to fluctuate from year to year. This provides the enterprises with a disincentive for efficiency because an enterprise which does well in one year is
likely to have its norms reduced in the following year. One reason for the
instability of the norms is that in many enterprises the figures for the increase in sales (or profits) and for profitability fluctuate sharply from year
to year, which fluctuations are not the result of changes in the efficiency
with which the enterprise is working, and it is felt to be unreasonable for
these sharp fluctuations to be reflected in the enterprise incentive funds.

The Interdepartmental commission attached to Gosplan has adopted a
regulation to deal with the problem.[18] The stable norms envisaged in this
regulation are scheduled to come into effect on January 1st 1970 and to be
the basis for planning the enterprise incentive funds for the forthcoming
five year plan period (1971–75). The stable norm relating profitability to the
incentive funds is to be based on profitability in 1969. The stable norm relating the increase in sales (or profits) to the enterprise incentive funds is
to be based on the geometric mean of the increase in sales for 1967, 1968
and 1969. (The reason for this difference is to reduce the weight of unrepresentative extreme values of the increase in sales.)

(a) Sitnin op cit p. 121. The economics of this is clear. Enterprise management is
faced by the problem

$$\text{Max} \quad B = a_1 y_1 + a_2 y_2 + \dots + a_n y_n$$

$$\text{S.T.} \quad y_1 \leq c_1 x_1 + c_2 x_2 + \dots + c_m x_m$$
$$\qquad\qquad\qquad \dots$$
$$y_n \leq c_1 x_1 + c_2 x_2 + \dots + c_m x_m$$

where $\bar{B}$ is the total bonus payment, y_i is the value of the i th bonus forming
index, a_i is the value of the i th norm, c_i is the intensity at which the i th
activity is operated and x_{ij} is the technology matrix.

Denote the optimal solution by $y*$. Then there exists a vector of shadow
prices $-p*-$ which minimises the dual problem. These shadow prices give the
optimal trade off possibilities open to the enterprise for small changes in its
activities. Suppose that the shadow price of 1 hour of unskilled labour used in
scrap metal collection is 2 roubles, and in increasing output 1/2 rouble; then
bonus maximising management will transfer marginal units of unskilled labour
to scrap metal collecting. If the value to society of the extra output foregone is
greater than the value to society of the extra scrap metal collected, then the
bonus system will have led the enterprise to a socially irrational decision. The
enterprise will only be led by the bonus system to a socially rational decision
in the special case in which $a_i = \bar{a}_i$, where $\bar{a}_i$ are the values of the bonus
parameters which lead the bonus maximising enterprise to socially optimal
values of $p*$, that is to shadow prices for the resources which reflect their
relative usefulness, for small changes, to society. In general the ministry (or
chief administration) will not have sufficient information to pick optimal values
of a_i.

It is possible to increase sales by extensive methods (by increasing the number of workers) and by intensive methods (by raising labour productivity). In order to discourage the former and encourage the latter the size of the incentive funds is to be adjusted to reflect the proportion of the increase in sales that results from raising labour productivity. Three methods of doing this are envisaged. In variant 1

$$MIF_p = [a\Delta S_{pi} + bP_p] \frac{WF}{100} \tag{11}$$

$$\Delta S_{pi} \simeq \Delta S_p - \Delta L_p \tag{12}$$

where ΔS_{pi} is the planned intensive increase in sales, that is

that part of the planned increase in sales resulting from an increase in planned labour productivity, and

ΔL_p is the planned increase in the labour force.

In variant 2

$$MIF_p = [ac\Delta S_p + bP_p] \frac{WF}{100} \tag{13}$$

$$c \equiv \frac{\left[\dfrac{\Delta S_{pi}}{\Delta S_p}\right]}{\dfrac{\sqrt[3]{\Delta S_{i\,1967} \cdot \Delta S_{i\,1968} \cdot \Delta S_{i\,1969}}}{\sqrt[3]{\Delta S_{1967} \cdot \Delta S_{1968} \cdot \Delta S_{1969}}}} \tag{14}$$

where ΔS_{it} is the percentage increase in intensive sales in year t, and

ΔS_t is the percentage increase in sales in year t.

In variant 3

$$MIF_p = \left([a\Delta S_p + bP_p] \frac{WF}{100}\right) c \tag{15}$$

In each variant the MIF_p is adjusted so as to encourage planned increases in intensive sales at the expense of planned increases in extensive sales. In the first variant, the formula for forming the MIF_p is the same as the original formula (1) except that now only the increase in planned intensive sales, rather than the total planned increase in sales, is one of the two fund forming indices. In the second variant that part of the MIF_p which depends on the increase in sales is adjusted so as to allow for the proportion of the planned increase in sales that is intensive relative to the average proportion of intensive increases in sales in 1967—69. In the third variant the entire MIF_p is adjusted to allow for the proportion of the planned increase in sales that is intensive relative to the average proportion of intensive increases in sales in 1967—69. Which variant is used depends on the circumstances of particular enterprises and ministries and is decided by the ministries (or chief administration).

The numerical values of the stable norms depend on which of the three variants of the formula for relating the MIF_p to the fund forming indices has been adopted. An example of the calculation of stable norms for 1970 and 1971–75 may clarify the method.

Table 8.6 *Data for calculation of stable norms for 1970*
(*in percentages*)

| | 1967 | 1968 | 1969 | | Averages used in working out the norms |
			Plan	Expected	
Growth of sales	110.0	109.0	107.0	108.5	108.6
Growth in labour force	103.5	103.0	101.5	102.0	102.6
Growth in intensive sales	106.5	106.0	105.5	106.5	106.0
Proportion of increase in sales that is intensive	65	67	78.7	76	70
Profitability	n.r.	n.r.	25	26	25
Proportion of *MIF* derived from					
(a) increase in sales	n.r.	n.r.	n.r.	n.r.	40
(b) profitability	n.r.	n.r.	n.r.	n.r.	60
MIF as percentage of *WF*	n.r.	n.r.	9.6	10.1	9.6
of which (a) for increase in sales	n.r.	n.r.	n.r.	n.r.	3.84
(b) for profitability	n.r.	n.r.	n.r.	n.r.	5.76

n.r. = not relevant

The stable norms are derived as follows :

First variant :

$$a = \frac{3.84}{6} = 0.643$$

$$b = \frac{5.76}{25} = 0.23$$

Hence if in 1970 the enterprise adopts a plan for a 6 per cent increase in intensive sales (its average for 1967–69) and a profitability of 25 per cent (the same as the plan for 1967–69) then its MIF_p for 1970 will equal its

145

MIF_p for 1969. The only way it can increase its MIF_p is by increasing its planned increase in intensive sales or its planned profitability. The idea is that whereas formerly these steps might have been risky (because they might have led to a reduction in the norms), now that the norms are (supposed to be) stable the enterprise has a strong incentive to raise its planned increase in intensive sales and its planned profitability above the levels achieved in the past.

Second variant:

$$a = \frac{3.84}{8.6} = 0.448$$

b is calculated as in the first variant.

This variant provides the enterprise with an incentive for raising its planned profitability, its planned proportion of sales that is intensive, and its planned increase in sales.

Third variant:

a is calculated as in variant 2, and

b is calculated as in variant 1.

This variant provides the enterprise with an incentive to raise its planned proportion of sales that is intensive, its planned profitability, and its planned increase in sales.

To what extent the norms will in fact be stable remains to be seen. [a]

8) '... the chief defect of the current system of organising material incentives is that the absolute majority of enterprises form the incentive funds on the basis of individual norms.' [19] When the norms are individual norms, that is norms that apply to one enterprise only, the crucial factor determining the size of the incentive funds is not the efficiency of an enterprise but the value of its norms. The Ministry (or chief administration) will try to set the norms in such a way as to eliminate differences in the size of the incentive funds of its enterprises resulting from factors outside the control of the enterprises. The Ministry, however, lacks the information necessary to distinguish between differences in the size of enterprise incentive funds resulting from factors from outside the control of the enterprises, and differences resulting from varying degrees of efficiency in the enterprises. Therefore, inefficient enterprises may well receive more favourable norms than efficient enterprises, penalising efficiency. Moreover, energies that should go to increasing efficiency go to persuading the Ministry (or chief administration)

(a) An official of the Ministry of non-ferrous metal of the USSR has argued that to work out stable norms for the enterprises in his industry according to the recommended rules is impossible, because the rate of growth of intensive sales and the level of profitability may vary considerably from those achieved in the past for reasons which do not depend on the work of the enterprises, such as changes in the volume of centralised investment or the declining quality of natural resources.
(*Ekonomicheskaya Gazeta* 1970 No. 15 p.7.)

to give soft norms.

A major objective of the reform was to depart from the system of individual plan targets and move towards a system in which enterprises are free to make their own decisions subject to certain uniform norms set by the planners. It is widely felt that the use of individual plan targets is bound to be less efficient than the use of economic levers. 'What is the advantage of economic methods of management over administrative methods? To use the language of cybernetics, the controlling signals of an administrative character are predominantly individualised, they are addressed to particular enterprises. However, no-one can know all the productive possibilities and reserves of an enterprise better than the collective of the enterprise itself. To the extent that with detailed regimentation there is no scope for creative initiative in the economy, these possibilities are far from fully utilised.'[20] For example, with individual plan targets, planning is often subjective in that success depends not on efficiency but on getting a slack plan. As long as the norms are individual norms these considerations continue to apply, and the intention of the reform is frustrated.

The reason why the norms are often individual norms is that there is a very wide dispersion of profitability (and increase in sales) rates between enterprises, and individual norms are used to equalise the circumstances (outside the control) of the enterprises. The position has been improved somewhat by the new wholesale prices introduced in 1967, and by the introduction of rent or fixed payments, but the problem remains. That the transition to the new system in 1966–69 was mainly on the basis of individual norms, was probably inevitable. What is now required is some method of eliminating differences in rates of profitability and increase in sales between enterprises resulting from factors outside the control of the enterprises, at any rate for groups of enterprises, so as to make the transition from individual norms to group norms. Various methods of doing this are used.

One method of doing this is by individual cost plus prices. By differentiating the price received by producers according to their costs it is possible for incentive funds to be formed even at those enterprises where costs are well above the average for that industry. The disadvantage of individual cost plus prices is that they provide no incentive for the efficient use of inputs.

Another method is to differentiate the rate of interest on capital which the enterprises have to pay according to the profitability of the enterprises. These payments, introduced as part of the reform, are in general 6 per cent, but in some cases are only 3 per cent and in some cases are zero. It has been suggested that this differentiation be extended, for example by introducing rates of 9 per cent and 12 per cent in the more profitable industries. It is clear that the extensive use of differentiated interest rates might have undesirable results. It would be another example of individualised norms, with their well known adverse effects. For example, although the system would be intended only to equalise differences in profitability resulting from causes outside the control of the enterprises, in practice it might well also equalise differences resulting from different levels of efficiency, i.e. penalise efficient enterprises and subsidise inefficient ones.

Another method, also introduced as part of the reform is the use of rent or fixed payments. (Rent payments are made in the extractive industries; fixed payments in manufacturing industry.) Fixed payments are established for enterprises where especially favourable natural and transport conditions give rise to differential rent, and for enterprises having a profitability higher than the average for their industry as a result of technical-economic conditions which do not depend on their activity. 'Experience indicates that the introduction of rent or fixed payments allows the problem of constructing group norms to be resolved satisfactorily. For example, the use of fixed payments as an instrument to regulate intra-industry profitability in the cotton industry allowed 270 enterprises transferred to the new system to be placed in 10 groups for the level of profitability and group norms for payment into the enterprise incentive funds to be established, which permitted a better founded approach to the formation of these funds.'[21]
At the moment the use of fixed payments is still rather limited. 'Therefore, bearing in mind the efficiency of fixed payments and the existence of economic conditions for their introduction in various branches of industry, at the present time the task of expanding the field of utilisation of fixed payments, increasing the number of industries and enterprises which pay them, which strengthens business like management, and raises the efficiency of production, is most topical.'[a] Fixed payments, if established separately for each enterprise involved, are yet another example of individualised norms. Sitnin has suggested that '... in the majority of industries, where the costs of individual enterprises show a wide dispersion, it would be desirable to construct a system of fixed payments in the form of a profits tax.'[23]

9) The purpose of the incentive fund is to provide enterprises with an incentive to adopt a taut plan. Nevertheless there have been repeated complaints that enterprises are still adopting slack plans. The reasons for this are that slack plans are an insurance against undesirable consequences of the administration uncertainty which characterises the Soviet economy, and the system of incentives for managerial personnel.

The plan for the following year, the final value of the current plan, and the timely arrival of inputs ordered through the supply system are all uncertain, and this creates an incentive for the enterprise to aim at a slack plan, as explained in the previous chapter. In addition, under a regime of unstable norms, uncertainty about the future value of the norms is a major disincentive to adopt a taut plan. Such a plan may merely result in a reduction of the norms in the following year. If the procedure outlined above to create a system of stable group norms is effective, then this source of

(a) The fixed payments are often calculated in such a way as to provide a disincentive for efficiency. What tends to happen is that: 'The basis for determining the fixed payments is not the additional profit, associated with better technical-economic conditions of production, but that part of the profit of the enterprise which is an excess of the average profit for the industry.'[22]

148

uncertainty will have been eliminated.

Although the method by which the incentive funds are formed provides an incentive to adopt a taut plan, managerial bonuses are still related to plan fulfilment and overfulfilment. The current bonuses paid to managerial personnel are paid for the fulfilment and overfulfilment of the plan for the fund forming indices (profitability and incremental sales) subject to certain conditions (such as fulfilment of the assortment plan) and subject to deductions from the bonuses if certain additional conditions are not met.[a] The rules governing the size of the managerial bonuses can be written

$$ B_{Man} \;=\; k \left[a + b(\Delta S_a - \Delta S_p) + c(P_a - P_p) \right] \frac{WF_{Man.}}{100} $$

where B_{Man} is managerial bonuses

WF_{Man} is the managerial wages fund.

$$ a, b, c > 0 \text{ if } \Delta S_a \geq \Delta S_p \text{ and } P_a \geq P_p \text{ and } d_i \geq \bar{d_i} $$

where d_i is the actual value of the ith necessary condition, and

$\bar{d_i}$ is the planned value of the ith necessary condition.

$$ a, b, c, \;=\; 0 \text{ if } \Delta S_a < \Delta S_p \text{ or } P_a < P_p \text{ or } d_i < \bar{d_i} $$

$$ k \;=\; 1 \text{ if } e_i \geq \bar{e_i} $$

where e_i is the actual value of the ith additional condition

necessary for receiving a full bonus, and $\bar{e_i}$ is the planned value of the ith additional condition necessary for receiving a full bonus.

$$ k < 1 \text{ if } e_i < \bar{e_i} $$

a, b and c are calculated in such a way that

$$ B_{Man} \propto MIF_a $$

Nevertheless it is clear that the method of calculating managerial bonuses is an example of relating bonuses to plan fulfilment and overfulfilment, and provides risk averting enterprise management with a strong incentive to

---

(a) The managerial personnel comprise the director, the chief engineer, deputy director, chief economist, head of the planning and economic department, chief accountant, head of the department of technical control and the head office officials (*rabotniki apparata upravleniya*).

The premia paid to the remainder of the engineering-technical personnel and employees may be for fulfilment and overfulfilment of the plan for the fund forming indices for the enterprise, but they may be related to other enterprise indices or to shop indices.

adopt a slack plan.[a] One per cent of underfulfilment means a complete loss of current bonuses, whereas a 1 per cent increase in the plan means only a small increase in the current bonus. In view of the fact that it is the sums actually paid (in particular to managerial personnel) rather than the sums entered in the enterprise's accounts, which provide an incentive, it is scarcely surprising that the reform has not led the enterprises to adopt taut plans. One way of dealing with this would be to form managerial bonuses in the same way that the incentive funds themselves are formed, that is to allow managerial personnel to receive current bonuses if the plan were underfulfilled provided that the plan was a high one relative to the extent of underfulfilment. In a revealing argument a Gosplan official has rejected this idea on the grounds that it would contradict the directive character of the plan, and weaken plan discipline. Rather than recognise that enterprise management has considerable room to manoeuvre within the framework of the plan and attempt to guide the enterprise in a socially rational direction by the use of economic levers, he prefers to 'strengthen plan discipline' and places particular reliance on the new procedure for working out stable norms. [24]

The result of all these factors is to provide a powerful incentive to adopt slack plans. The loss from each one per cent of underfulfilment (reprimands, inspection by higher bodies, loss of managerial bonuses, reduction in the enterprise incentive funds) being much greater than the gain from each 1 per cent by which the plan is increased (30 per cent or more of the marginal increments to the enterprise incentive funds and marginal increments to the managerial bonuses). It is scarcely surprising that risk averting enterprise management should be keener to avoid underfulfilment than to adopt a taut plan, which may turn out to be underfulfilled because of factors outside the control of enterprise management, and which may simply make the following year's work more difficult.

10) In his classic study *Overcentralisation in economic administration* (1959) Kornai argued that the administrative economy forms an integrated economic mechanism and that simply to introduce profits as a criterion for guiding and evaluating the work of enterprises would be unsatisfactory. What was required, he argued, was a comprehensive system of reforms leading to the creation of an alternative economic mechanism.

'Some people are inclined to regard profit as the 'miracle producing index', which is itself capable of solving our troubles. They evisage the provision of financial incentives to make profits in a manner analogous to the way we have hitherto encouraged attempts to increase total production value. They propose that, henceforth, 100 per cent fulfilment of profits plans be made the basis of premium payments, with additional

---

(a) The current bonuses paid to managerial personnel are not the only bonuses still related to plan fulfilment and overfulfilment. Bonuses for inter-enterprise socialist competition are formed similarly. In addition, as pointed out in the previous chapter, the judgement of the manager's superiors about the quality of his work is still often related to plan fulfilment and overfulfilment.

payments becoming payable in respect of higher profits. But they propose no change in our economic mechanism in other respects, and are content to leave our system of planning, of prices of renumerating top management etc., more or less as they are today ...

More is required: we need a *unified system of comprehensive reforms* ... [a]

Some people may consider that the experience of the Soviet Union (and of Poland, Czechoslovakia and Hungary) corroborates Kornai's analysis. Features of the existing economic mechanism which prevent profit from being a stimulus for efficiency are the existing price system (which inter alia gives rise to the 'assortment problem'[b]), the lack of competition between enterprises (the introduction of competition between enterprises for orders was an integral part of the new economic mechanism introduced in Hungary as from 1 January 1968 and has been suggested in Soviet discussion), and the permanent sellers' market.

It is clear that the system of enterprise incentive funds requires further improvement. A large number of suggestions for improving it have been made. Some economists have queried the use of incremental sales as a fund forming index. Novozhilov has suggested that this confuses costs and benefits in a way analogous to the confusion between costs and benefits engendered by the notorious gross output index.[25] Vaag has pointed out that the maximisation of sales may have adverse effects on efficiency.[26] Many economists have suggested that instead of relating the enterprise incentive funds to profitability and incremental sales they should simply be related to the enterprise's profits. A number of variations on this theme have been suggested. In one variant enterprise incentive funds would be formed by relating norms to the enterprise's net profits. In another variant, supported by TSEMI, all the profit left to the enterprise after it had met its obligations to the state, would belong to the enterprise. A number of experiments with a variety of different methods of forming the enterprise incentive funds are proceeding. The 1968 all-Union conference on improving the planning system recommended that: 'In experimenting with the formation of incentive funds directly from profit it is desirable to test the advantages of the following variants: per rouble of net profit and per rouble of sales; per rouble of net profit in the base year and per rouble of incremental profit.' The first variant has found expression in the method worked out by the department for the introduction of the new methods of planning and incentives of Gosplan USSR, which is being experimented with in a number of enterprises in various ministries. It can be written:

$$MIF_p = aPR_p + bS_p$$

In order to discourage increases in extensive sales, S_p is defined as $S_{t-1} + \Delta S_{pi}$. a and b are calculated in such a way that half the MIF_p

(a) J. Kornai, *Overcentralisation in economic administration* (1959) pp. 229–236·
   The New Economic Mechanism introduced in Hungary as from 1 January 1968 is a comprehensive system of reforms of the type Kornai advocated.

comes from the first term and half from the second term. If profitability is dropped as a fund forming index, this would tend to turn the rate of interest on capital paid by the enterprises to the state into the lower bound of returns acceptable to an enterprise on an investment. As this rate is only 6 per cent (and sometimes lower) the Gosplan variant envisages raising the payment for capital to 12 per cent. As an experiment 95 enterprises have been working on this system since the second half of 1968. The second

(b) The 'assortment problem' arises because the economic mechanism, and in particular the price system, is such that the rate of transformation of one output into another for bonus maximising enterprises is different from the relative social valuations of the outputs.

The two goods can be represented as in figure 8.1.

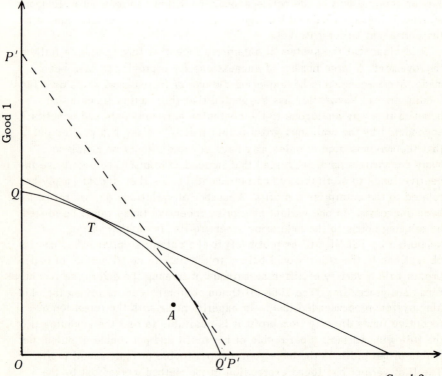

Fig. 8.1 *The assortment problem*

The production possibility area for the enterprise is OQQ'. The plan is A. Prices are such that the value of output (and profit and bonus) are maximised at T. At T the assortment pattern (i.e. the relative quantities of goods 1 and 2 produced) is radically different from that at A. Only the optimal plan price $p'p'$ will lead the bonus maximising enterprise to the socially optimal assortment pattern.

Repeated press articles have made it clear that this problem is an important one. At the moment it is often dealt with by reducing the MIF if the plan for the more important items of output is underfulfilled and by making managerial bonuses conditional on fulfilling the assortment plan.

variant has been elaborated by the Institute of Economics of the USSR
Academy of Sciences and in 1969 was tried out in seven plants of the USSR
Ministry of instrument making, means of automation, and control systems. It
can be written:

$$MIF_p = aPR_{t-1} + b\Delta PR_p$$

where PR_{t-1} is the profit earned by the enterprise in the year
preceding the planned year.

Both variants drop the link between the *MIF* and the *WF*. Both variants
drop profitability as a fund forming index. In one the two fund forming
indices are profits and sales, in the other profits in the year preceding the
planned year and incremental profits.

It has been suggested that relating part of the *PDF* to the value of the
capital stock is undesirable because it provides the enterprise with a disincentive for the efficient use of its capital stock, and that that part of the
formula for forming the *PDF* should be altered.

Ya.G. Liberman has suggested moving from incentives for taut plans to
incentives for actual high results. 'In the majority of cases encouraging
'taut' plans is in practice pointless. The limits of the increase in the plan
for sales is determined not so much by the productive possibilities of the
producer, as by the demand of the consumer, and for most industrial products
this demand is exhausted or near to exhaustion ... Why is it necessary to
encourage "taut" plans, and not a direct increase in output, lowering its
cost and raising its profitability?'[27] For incentives for actual high results
to encourage efficiency, it is necessary to find indices which measure
efficiency. Ya.G. Liberman suggests relating material incentives to profit
(suitably measured).

'It is well known that in the discussion which preceded the September
(1965) Plenum of the CC CPSU some economists and managers suggested
that profit should be the single and universal index for the evaluation of
the work of enterprises. The majority of Soviet economists, however,
came out against this suggestion, and when the reform was being worked
out it was not accepted.'[28]

There are four groups of reasons for objecting to enlarging the role of profit
in Soviet industry. First, one may object to the distributive consequences
of such a move. Secondly, there is the fact that 'profit' as currently measured
by Soviet accountants is an exceedingly imperfect measure of efficiency.
For the purpose of forming the enterprise incentive funds 'profitability'
(*raschetnaya rentabel' nost'*) is defined as the ratio of 'profit' (*raschetnaya
pribyl'*) to the sum of fixed and circulating capital. *Raschetnaya pribyl'* is
not the same as the net income remaining to the enterprise, because a large
part of it has to be paid over to the state (the so called free remainder of
profit), and is largely determined by factors (such as the value of output,
and the assortment plan) which can in no way be regarded as measures of
efficiency. The valuation of fixed capital is rather conventional bearing in

mind that it is simply historic cost without allowance for depreciation. Comparing two alternative production plans feasible for an enterprise it is quite possible for one to be more profitable but the other more socially desirable because of different ratios of profit to turnover tax in the net income.[a] For profit to serve as a reasonable good synthetic success indicator in the Soviet Union would require, inter alia, a comprehensive re-organisation of the financial relations between the state budget and the enterprises of the type suggested by Ya.G. Liberman.[29] Thirdly, there is the fact that the reasons for the inadequacy of profit as a measure of efficiency are deeper than simply measurement problems, important as the latter are, and relate to the entire economic mechanism. In particular, with the existing price system it is extremely difficult to consider profit as a measure of efficiency. Those officials who oppose the transition to one fund forming index (profit) or even allowing an enterprise to retain all the profits remaining to it after it has met its obligations to the state, are firmly grounded in reality. As Kotov has argued, 'the volume of profit, and consequently the level of profitability to a considerable extent depends not only on the results of the work of an enterprise, but also on a number of other factors ... Consequently the level of profitability, the relationship of profit to capital, by itself is insufficient to answer the question whether this level represents the maximum results for the minimum cost.'[32] It is for this reason that the Gosplan variant uses not only profit but also sales as a fund forming index. Even those economists who advocate the transition to one fund forming index (profit) recognise that with the existing economic mechanism this can not be done immediately. As one of them puts it, 'Are the fears connected with the transition to one chief fund forming index justified? Yes, if this method were to be used today, in contemporary conditions of the work of industry, that is with the existence of many as yet unresolved questions in the fields of planning, supply, price formation and incentives.'[33] Hence those economists who advocate the transition to one fund forming index (profit) or even allowing the enterprise to retain all its profit after it has met its obligations to the state, regard such measures as only part of an integrated system of reforms. Fourthly, there is the possibility that, given the use of profit as a synthetic success indicator only makes sense as part of the transition from the administrative economy to the *khozraschet* economy, one may not wish to make the transition to the *khozraschet* economy. Karagedov has argued that such a transition might

---

(a) Turnover tax as an element of net income separate from profit is largely a re-flection of the two tier price system.
   The question of merging profit and turnover tax was raised, and dismissed as 'premature', a number of years ago by Petrakov.[30] The question has also been raised by the Kondrashevs who consider that the time has not yet come to merge the two, but that steps in that direction should be taken now. [31] The Kondrashevs poke fun at economists who take it for granted that enterprises should maximise 'profit' but who do not consider the meaning of this category in an economy where half the net income is collected by a turnover tax derived mainly from the light and food industries.

introduce into the Soviet economy the harmful effects of monopolies and cyclical fluctuations.[34] An official of Gosplan USSR has explained that 'market socialism' is unacceptable because 'in practice it means a weakening of the role of the socialist state and the party of the working class in the management of the economy.' [35]

Conclusion

1) An integral part of the reform in the Soviet economy was the replacement of the enterprise fund by three enterprise incentive funds, which embody two innovations, incentives for adopting a taut plan, and the use of profitability and incremental sales (or incremental profit) as fund forming indices. The main purpose of these funds was to provide the enterprises with an incentive to adopt taut plans.

2) The creation of the enterprise incentive funds has not succeeded in this purpose.

3) The idea of providing incentives for the adoption of taut plans makes sense in the administrative economy. In the *khozraschet* economy, on the other hand, it makes sense to provide incentives for actual high results.

4) For a number of years prior to the September (1965) Plenum the increased use of profit as an index in planning was discussed. This suggestion was adopted to the extent that the enterprise incentive funds are formed out of profit (except for that part of the *PDF* which is financed by depreciation and the sale of superfluous equipment) and profitability is one of the two fund forming indices (and incremental profit is sometimes the other). The purpose of enhancing the role of profit is fourfold, to serve as a source of material incentives for raising efficiency, to serve as a source of finance for welfare purposes and for decentralised investment, to act as a criterion for guiding the enterprise to efficient decisions, and to act as an index which enables the enterprise's superiors to assess its efficiency.

5) The system adopted in many cases does not provide the workers with a significant incentive for efficiency because the size of the material incentives paid out of the *MIF* to the workers is not substantial relative to their wages and to the bonuses they receive out of the wages fund.[a] The system provides managerial personnel with an incentive to adopt slack plans because they receive bonuses for plan fulfilment and overfulfilment.

6) The use of profit as a criterion for guiding and evaluating the work of enterprises is not very sensible given the existing economic mechanism, and in particular the price system, which creates the assortment problem.

(a) In a questionaire answered in 1969 by the directors of 241 enterprises in Siberia and the Far East, the question, Does the size of the incentive funds at your enterprise create sufficient material incentives for the workers? was answered as follows:

Yes	52 per cent
No	48 per cent

(*Ekonomika i organizatsiya promyshlennogo proizvodstva* 1970 No. 1 p. 104.)

7) Soviet officials are well aware of these problems, and measures for the further improvement of the system are currently being actively discussed and will probably be announced soon.

8) In *Overcentralisation in economic administration* Kornai ridiculed the idea that profit was a miracle producing index, and argued that what was required in order to overcome the problems of the administrative economy was not the transition from one index for guiding and evaluating the work of enterprises (gross output) to another (profit) but the transition from one economic mechanism to another. Soviet experience to date corroborates Kornai's thesis. It will be interesting to see whether the forthcoming alterations to the incentive funds system are actually successful in overcoming the problems, or whether they simply provide further corroboration of the Kornai thesis.

9) In the discussion of the use of profit as an index in planning, the supporters of the theory of the optimally functioning economic system are not unanimous. Exaggerated views about profit as a guide to efficiency have been attacked by Pugachev [36] and Vainshtein, [37] both research workers at TSEMI, and by Karagedov [38] of the Institute of Economics and the Institute of Economics and the Organisation of Industrial Production of the Siberian Branch of the USSR Academy of Sciences. Karagedov, who is thoroughly acquainted with Western literature on the subject, has observed that 'The economic reform in the USSR has sharply increased the role of profit as an index in judging the economic efficiency of enterprises. Theoretical interest in this category has grown and the problem of profit has given rise to a lively discussion in our literature. If until recently there dominated a nihilistic attitude to this category, now one can observe the opposite tendency — an exaggeration of its role. One encounters statements about profitability as the only, universal criterion of the efficiency of enterprises.' Karagedov's analysis leads him to the view that 'In our opinion the imitation of profit guided perfect competition is far from being the only or even the best way of constructing a model of the optimal regime for the functioning of a planned economy. A real alternative to the spontaneous market economy is not a trimmed variant of it, but the utilisation of the new in principle methods of the optimisation of the process of economic development opened up by the socialist system, based on the possibilities of centralised planning.' Karagedov concludes that profit has an important role to play as an index summarising the work of an enterprise, but even in theory cannot be the only index, and that given the existing economic mechanism its importance must be even more limited.

It is clear that in the administrative economy profit can not, in general, be regarded as a measure of efficiency. Profit does have a useful role to play in the administrative economy as part of the financial control over enterprises and as a source of finance for material incentives and decentralised investment, but to regard it as the sole criterion for guiding and evaluating the work of enterprises is not very sensible, and even to expand its role as a measure of efficiency makes little sense, given the price system which creates the assortment problem. In the *khozraschet* economy, on the other hand, profit has a bigger role to play. The reason for this is that the difference between income and expenditure (profit) is the natural criterion for guiding and evaluating the work of enterprises in an economy where indirect centralisation has replaced direct centralisation as the main source of information about the needs of society available to enterprise management, in the same way that plan fulfilment is the natural criterion for guiding and evaluating the work of enterprises in the administrative economy, and is the source of finance for decentralised investment and material incentives. Various variants are possible. For example one might regard the sum of profit and wages as the synthetic success indicator, or the ratio of profit to wages as the measure of efficiency. Which variant makes sense depends on the institutional setting e.g. whether the enterprise is free to adjust the size of its labour force and the wages paid to each person. What is important is not the 'proof' that profit is a perfect measure of efficiency, but the simple fact that some value criterion which sums up the work of an enterprise should be regarded as the synthetic success indicator in an economy where value relations are of great importance. Of course, even in the *khozraschet* economy, profit is a very imperfect measure of efficiency, and there would be many cases (such as urban public transport) where it would be perfectly rational to organise loss making enterprises, but then the search for an ideal measure of efficiency to be actually applied in all cases is a fruitless enterprise.

The fact that the choice between the administrative economy and the *khozraschet* economy raises issues outside the field of technical-economic considerations, but that this choice, once made, determines all such questions as the role of profit as an index in the activities of the enterprises, has been carefully explained by Khanin. 'The choice of this or that economic mechanism is determined by the level of the productive forces, the character of the tasks standing before society, the external and internal socio-economic conditions and so on. Once the economic mechanism is chosen, its internal logic by itself determines the interrelations and construction of its separate parts. All the contradictions of this logic will be discarded sooner or later. The type of economic mechanism determines everything: the rights and obligations of the enterprises and the higher organs, the character of the relations between enterprises, the role, organisation and methods of work of the financial-credit and monetary system, external and internal trade, the method of price determination, the relationships between productive collectives, the criteria for selecting cadres and the requirements they have to meet, the methods of maintaining labour discipline and so on.'[39]

10) Those supporters of the theory of the optimally functioning economic system who do consider that profit is the appropriate local optimality criterion in an optimally functioning economic system recognise that this requires optimal prices and optimal payments for the use of resources. It is reasonable to assume that in the preparations for the reform proposals endorsed by the September (1965) Plenum TSEMI supported the use of profit,

but only as part of a system of reforms including payment for the use of capital goods and natural resources and an improvement in price formation.

11) Once the decisions of the September (1965) Plenum were announced, TSEMI was quick to realise the unsatisfactory results that would come about from emphasising profit as an index of efficiency in an otherwise unchanged economic mechanism. In the 1966 debate on optimal planning a deputy director of TSEMI explained that:

> 'we say: comrades, if you want to introduce profit, then it is necessary to reconstruct the whole system of prices, the system of incentives, in short to alter a great deal in the existing forms and methods of economic management. If this is not done, then the introduction of profit will bring about no effect whatsoever.' [40]

In an article published in March 1970 Academician Fedorenko pointed out that already in 1966 TSEMI had criticised the system adopted and suggested an alternative. [41] As published TSEMI's alternative was as follows:

> 'In our opinion the following scheme for evaluating the work of economic units would be more correct. Every enterprise receives norms of payment for resouces (productive capital, natural-transport conditions, labour resources) and also output prices. The norms of payment for resources are established at that level which balances supply and demand for them on the scale of the national economy for the planned period. On the same principle output prices are calculated, essentially they characterise the marginal limits of socially necessary costs on this or that product and themselves determine those enterprises which should produce the given type of product.
>
> Comparing income with costs (including payment for capital goods, rent and so on) the enterprise works out its final profit. At those enterprises where costs are very high, there will be a loss. They will have to diversify, reconstruct or close down (depending on which is more desirable). In an extreme case there will be left only those enterprises which cover current costs, including payments to the state (including payments for land and labour resources).
>
> If the profit of the enterprises is sufficient to pay for capital and labour resources, and rent payments, then they will cover all costs. (We do not exclude some modification of this scheme, in which part of the social payments are retained by the enterprise as its own source of finance for development and premia, received even on condition of plan fulfilment.)
>
> If the enterprise collective works better than envisaged by the norms, then it will receive above the plan profits. From this one could establish norms for payment into incentive funds, and the remainder pay into the budget. Alternatively, one could introduce a tax on above the plan profit, and the remainder pay into the incentive funds. The losses of productive units should be met out of these funds and from credits. Obviously the transition to a system of economically well founded payments for resources

requires considerable time in connection with the necessity for detailed elaboration of the method for caluclating them. But it is possible already now to begin the preparations for an experiment.'[42]

What this appears to describe is a system in which the authorities fix payments for the use of resources (capital goods, natural resources and labour) and prices for output at levels which balance supply and demand. The enterprises then determine their own production plans, guided by profitability. Net profit (after meeting all costs) would only arise for those enterprises that did better than envisaged by the norms.

12) The fact that this alternative was put forward in 1966, and that by September 1970 no substantial modifications to the system adopted in 1965 had been introduced, suggests that TSEMI's influence on policy is limited.

13) TSEMI's proposal for reconciling the interests of the enterprises and the national economy as a whole has come in for strong criticism both from advocates of the transition from the administrative economy to the *khozraschet* economy, who think that it is undesirable and possibly unfeasible, and from supporters of the status quo, who regard its emphasis on the role of prices as all too reminiscent of 'market socialism'.

The first line of argument has been clearly put by Ya.G. Liberman,[43] who would like current planning to be largely confined to the establishment of certain financial obligations of the enterprises to the state budget, and for the planners to concentrate on the macro-economic variables, rather than on the imitation of market processes.

The second line of argument was clearly put by Batyrev at the 1966 debate on optimal planning.[44]

'Advocates of the discussed conception treat the system of "optimal prices" as a mechanism for automatic regulation, the action of which, allegedly is sufficient to ensure that the partial decisions of the separate enterprises made in the course of fulfiling the plan coincide with the interests of society as a whole ... The question at once arises, is it possible for the separate enterprises to ensure the proportionality of social production, if the planned management of their activity is limited to the establishment of aggregated prices, creating definite incentives, and for everything else reliance is placed on the competitive market mechanism? Obviously not. It is well known that the competitive market mechanism means a constant deviation from the objectively necessary proportions and the establishment of the necessary proportionality only as a result of mutually cancelling deviations. The construction of prices, even on the assumption that in them are embodied incentives for the best satisfaction of social requirements and economy in costs, does not alter this feature of the market mechanism. An enterprise, having only prices and the profit motive to orient it can only find the optimal structure of production, the scales on which it should be expanded, by "firing across the range" [i.e. trial and error]. Inevitably there will arise disproportions, socialist cycles, caused by the necessity for growth in some cases and the necessity for decline in other cases.

The fixing of prices, even in aggregated terms, does not improve the position and may even worsen it, because the market mechanism of regulation without the fluctuation of prices and the migration of capital, cannot overcome the difficulties which would arise. If we start on the path of developing the fluctuations of prices under the influence of deman and supply, then from the conception of "optimal prices" nothing remains, because the prices could, allegedly, serve as the instruments of the automatic regulation of the economy only because the criterion of optimality had been embodied in them, i.e. they were firmly fixed prices.'

Batyrev went on to argue that the inadequacy of the policy suggestions of the optimal planners was no accident.

'The replacement of direct planned management and the utilisation in addition of market forms by the mechanism of automatic regulation by means of the so called optimal prices would have an adverse effect on maintaining the proportions of the economy fixed in the plan and would establish obstacles on the road to real optimal planning. And this is natural. The departure from correct Marxist theoretical positions can not but show itself in the practice of socialist economic management.'

It is not surprising that corresponding member of the Academy of Sciences Pashkov referred to 'the theory of prices of the optimal plan' as a 'definite political-economic conception' [45] i.e. a proposal that went beyond the boundaries of planning techniques.

In 1969 TSEMI published a scheme for reconciling the interests of the enterprises and the national economy as a whole which can be regarded as a three level tatônnement process for both quantities and prices. [46]

'In accordance with the general contours for the planned period the lower levels of the national economy (enterprises, associations) submit to higher organs (industries) the initial information about their productive possibilities in the form of input coefficients and the corresponding resource constraints.

At the level of the industry these initial data are aggregated, in which process account is taken of intra-industry links. As a result of this conditions of growth for the industry as a whole are described by a comparatively small number of aggregated products and resource constraints.

The industrial input coefficients and constraints, the interindustry links and the national economic criterion of optimality form the initial data for the compilation of the optimal national economic plan. In this each industry receives its output volume and resource requirements resulting from the solution of an extremal problem at the national economic level in the aggregated nomenclature of national economic planning. The system of optimal prices, arising from the solution of the national economic extremal problem, are also determined in this nomenclature.

Starting from the volumes of production and consumption received in the nomenclature of the national economic plan and the prices corresponding to this nomenclature the industries establish contact among themselves and disaggregate the physical indices and prices to the nomenclature of industrial planning. In this case each of them maximises its local industrial criterion of optimality, which is established for it starting from the interests of the whole national economy. In other words, each industry strives for the best realisation of its links with the other industries. Simultaneously in the process of control the industry disaggregates the indices received from above, that is returns to the earlier compressed mass of primary information about the productive possibilities of all the enterprises of the industry, and the working out of aggregated plans for the enterprises. This is connected with the solution of the corresponding problems of optimal planning using computers.

Finally, the enterprises, having received the plans and prices in the nomenclature of industrial planning, disaggregate their productive programmes and prices into concrete types of products by means of direct contacts between suppliers and producers. In addition, they maximise the corresponding local criteria of optimality and themselves strive to organise direct contacts in the best way.

At this stage the compilation of an approximately optimal and balanced national economic plan is finished. A fuller optimisation can be obtained by multiple repetition of the process described by carrying out many iterations.'

The problems to which the increased emphasis on profit in an otherwise unchanged economic mechanism gave rise were familiar to TSEMI already in 1966. TSEMI put forward a proposal for overcoming them by applying the theory of the optimally functioning economy. The proposal was a three level planning scheme of the type analysed by mathematical economists throughout the world. [47] The feasibility, desirability and acceptability of this scheme are all extremely doubtful. Within this general framework TSEMI has advocated the expansion of wholesale trade and greater flexibility of prices.

14) The proposition that 'experience has clearly demonstrated the progressive nature of the new system of management' and hence that optimal planning is not simply a branch of applied mathematics which enables the methods of economic calculation to be improved, but which has no implications for the economic mechanism; but that its conclusions (such as 'the significance of profit as an index') can help to improve the economic mechanism, is an assertion for which there is no evidence.

15) Experience with the reform so far suggests that the ideas of the optimal planners, derived from linear programming and systems engineering, throw less light on the question of economic reform than the ideas of Kornai, derived from studying how the economic mechanism works.

The fact that the administrative economy forms an integrated economic mechanism, and that if it is desired to overcome its problems, and the costs of doing this are accepted, then what is required is the transition to an alternative economic mechanism, was clearly seen by Kornai in 1956 and by Khanin in 1970, both of whom based themselves on a study of how the administrative economy functions. It was not appreciated by Kantorovich, who lent his name to the reform announced at the September (1965) Plenum which failed to live up to the hopes of its keenest supporters precisely because it ignored this cardinal fact, which is clear to those who have studied how the administrative economy functions, but which is not obvious to those who base themselves on the analysis of the conditions for the existence of optimal solutions to certain classes of extremal problems. It would, however, be unfair to be too critical of TSEMI. Looked at from a purely intellectual viewpoint, the theory of the optimally functioning economy is clearly less helpful as a guide to economic reform than Kornai's theory of the administrative economy as an integrated economic mechanism overcoming the problems of which requires the transition to an alternative economic mechanism. One must bear in mind, however, that TSEMI is putting forward policy proposals in the USSR, and not taking part in a seminar. TSEMI did publicly state already in 1966 that to give greater emphasis to profit in an otherwise unchanged economic mechanism would be fruitless, and it has emphasised the importance of wholesale trade and flexible prices at a time when the prevailing official attitude towards these was sceptical. In the discussion which followed the December (1969) Plenum between those who argued that the problems of the reform indicated the dangers of expanding *khozraschet,* and those who argued the need to deepen the reform, TSEMI backed the latter. Furthermore, TSEMI has established a laboratory for the study of problems of *khoyraschet* in an optimally managed socialist economy; its 1970 book indicates substantial contact with reality, and it may well be that in the future TSEMI will be able to formulate some relevant proposals.

9. Can the optimal planners help improve the methods of economic calculation?

'The third objection [to the use of mathematical methods in planning] is that in a number of cases the initial data are doubtful and are known only very approximately ... and therefore calculations based on these data may turn out to be incorrect.

In this connection it is necessary first of all to say that it is necessary to use these self same data for any other method of choosing the plan and there is no reason to think that their doubtfulness and lack of precision play a bigger negative role for a plan chosen in the most effective way, than for an arbitrarily chosen plan ...

The fourth objection is that the saving resulting from the transition from the usually chosen variant to the best, is comparatively small, in many cases in all 4–5 per cent.

In this connection it is necessary to say, first, that the use of the best variant does not require any additional cost, besides the quite insignificant cost of the calculations. Secondly, one may expect the application of the method not in one random question but in many, possibly in the majority, of branches of the national economy, and in this case not only 1 per cent but every 1/10 of a per cent is an immense sum.'

L.V. Kantorovich[1]

The widespread discussion of the use of mathematics in economics at the end of the 1950s immediately gave rise to a number of experimental applications of linear programming to planning in order to test whether its use really could lead to a substantial increase in efficiency. In 1958 and 1959 the Institute of Complex Transport Problems carried out a number of experiments in working out least cost plans for the movement of freight by rail and lorry. In 1961 a draft optimal fuel balance for the USSR for 1980 was worked out. From March 1962 operational plans for the optimal shipment of freight were prepared regularly by the Computing Centre of the USSR Academy of Sciences for Mosnerudsbyt, a Moscow marketing organisation. From 1962 a large number of calculations of optimal perspective plans for sectors of the economy were drawn up by the Laboratory for economic-mathematical methods (subsequently the Institute of Economics and the Organisation of Industrial Production) of the Siberian branch of the USSR Academy of Sciences, under contract to various official bodies. For example a plan for the development and location of the coal mining industry of the RSFSR till 1975 was calculated, which involved 13 per cent less investment than Gosplan RSFSR's draft plan, while increasing output by 2.7 million tons and cutting current costs by 2 per cent. In the middle of the

1960s specialists from the Institute of Mathematics of the Siberian Branch of the USSR Academy of Sciences prepared optimal plans for individual state farms in the Altai krai, and TSEMI carried out a number of experimental applications of linear programming to agriculture in the Moscow region. In particular, the results of the calculation of an optimal plan for the transportation of potatoes and vegetables within the Moscow region in 1966, that were obtained by TSEMI jointly with the Moscow Regional Planning Agency, were approved for use in the preparation of the state plan. The problem relating to the transportation of potatoes contained approximately 75 000 variables and 563 constraints. It referred to 348 delivering units and 215 consuming organisations. Two variants of the plan were prepared, one in which an average reduction in the distance of potato deliveries from 68.7 kms to 54.6 kms, that is of 20.5 per cent, was achieved, and a second variant which took account of certain additional constraints and achieved a reduction in the average distance to 59.6 kms, that is of 13.3 per cent.

Two applications of linear programming in Soviet planning, the working out of optimal production schedules for rolling mills and tube mills in the steel industry, and the calculation of optimal plans for the development and location of a number of industries, are particularly interesting, because they have actually been applied in planning and their intrinsic economic importance is substantial, and these will be described in detail below.

Optimal production scheduling of rolling mills and tube mills in the steel industry

Linear programming was discovered by Kantorovich in the course of solving the problem presented to him by the Laboratory of the All-Union Plywood Trust of allocating productive tasks between machines in such a way as to maximise output given the assortment plan. [2] From a mathematical point of view the problem of optimal production scheduling for rolling mills and tube mills is very similar to the Plywood Trust problem, the difference being the huge dimensions of the former problem.

The problem arises in the following way. As part of the planning of supply Soyuzglavmetal, after the quotas have been specified, has to work out attachment plans and production schedules in such a way that all the orders are satisfied and none of the producers receives an impossible plan. Traditionally this was done by production schedulers (*bronirovshchiki*). They received the orders, on each of which was the address of the consumer and the content of the order (the type of rolled metal, the standard, the type of steel, the profile, size and quantity per month). In the order also is the railway code, the code of the territorial supply organ to which the consumer belongs, and some other data. The production scheduler placed on each order the number of the supplier plant and the number of the mill, keeping a file on each mill so as not to overload them. The production scheduler started work with a preliminary plan of mill loading which took explicit account of constraints ('not more than N tons') respecting certain types and sizes. There was no guarantee that the attachment plans and production schedules worked out in this way were optimal. Indeed, there was a presumption that they were not. The optimal planners considered that here was a typical case where the application of optimising methods could bring about useful savings, and in the 1960s an extensive research programme was initiated by the department of mathematical economics (which is headed by Academician Kantorovich) of the Institute of Mathematics of the Siberian Branch of the USSR Academy of Sciences, to apply optimising methods to this problem. The chief difficulty was the huge dimensions of the problem. About 1 000 000 orders, involving 60 000 users, more than 500 producers, and tens of thousands of products, are issued each year. Optimal production scheduling was first applied to the tube mills producing tubes for gas pipelines (these are a scarce commodity in the Soviet Union). The optimal production schedules gave an additional output of 60 000 tons of tubes and a reduction in transport costs of about 15 per cent, compared with production schedules and attachment plans worked out by the traditional methods. By the second half of 1969, the production schedules and attachment plans for more than twenty million tons of rolled metal were planned by this method, and Kantorovich envisages the application of the method to other types of metal products, e.g. sheet steel, and to other industries, e.g. the paper industry. [a]

Kantorovich and Gorstko have given the following simple algebraic formulation and numerical example to explain how it is possible to calculate an optimal production schedule, and organise an optimally functioning economic system, in the steel industry. [3]

There are m enterprises at which it is necessary to produce n products in the assortment $k_1 \ldots k_n$. The production possibility of the i th enterprise for the j th product per unit of time is a_{ij}. It is assumed that $\max_i a_{ij} > 0$, i.e. that each product can be produced by at least one enterprise. It is required to determine the proportion of the time of each enterprise devoted to the production of each output in such a way as to maximise the volume of output given the assortment plan. In other words the situation is that there is a shortage of the outputs, productive capacities are limited and should be utilised in the most efficient way.

Let x_{ij} $(i = 1 \ldots m; j = 1 \ldots n)$ be the share of the working time of the i th enterprise devoted to producing the j th product. Then the search for the optimal plan can be represented by the problem of finding numbers x_{ij} which satisfy the conditions

$$x_{ij} \geqslant 0 \tag{1}$$

(i.e. the share of an enterprise's time devoted to a particular commodity can not be negative)

$$\sum_{j=1}^{n} x_{ij} \leqslant 1 \tag{2}$$

(a) This use of linear programming is analogous to the use of linear programming for production scheduling by Tube Investments.

(i.e. for each enterprise, the total time spent in producing the products can not exceed the time available)

$$y_j = \sum_{i=1}^{m} a_{ij} x_{ij} \tag{3}$$

(i.e. the output of each good is the sum of the output of all the enterprises)

$$Z = \min_{j} \frac{y_j}{k_j} \tag{4}$$

(i.e. the assortment plan is satisfied)

$$Z \text{ achieves a maximum} \tag{5}$$

The optimal plan is characterised by the existence of shadow prices $q_1 \ldots q_n$ for the outputs (or more precisely, for the work involved in manufacturing them, i.e. the value added) and $d_1 \ldots d_m$ for the working time of the enterprises, such that

$$q_j a_{ij} = d_i \qquad \text{if } x_{ij} > 0$$

(i.e. if the ith enterprise produces the jth product, then the shadow price received per unit of time for the product is equal to the shadow price of each unit of the enterprise's time)

$$q_i a_{ij} \leqslant d_j \qquad \text{if } x_{ij} = 0$$

(if the ith enterprise does not produce the jth product in the optimal plan, then the shadow price of the output which it would have been possible to produce per unit of time at that enterprise, does not exceed the shadow price of a unit of time on the ith enterprise)

$$q_j = 0 \qquad \text{if } y_j > k_j z$$

(if the product is produced in excess of requirements than its shadow price is zero)

$$\sum_{i=1}^{n} x_{ij} = 1 \qquad \text{if } d_i > 0$$

(if the shadow price of a unit of time at any enterprise is positive, then the enterprise is fully occupied).

The usefulness of this result can be illustrated by means of a simple numerical example.

Table 9.1   *Data for production scheduling problem*

Enterprise	Monthly production possibilities (units)		Monthly fixed costs (roubles)	Cost of manufacture		Cost of materials (roubles)		Total cost	
	1	2		1	2	1	2	1	2
A	4000	2000	44 000	11	22	6	4	17	26
B	6000	4000	60 000	10	15	6	4	16	19
C	5000	5000	40 000	8	8	6	4	14	12

The meaning of this table is as follows. Take the second row. Enterprise B can produce per month either 6000 items of output 1 or 4000 of output 2. Its monthly fixed costs are 60 000 roubles, which means that the cost of manufacturing a unit of output 1 (excluding the costs of materials) is 10 roubles, and of output 2 is 15 roubles. The cost of materials is 6 roubles per unit of output 1 and 4 roubles per unit of output 2, so that total cost per unit is 16 roubles for output 1 and 19 roubles for output 2.

It is required to work out production schedules for the enterprises in such a way as to maximise output subject to the requirement that the output of the two goods be equal. Because there are only two goods, the optimal plan and associated shadow prices can easily be calculated by comparing opportunity costs. Imagine all the enterprises are producing only output 1. It is necessary to switch some productive capacity over to producing 2. The lowest opportunity cost of output 2 is 1 (in enterprise C). Switching this enterprise over to output 2 gives an output of 10 000 units of 1 and 5000 of 2. It is necessary to switch further productive capacity over to 2. The lowest remaining opportunity costs of output 2 is 3/2. If we switch enterprise B wholly over to output 2, there will be a surplus of 2. Hence we switch over only half the productive capacity, and relative shadow prices are 2:3. Output of each good in the optimal plan is 12% higher than in the naive plan in which the assortment plan is observed by each enterprise. The optimal plan can be set out in the following table.

Table 9.2   *The optimal production schedule*

| Enterprise | Work of enterprise (in months) | | Annual output (in thousands of units) | | Value of output/ month in shadow prices if | |
					output 1 produced	output 2 produced
A	12	–	48	–	8 000	6 000
B	6	6	36	24	12 000	12 000
C	–	12	–	60	10 000	15 000

In the optimal plan each enterprise produces those items which maximise the value of its output, valuing the output at shadow prices. (For one enterprise output is equally profitable whichever item is produced.) The valuations of monthly output which correspond to the optimal plan are underlined in the table.

Not only can the application of linear programming to the problem of production scheduling result in a compilation of an optimal plan (in cases essentially similar to, but much more complex than this simple example) but the shadow prices associated with the optimal plan can be used to enable the economy to function in an optimal way. This can be shown as follows.

Assume that the price of the outputs is made up of three parts, the cost of manufacturing them, the cost of materials, and the net income of the producer. Let the price of one set of output (one unit of output 1 and one unit of output 2) be 40 roubles. Material costs are $6 + 4 = 10$ roubles. Thus the price being paid for manufacturing a set is $40 - 10 = 30$ roubles. The shadow prices of manufacturing (i.e. the opportunity costs) are in the ratio 2:3, so that the shadow price of manufacturing each article is 12 and 18. As the price of each item is made up of material cost plus manufacturing cost, this enables the price of each item to be determined. The price of output 1 is $6 + 12 = 18$ roubles, and of output 2 is $4 + 18 = 22$ roubles. The financial results of the optimal plan can now be expressed in table 9.3.

The quasi rents are determined by comparing the income of an enterprise with outgoings. For example take enterprise C. In the optimal plan it produces only output 2. Costs/unit are $8 + 4 = 12$, the price is 22, hence income/unit is 10, and monthly quasi rents $5\,000 \times 10 = 50\,000$. If the enterprise actually has to pay this sum to the state then *khozraschet* will be reconciled with the plan. An enterprise guided by *khozraschet* will make socially rational decisions. If enterprise C has to pay 50 000 roubles/month to the sate, then the output of 1 is clearly loss making ($24 > 18$), whereas the output of 2 is non-loss making ('profitable'). The calculation of quasi rent payments prevents differences in technical conditions affecting incomes, and turns avoidance of losses ('profit') into a guide to efficient decision making. It enables enterprises to make socially rational decisions by comparing costs and benefits in money terms. Suppose that engineers at C discover a way of producing an additional output of 2 with a cost of manufacture of 12 instead of 8. Would it be socially rational to utilise this method and increase output? If the decision were made by looking at the effect on costs, then it might seem that the answer should be no, because costs will be increased ($12 > 8$).[a] Using the shadow prices it is clear that the answer is yes, because the cost of manufacturing the additional output (12) is below the shadow price of manufacture (18). The use of the additional productive possibility enables production to be rescheduled, the output of both products to be higher, and the income of all the enterprises to be higher, than in the

(a) It is true that the enterprise would know that it was in its own interest to produce the additional output, because marginal cost (16) would be below marginal revenue (22), but it would have no means of knowing whether or not this was socially rational.

Table 9.3 *Financial results of optimal plan*

Enterprise	Monthly fixed cost (roubles)	Monthly quasi rent [a]	Cost/unit, in roubles							
			Output 1				Output 2			
			Cost of manufac-turing	Income from each article	Material costs	Full costs	Cost of manufac-ture	Income from each article	Material cost	Full cost
A	44 000	4 000	11	1	6	18	22	2	4	28
B	60 000	12 000	10	2	6	18	15	3	4	22
C	40 000	50 000	8	10	6	24	8	10	4	22

(a) Kantorovich and Gorstko use the term *prokatnaya otsenka*.

optimal plan calculated on the basis of the initial information.[a] It was pointed out in the previous chapter that the present method of calculating fixed payments is often a disincentive for efficiency. The shadow prices associated with the optimal plan enable optimal fixed payments (Marshallian quasi rents) to be calculated which would act as a guide to efficient decision making.

Evaluation

It is important not to confuse optimal plans drawn up in real situations with the optimal solutions to simple examples in textbooks. It is clear that the former are optimal only in a conventional sense. To deal with the huge size of the problem, much of the information is aggregated, many important factors are neglected (for example the cost of transporting the billets from which the required production is rolled is often not taken into account) and a large proportion of orders are changed between the submission of orders and the receipt of the metal.[b] Furthermore, the production schedulers have detailed knowledge of the real needs of consumers and the real possibility of producers, which may well be more reliable than the information available to the compilers of 'optimal' plans. For example in practice there is some substitutability in requirements and for some scarce products the production scheduler can suggest acceptable alternatives to the consumer in a way not open to the compilers of 'optimal' plans. Nevertheless, it would be a mistake to overemphasise the problems. It does seem that the introduction of optimising methods into the work of attachment planning and production scheduling for rolled metal products has led to the drawing up of plans which provided a useful increase in output and reduction in transport costs compared to the plans drawn up by the production schedulers without the help of optimising methods.

Although the optimal plan calculations have been implemented, it would appear that the shadow prices associated with the optimal plan, which Kantorovich considers should be utilised in the way explained in the example given above, are not being used.

(a) This example, which is given by Kantorovich and Gorstko, is not all that convincing, for two reasons.

First, the increase in the output of both products depends on enterprise B switching some capacity from 2 to 1, and B has no *khozraschet* reason for this.

Second, suppose that engineers at C discover a way of producing an additional output of 2 for a cost of manufacture of 20. Using the shadow prices it would seem that the additional output should not be produced (20 > 18), although if the object is to maximise output given the assortment plan, then it would be socially rational to use this method, and there would be a clash between *khozraschet* and the plan in which is would be socially rational to ignore *khozraschet*.

(b) This is a serious problem. A major reason for it is that, as explained in chapter 6, orders for inputs have to be sent in before the production plan is known.

170

Optimal planning of the development and location of industries

A major field for the application of linear programming to improving the methods of economic calculation has been in working out optimal plans for the development and location of industries, notably in the building materials sector of the economy. This is an application of the open transport problem (first suggested by Yudin and Gol'shtein in 1960) to a future date, in which it is assumed that the demand for the product concerned is known, and it is sought to satisfy this demand at the lowest cost (transportation, production and capital) and where the variables are the existing enterprises which should be expanded, the existing enterprises which should carry on producing as in the base year, the existing enterprises which should be closed down, the places where new enterprises should be constructed and their capacity, and the shipment scheme.

Perhaps the easiest way of explaining what has been done in this field is by summarising one such study which has been applied in planning practice, the calculation of an optimal plan for the cement industry. [a]

Economic background

The cement industry is growing fast. In 1965 output was 12½ times greater than in 1940. The cost of production of cement shows a wide dispersion by regions, ranging from 78% of the all-Union average in the Ukraine to 136% of it in Central Asia. (This and subsequent data refer to 1965.) The efficiency of fixed capital measured in terms of output per thousand roubles of fixed capital, shows a wide dispersion by size of enterprises. 46% of output is produced in plants with an output greater than 50 tons p.a. per thousand roubles of fixed capital, and 12% is produced in plants with an output of less than 30 tons p.a. per thousand roubles of fixed capital. 7 regions which in 1960 produced 47% of the cement are cement surplus regions, 9 regions with 31% of production are deficit regions, and the remaining regions have a surplus some years and a deficit in others.

At present transportation of cement is non-optimal. For example some cement is sent from Central Asia to the Urals and even to the Volga which themselves are surplus regions and export cement to Kazakhstan and Central Asia. In 1964 transport from producers to consumers was 29.75 milliard ton kms. The optimal transport scheme, calculated on the computer Ural 2 using the closed transport model, reduced this by 8.95 milliard ton kms, i.e. about 30%. The saving in railway charges was 20 million roubles.

The poor organisation of the running in of new plants increases costs. For example, the average cost of cement in 1965 at 10 factories brought into operation in 1959–65 was 24% higher than the all-Union mean.

When siting cement plants the basic need is deposits of carbonaceous

---

(a) For an analogous study of the Brazilian steel industry see D.A. Kendrick, *Programming investment in the process industries* (Cambridge Mass 1967) and Kendrick's article in *Economics of Planning* 1967 No. 1. Whereas the Soviet calculations have been used in planning, Kendrick's calculations have remained purely paper calculations.

rocks (such as limestone) which can be worked by open cast methods not more than 20–30 kms from a railway.

Initial data

'For the calculation it is necessary first of all to determine:

(a) the perspective requirements for cement in each region of the country,

(b) the points where it would be possible to construct cement plants,

(c) the current cost, the quality of production and the investment cost of each plant and each variant of capacity,

(d) the distance and cost of transporting cement from production points to consumption point.

The totality of these indices forms the initial data which is fed into the computer. The reliability of the results depends on how correctly these indices are determined and it is precisely in the calculation of the initial data that the greatest difficulties exist.'

Loginov & Astanskii[4]

The perspective requirement for cement will be determined by the volume of building work, with allowance for technical progress. The volume of building work over the next ten years is not known. What is known is only that the demand for cement will continue to increase. Therefore the optimal plan was calculated not for any definite future year, but for certain volumes of cement requirements at some unknown dates in the future. The 1965 output was 72 million tons, and the optimal plans worked out for requirements of 100, 125 and 150 million tons p.a.

In the calculations it was assumed that 42 existing plants producing c 30 million tons of cement p.a. could not be further expanded (e.g. because of a shortage of raw materials); 45 plants with a capacity of c 57 million tons could be expanded with varying degrees of efficiency, and by the end of 10–12 years could be expanded by 75 million tons to 132 million tons. In addition 34 possible new plants, with a capacity of 76 million tons were considered. Total possible capacity was more than twice estimated requirements in 1970, and about 60% greater than the 150 million ton requirements figure, which gave substantial opportunities for optimisation.

Estimates of future current costs were made.

The basis for calculating anticipated investment costs was the data of typical designs corrected to allow for local conditions especially for the expansion of existing enterprises where the savings from the utilisation of existing infrastructure is often insufficiently taken into account. In order to make capital and current costs comparable a norm of investment efficiency of 0.17 (which corresponds to a recoupment period of 6 years) was used.

There are several different ways of calculating transport costs, and variant calculations were undertaken.

172

Mathematical formulation of problem

Knowns

(a) capacity and location of existing enterprises, possible variants of construction of new plants; for each variant cost/ton of cement and/ton of cement of standard quality.

(b) consumption points and requirements at each one.

(c) the cost of transporting 1 ton of cement from each factory to each consumption point.

Required to find

(a) existing factories which are efficient and which should be used at their existing and perspective capacities.

(b) location of new plants

(c) ouput of cement at each plant, and

(d) transportation scheme

which minimise total costs.

Included in the calculations were 121 productive enterprises, embracing 166 positions (45 factories had two capacity variants considered) with a total capacity of 243 million tons of standard cement; 149 consumption points; and three variants of requirements, 100 million tons, 125 million tons, and 150 million tons.

Introduce the following notation:

i is an index signifying a production point $(i = 1 \dots m)$

m is the number of production points

j is an index signifying a consumption point $(j = 1 \dots n)$

n is the number of consumption points

r_i is an index signifying a variant of capacity at the ith production point $(r_i = 1 \dots k_i)$

k_i is the number of capacity variants at the ith production point

$a_i^{r_i}$ is the quantity of cement which can be produced at the ith point using the r_i^{th} capacity variant

b_j is the requirement for cement at the jth consumption point

$C_i^{r_i}$ is the current cost per unit of cement produced at the ith production point using the r_i^{th} capacity variant

$K_i^{r_i}$ is the capital cost per unit of cement at the ith production point using the r_i^{th} capacity variant

T_{ij} is the cost of transporting a unit of cement from the ith production point to the jth consumption point

E is the coefficient of investment efficiency (the reciprocal of the recoupment period)

X_{ij} is the unknown quantity of cement to be delivered to the jth consumption point from the ith production point

173

X_i is the unknown capacity of the ith production point

The problem is to find values of X_{ij} and X_i such that total costs

$$\sum_{i=1}^{m} \sum_{j=1}^{n} X_{ij} \, T_{ij} + \sum_{i=1}^{m} X_i \, (C_i + E \, K_i)$$

(where C_i and K_i are the current and capital costs corresponding to the chosen capacity variant X_i) are minimised subject to the conditions

$$\sum X_{ij} \leqslant X_i \qquad\qquad i = 1 \dots m \qquad\qquad (1)$$

(i.e. the total quantity of cement delivered to all the consumption points from the ith production point, can not exceed the capacity of the ith production point)

$$\sum_{j=1}^{n} X_{ij} = b_j \qquad\qquad j = 1 \dots n \qquad\qquad (2)$$

(i.e. the total quantity of cement received by the jth consumption point from all the production points equals the given requirements at that point)

$$\sum_{i=1}^{m} X_{ij} \geqslant 0 \qquad\qquad i = 1 \dots m; \; j = 1 \dots n \qquad\qquad (3)$$

(i.e. the deliveries must be non-negative)

$$X_i = \text{one of the values of } a_i^{r_i} \qquad\qquad (4)$$

For the results to be interesting it is also necessary that there should be values of $a_i^{r_i}$ for which

$$\sum_{i=1}^{m} a_i^{r_i} > \sum_{j=1}^{n} b_j$$

(i.e. the quantity of production which it is possible to produce must exceed requirements — preferably substantially)

Analysis of results

A feature of these calculations was the great use made of sensitivity analysis. Calculations made in 1963 showed that the decision to build new plants (as opposed to the expansion of existing ones or maintaining existing inefficient plants) was very sensitive to the norm of investment efficiency used. On the other hand the results were not very sensitive to different ways of calculating transport costs, and different regional breakdowns or requirements for cement.

Unless a constraint was introduced that all the existing enterprises should remain open, a number of them were closed down in the optimal plan. In some variants this condition was introduced, in some it was not.

Utilisation of the results in planning

The results of the calculations were a list of enterprises which should be closed down, a list of enterprises which should be maintained at their existing capacity, a list of enterprises which should be expanded, and a list of places where new enterprises should be built, in order to meet the specified output targets. Important features of the results were that it was shown that it is desirable to concentrate the production of cement in a small number of large factories rather than treat cement as a local material the production of which should be scattered all over the country (despite an influential opinion to the contrary in cement industry circles); that the development of the cement industry should proceed mainly by means of expanding existing plants rather than building completely new ones; and that some cement factories built within the last 10—15 years have such high current costs that they should be closed down. (Some existing cement plants are so inefficient that the investment required to replace them by well sited modern plants would be recouped in two years.) These calculations were done in stages in 1962—69 and served as a basis for the plans for the cement industry in the five year plans 1966—70 and 1971—75. 'Unfortunately they only served as a basis. Finished, completed plans we were not able to compile. The imprecisions, conventionalities and debatability of many aspects of the work, not to speak of the fact that some people are unaccustomed to the new methods, provided a basis for the directing organs to reject some of the results (for example the conclusion about the need to liquidate some enterprises).'[5]

The fact that the 'optimal plans' are not simply accepted and implemented, but are regarded merely as material useful for the planning officials when they come to make decisions, is regarded as unsatisfactory by some of the research workers who do the calculations.

'Even many specialists picture the situation this way: a calculation is a calculation, but the plan must be based on something or other else, in addition to this. It is recommended that first a calculation be undertaken, then the results analysed, and then a decision be made in the light of various circumstances. In other words, it is advised that the decisions be taken after the calculation, but at the same time it is assumed that the decisions may deviate from the results of the calculations. In essence, this is a variant of the well known proposition that a calculation should give "material" for competent administrators, who are the ones who should "decide the question".

The basic idea, however, of the application of economic-mathematical methods is that "questions should be decided" by calculations, and not represent a willfull act.'[a] [6]

Evaluation

There are a large number of problems connected both with posing and solving problems of the optimal developments and location of industries. Such calculations are obviously easier for an industry which produces a relatively homogenous product, such as cement, than for industries producing a very heterogenous collection of products. Reliable estimates of regional and total future demand for a product are difficult to compile, especially if there

(a) This line of argument is understandable, but quite unacceptable, because the variables which the 'optimal plans' optimise are only a small subset of the variables whose values are of interest to policy makers, and the initial data is unreliable (and approximate methods of calculation are often used).

are now or may in the future come into existence, substitutes. The calculations take no account of social factors which may be the most important
ones in some location decisions, for example the need to provide work for
women in coal mining areas. The relationship between the output of a plant
and its cost is often non-linear. It is normal in this kind of calculation for
some of the savings to result from the closing down of existing inefficient
enterprises. In so far as these enterprises remain open (on socio-political
grounds or disbelief in the relevance of linear calculations) then part of the
savings claimed are spurious. Further, it is not clear that the increases in
efficiency resulting from the use of this method are substantial compared to
the short run savings that could be obtained by improving the way that the
economy functions (e.g. a reduction in the construction and running in
periods for new plants) or the long run savings resulting from technical
progress.

The harshest attack on the compilation of optimal plans for the development and location of industries has come from Gerchuk, who has argued that
this work is misguided in principle because problems of perspective planning
can not fruitfully be regarded as linear programming problems.[7]   In this
connection it is very important to bear in mind I.Ya. Birman's observation
that 'It is necessary once more to underline the fact that the basic practical
results of the work were achieved not only and not so much thanks to the
new methods of calculation and electronic technology as to the strict adher-
ence to the principle of the single criterion of optimality, the comensurability
of current and capital costs, the correct (within the limits of the possible)
determination of the initial indices and so on.'[8] In other words, Birman
argues, the main reason for the savings resulting from the optimal plans
compared with the plans drawn up by the traditional methods is that the
former are drawn by research teams headed by distinguished economists such
as A.G. Aganbegyan and I.Ya. Birman who pay more care to the economic
aspects of investment planning than did the people who drew up plans by
the traditional methods. This is a very plausible argument. Numerous
alternative ways of calculating transport costs existed before the optimal
planners came on the scene. They, however, were concerned about this, and
devoted considerable efforts to working out the 'right' way of calculating
transport costs, and there now exist the figures for transport costs worked
out by the Institute of Complex Transport Problems, which meet the requirements of perspective planning.

From a practical point of view the crucial question is, how much cheaper
is the output resulting from an optimal plan than the same output produced
by a non-optimal plan? Although the optimal planners cite figures for the
saving (which always show substantial savings) it is difficult to see how
this question can be answered, because it is not possible to implement two
alternative plans simultaneously, and the usual comparison between the
indices of the optimal plan and the indices of a traditional plan, showing
that the former achieves the same output as the latter for a cost 10–15%
lower, implies the very strong assumption that the degree of divergence

176

between the plan and the outcome is the same for the optimal plan as for the traditional plan. (An *ex post* comparison, using actual, rather than assumed, values of the initial data, would be more useful.)

Nevertheless, Gosplan USSR not only accepted the cement calculations as a basis for planning the cement industry, but already in the spring of 1966 issued a special order requiring the compilation of optimal plans for the development and location of the industry in several tens of industries, and at the beginning of 1968 when work on the 1971—75 five year plan was being organised, it was envisaged that the plans for 74 branches of industry accounting for three quarters of the capital stock in industry would be compiled only by the optimal methods. It would seem that the calculation of optimal plans for the development and location of industries is a useful addition to the techniques available to the sectoral planners, the significance of which should be neither exaggerated nor belittled.

Conclusion

The ideas of the optimal planners for improving the methods of economic calculation have given rise to a large number of experimental calculations, and some applications of their ideas, for example in the planning of transport and agriculture. One important application has been in production scheduling in the steel industry. Another has been the working out of optimal plans for the development and location of the cement and other industries.

Close examination of this work reveal that optimal planning as an exercise actually carried out by planners is far removed from optimal planning as explained in lecture rooms and textbooks. The data is unreliable, and the methods of calculation often approximate. Nevertheless it would be misleading to overemphasise the shortcomings of this work. As Kantorovich pointed out in the quotation which heads this chapter, the same unreliable data is used for plans drawn up by other methods. Further one of the features of the Soviet work is the widespread use of sensitivity analysis to spot where variations in the initial data have the most effect on the results, and this enables efforts to be devoted to trying to improve them. As a practical activity optimal planning is concerned with obtaining bad answers to questions to which worse answers are obtained by other methods.

It would be a mistake to suppose that the compilation of optimal plans is an alternative to the expansion of *khozraschet*. In a report on a conference on optimal plans for the development and location of industries I.Ya. Birman asked 'Why have the new methods and tools not yet become basic in industrial planning? What prevents this? Mention was made at the conference of certain imperfections in the mathematical apparatus, the limited potential of the electronic machines available, the complexity of obtaining authentic calculations of the initial indices and the debatability (as a consequence of incomplete elaboration) of many methodological propositions. And yet none of this is the main trouble.

The main trouble consists in the fact that the solution to this economic problem is being pursued not by economic but by administrative methods.

For example, the USSR Ministry of the Building Materials Industry is supporting work on optimal perspective planning. It is probable that more practical computations have been made for the branches of this industry than for any other. But under the existing situation, the ministry has little stake in whether or not the results of these computations are implemented in economic practice.

Of course, everyone must be concerned for the welfare of the state. However, if the optimal computations result in a reduction, by tens of millions of roubles, in the requirements for capital investments, the ministry's allocation quota will simply be lowered by this sum. There will be no immediate benefit for those who did the calculations and who introduced the optimal plan. For the ministry, the savings on the haulage of building materials effected through improvements in the siting of enterprises are no more substantial. It is another department — Gossnab — that obtains these savings.

Is it for this reason, perhaps, that the ministry is delaying the creation of a computer centre and is contributing little to the further development of research and the introduction of its results?

Orders and circulars will correct nothing here : the USSR Ministry of Ferrous Metallurgy, for example, despite a special order from Gosplan, is doing nothing at all about optimal planning. It is necessary to create economic conditions in which both the ministries and the planning agencies will have an interest in the optimisation of industrial plans.'[9]

Soviet specialists consider that the possibility of the large scale application of optimal planning methods is one of the advantages of socialist planning, and is one of the areas where the conflict between the social character of the productive forces and the individualistic nature of the capitalist mode of production reveals itself. Whereas in the Soviet Union there is a design institute for each industry which can calculate optimal plans for the development and location of the industry (such as Giprosteklo in the glass industry) and a ministry to implement them, in capitalist countries optimal planning can only be carried out within the public sector or on the scale of the firm, and when it is carried out by firms costs and benefits which accrue to other economic units ('external effects') are ignored. Whereas in the Soviet Union optimal plans are being worked out for the utilisation of steel mills, in capitalist countries steel plants often work well below capacity because the capitalist system is unable to ensure the efficient allocation of resources.[a]

(a) The reader unfamiliar with the idea of the capitalist system as an obstacle to the efficient allocation of resources may find the following example helpful. Under capitalism, in order to attract resources into research it is necessary to turn inventions into private property (by means of the patent system). This ensures their non-optimal utilisation.

10. Conclusion

For many years a debate has been going on in the Soviet Union about the importance of the efficient allocation of resources, in which a tiny group of economists has urged that the economic mechanism and the methods of economic calculation should be such as to ensure the efficient allocation of resources, and policy makers have failed to accept this argument. This debate flared up in the 1960s when concrete proposals were put forward by TSEMI aimed at transforming the Soviet economic system into an optimally functioning economic system. The views of the economists concerned with the efficient allocation of resources were clearly explained by Yushkov in his 1928 paper.

> 'It would be a serious mistake to think that the existence of a planning apparatus, by itself, is sufficient to resolve the question of the transition to a higher stage of the utilisation of resources. The latter will be achieved only on the basis of a difficult struggle for the creation of the methodology of planning.' [1]

Liberals believe that the efficient allocation of resources is impossible under socialism, and market socialists that it is possible only by mimicking perfect competition. Marxists have traditionally believed that socialist planning is bound to be more efficient than the anarchy of production prevailing under capitalism, because the socialist mode of production eliminates the conflict between the productive forces and the productive relations which characterises capitalism (which reveals itself in such phenomena as strikes, low labour productivity, lack of effective demand, insufficient finance for research and development and geological exploration, and chronic open inflation). Yushkov, arguing against this last position, accepted that it is indeed possible to have greater efficiency under socialism than under capitalism (i.e. to make 'the transition to a higher stage of the utilisation of resources'). He insisted, however, that to turn this possibility into reality required a difficult struggle to establish the appropriate economic mechanism and to work out the appropriate methods of economic calculation — precisely the position taken by TSEMI forty years later.

The arguments of the Lausanne school have traditionally been used as arguments for unlimited private enterprise. Many of the Soviet optimal planners regard the valid kernel of the doctrines of the Lausanne school (the propositions that a number of planning problems can fruitfully be treated as extremal problems, and that the optimal solutions to certain classes of extremal problems are characterised by the existence of numbers that can be given an economic interpretation) as arguments for full *khozraschet* and the use of techniques for obtaining optimal solutions to planning problems, in a socialist economy where the main proportions of the economy are determined by the party in accordance with its political and economic objectives. This was true for Yushkov, and is true for Kantorovich. The latter has explained that:

'if in the question of what to produce (final product) economic calculation plays a secondary role, then in the question of how to produce, in the choice of the most economic methods of obtaining the required product these indices are highly important.

In this way the basic character and direction of long term investment can be determined only in the plan by the general political and economic decisions.

At the same time, in the process of working out the plan, resulting from the general line [of the party], the calculation of efficiency should play a very important role, in particular in the consideration of more partial, but also important questions such as the choice of which raw materials and technological processes to use, the type of enterprise, the degree of concentration and specialisation and so on. Of course these questions also must be solved taking into account the general plan.' [2]

In the introduction to this study the debate was set in its context within the history of economic thought both inside and outside the Soviet Union. In the first chapter the history of the current discussion was outlined, and the chief issues explained. The study went on to outline the theory of optimal planning and functioning, and explained that this theory provides a framework for a large volume of research both on improving the methods of economic calculation and on improving the economic mechanism.

In chapter 3 the way that Kantorovich generalised his economic interpretation of the linear programming problem from a limited group of problems of the organisation of production to national economic planning, both current and perspective, was described. It was then explained how the study of linear programming leads to proposals for reforming the economic mechanism. The idea that welfare economics is a 'risk' to a socialist economy was then criticised on the ground that the result on which this belief is based – the basic theorem of welfare economics– has a very limited domain of validity. It was argued, per contra, that the theorem is a help to a socialist economy because it directs attention both to a useful, though frequently over-rated, group of tools of economic management, trade, flexible prices, and payment for the use of natural resources, in a phrase, full *khozraschet*, and to the need for the rational organisation of production.

The views of the supporters of the transition to an optimally functioning economic system are based not only on the implications for the economic mechanism of the study of linear programming, but also on a critique of the traditional planning techniques and the way that the traditional economic mechanism functions. In chapters 6 and 7 some of the non-optimalities of the existing system of planning were explained. These are important in themselves. In addition, they explain the references by the optimal planners to

180

the 'unscientific' nature of the traditional planning techniques and the need to make the transition from the first to the third stages of planning. Moreover, they provide an explanation of the views of those supporters of the theory of the optimally functioning economy who consider that it as least as important to optimise the economic mechanism as to attempt to introduce optimal methods of economic calculation in an otherwise unchanged economic mechanism. Only in an economy with the waste generated by the use of the balance method for the planning of current production could a large scale campaign for the efficient allocation of resources come into existence.

In chapter 8 the relevance of the ideas of the optimal planners for improving the economic mechanism was examined by means of a detailed study of the enterprise incentive funds, which are the way that the conclusion about the importance of profit which emerged from the economic discussion of 1955 to 1965 was put into practice. It was concluded that the experience of this system provides no support for the Kantorovich—Gorstko assertion that the experience of the new system demonstrates the usefulness of the theory of optimal planning as a source of ideas for reform of the economic mechanism. What a study of linear programming can do is to provide a theoretical demonstration of the desirability of full *khozraschet* which is invaluable pedagogically and which carries more weight (because of its mathematical basis) with engineers and practical men than either Yushkov's arguments or the arguments put forward in the discussion of the role of the law of value which took place in the 1950s.[3]   Whether these ideas are relevant to economic policy at any particular time depends on a political analysis of the costs and benefits of different economic mechanisms relative to the goals of policy. Transforming these general ideas (such as the desirability of full *khozraschet*) into workable policies requires careful economic analysis, such as that provided by Kornai, Khanin and Ya.G. Liberman. In chapter 9 the efforts of the optimal planners to improve the methods of economic calculation were briefly surveyed.

The question of the efficient allocation of resources is an interesting one for three reasons. First, it really is possible to organise the economy in such a way as to generate substantial waste (as explained in chapters 6 and 7). Secondly, it is possible to increase the efficiency with which resources are allocated by using the appropriate methods of economic calculation (as explained in chapter 9). Thirdly, the study of the conditions for the efficient allocation of resources provides arguments for the expansion of *khozraschet* which some people find more convincing (because of their mathematical basis) than other arguments for the expansion of *khozraschet* (for example those concerned with bureaucratisation or individual freedom).

Accordingly it would seem that those economists who argued that the problem of the efficient allocation of resources was purely 'formal'[a] , or that mathematical analysis of the problem was 'barren',[b] were mistaken,

(a) P. Sweezy, *Socialism* (New York 1949) pp. 237—239. Sweezy subsequently altered his position, as is clear from chapter 9 (The utilization of resources) of L. Huberman and P. Sweezy, *Socialism in Cuba* (New York and London 1969).

(b) M. Dobb, *Political economy and capitalism* (1945) p. 129.

and that those economists who emphasised its importance, such as Yushkov, Kantorovich, Novozhilov and Wiles,[a] had a valid point. Economists of the Lausanne school can, however, fairly be criticised for identifying the problem of the efficient allocation of resources with economics as a whole. This ignores Kantorovich's distinction between the two ways of raising efficiency in production planning, and identifies the whole of economics with one of the two ways. Moreover, the central question of production planning is that of economic growth, and although it is perfectly possible to generalise the problem of the efficient allocation of resources to include economic growth, there is a danger that some important features of economic growth are distorted by this approach. For example, Debreu's way of dealing with changes over time is to consider an economy with futures market for all commodities for all dates. On the other hand, the Pasinetti model, which ignores the question of the efficient allocation of resources, does deal with the main features of the growth process. Similarly, the identification of economics with the problem of the efficient allocation of resources ignores the fact that the central question of economic policy is maintaining and expanding freedom by appropriate policies in such fields as negative freedom, working conditions, employment, education, housing, medical care, and the environment. Economists of the Lausanne school can also be criticised for confusing analysis of the conditions for the efficient allocation of resources with a descriptive theory of capitalism. (It is rather striking that the economic system whose apologists claim that it is guided by the price mechanism to the efficient allocation of resources, is the one which is obliged to waste resources in order to reduce the rate of increase of prices.) Furthermore economists of the Lausanne school can be criticised for being more interested in apologetics than in developing operational techniques for actually solving problems of the efficient allocation of resources, and considering the conditions for the application of these techniques. Soviet specialists on optimal planning consider that a necessary condition for the efficient allocation of resources is the social ownership of the means of production. It is no accident that linear programming, the most widely used technique for ensuring the efficient allocation of resources, was discovered not in an atomistic, competitive, economy, but by a mathematician in a socialist economy in order to solve a planning problem, and was subsequently rediscovered by mathematicians concerned with solving the planning problems that arise in the New Industrial State. Soviet specialists on optimal planning consider that a sufficient condition for the efficient allocation of resources is that their views on how the economy ought to function and how economic calculations ought to be performed, be accepted by policy makers and implemented in practice.

Believers in the doctrines of the Lausanne school grossly exaggerate the importance of the question of the efficient allocation of resources, and imagine, inter alia, that allocative efficiency provides a universally acceptable non-ideological criterion for judging economic systems. For example

(a) P. Wiles, *The political economy of communism* (Oxford 1962) pp. 95—96.

182

Ward has argued as follows.

'Consider an economy consisting of a number of families and a number of firms. Each family has a consistent pattern of preferences, and each firm is capable of transforming goods in a given pattern of alternative ways. The state by some process has arrived at a set of goals for society, goals which can be expressed, at least in part, in terms of the amounts of goods provided by society to each family. Having nationalized the means of production, the state wants to find the best allocation of resources in terms of this criterion, accepting as a constraint that nationalization means at the very least that there is no market, in the ordinary sense, for producer goods.

It is hard to find any loading of the ideological dice in this formulation of the problem faced by a socialist economy.' [4]

This criterion is extremely controversial and very far from being 'unideological'. For a liberal, the criterion for ranking economic systems is not efficiency, but the extent to which they provide for individual freedom. As Popper has explained:

'In regard to hedonism and utilitarianism, I believe that it is indeed necessary to replace their principle: *maximise pleasure*! by one which is probably more in keeping with the original views of Democritus and Epicurus, more modest and much more urgent. I mean the rule: *minimise pain*! I believe (cp chapters 9, 24 and 25) that it is not only impossible but very dangerous to attempt to maximise the pleasure or the happiness of the people, since such an attempt must lead to totalitarianism.' [5]

Similarly, Milton Friedman has stated that:

'As liberals, we take freedom of the individual, or perhaps of the family, as our ultimate goal in judging social arrangements.' [6]

Liberals are happy to claim that the administrative economy is inefficient. Their main objection to it, however, is not that it is inefficient, but that it puts too much power into the hands of the state.

Marxists, like liberals, reject allocative efficiency as a criterion for ranking economic systems. Whereas the liberal criterion for ranking economic systems is individual freedom, the Marxist criterion (to the very limited extent that it is possible to speak of a 'Marxist criterion for ranking economic systems' independent of the concrete historical circumstances of particular countries at particular times) is democracy, the extent to which people have control over their lives, and in particular the extent to which workers have control over their working lives. As A.M. Birman has explained:

'What is the basic, organic defect of capitalist society and why are we absolutely convinced that the internal laws of development of this society are leading to its destruction? You see before our eyes there is taking place in the capitalist countries a rapid growth of technology, to a definite extent the living standards of the working people are being raised, the population is increasing.

The classics of Marxism—Leninism have given an exhaustive answer to this question. Its truth is being confirmed by life.

The essence of the matter is that in capitalist conditions mankind is divided into two antagonistic-hostile camps — the ruling minority and the enslaved absolute majority. The external form of the enslavement has changed as a result of the class struggle. The contemporary worker-engineer in the USA or England does not work for 12—14 hours a day, is very well dressed, may have his own car and house — but all the same he is being enslaved.

What does his enslavement consist of?

The worker is being exploited because he does not play any part in the control of production. His opinion is not asked when enterprises are created, it does not interest the bosses at work either. And only if it is necessary to close the enterprise, the owners have to face the despairing resistance of the workers: sitdown strikes, refusals to leave the enterprise and so on.

The workers are used only to the extent that they bring profit. When there is overproduction there is a dilemma, either to lower prices or to throw the workers on to the streets. There is one and only one answer. Therefore the millions of workers are not interested in the improvement of production under capitalism. The words of Marx, that under conditions of capitalism the worker is as indifferent to the results of his work as the horse is indifferent to being bridled by a dear bridle or a cheap one, remain true and correct.' [7]

The reason why believers in the doctrines of the Lausanne school regard allocative efficiency as the criterion for ranking economic systems is quite clear, because analysis of the conditions for the existence of optimal solutions to one class of problems of the efficient allocation of resources provides arguments for their policy views — striking testimony to the 'unideological' nature of the criterion. The reason for the importance of allocative efficiency in the theory of the optimally functioning socialist economy is that in an economy where policy is determined by the party, economists are confined to suboptimisation. The decision to build a giant car plant was made within the central organs of the party, but the choice of the most efficient location for it (Tol'yatti) was one on which TSEMI's advice was sought.

The current discussion in the Soviet Union is a revival of arguments which were first put forward in 1928 and 1943[(a)] , which were ignored when they were put forward, and decisively rejected by Stalin in 1952. Yushkov, applying the conception of the efficient allocation of resources to a socialist planned economy argued that it meant full *khozraschet* plus the use of methods for ensuring the most efficient allocation of scarce investment resources. Kantorovich discovered a new method of obtaining optimal solutions to a class of extremal problems, pointed out that this method

(a) The reference is to Yushkov's paper and to Kantorovich's lecture to the Institute of Economics in which he put forward the main ideas of his 1959 book.

could be used to obtain optimal solutions to many problems of the organisation of production, and noted that the optimal solutions to this class of extremal problems are characterised by the existence of numbers that can be interpreted in such a way as to provide a theoretical basis for *khozraschet*. This line of argument is controversial, and its impact both on the economic mechanism and on the methods of economic calculation, has been very limited. The ideas about the economic mechanism of those Soviet economists who are concerned with the question of how to construct an economic mechanism that would provide for the efficient allocation of resources, range from Kantorovich's proposals for establishing an optimally functioning economic system in the steel industry, via TSEMI's proposals for establishing an optimally functioning economic system in the economy as a whole, to the ideas of those economists who advocate the transition to the *khozraschet* economy. (It is important to note that those who advocate optimal planning are not identical with those who are concerned about the efficient allocation of resources. The ideas of the Ukrainian Cybernetics Institute, the Institute of Management Problems, and the Institute of Economics and the Organisation of Industrial Production, are not based upon an analysis of the conditions for the efficient allocation of resources, and some of those most concerned about the waste generated by the administrative economy simply advocate the transition to the *khozraschet* economy.)

It is very important to understand that the reason why the Soviet government has persistently rejected the conclusions about the economic mechanism of those who study the conditions for the efficient allocation of resources is not that the government is 'irrational' nor that it suffers from 'bureaucratic conservatism', but that these conclusions have been irrelevant to the real historical conditions which confronted the party. In 1928, when Yushkov's article was published, the central question of economic policy was the grain question, how to extract from the peasants sufficient grain to feed the towns, the army, and to finance the imports necessary for the industrialisation programme of the party. Stalin's exasperation with those who contributed to economics rather than assisting with the solution of immediate problems, was understandable. The advocacy of full *khozraschet* in 1928 was about as relevant to Soviet economic policy as the advocacy of the market by Hayek in 1939 was relevant to British economic policy at that time.[8] Whereas economists of the Lausanne school have always conceived of the economic mechanism as something for which one can formulate general rules independent of the real historical situation, in fact, in any given historical situation there are certain things which are on the historical agenda and certain things which are not. (What is, and what is not, on the historical agenda at any given time is determined by the concrete political, social, economic and technological situation.) What made the ideas of the optimal planners relevant in the 1960s, in a way that the ideas of Yushkov were not relevant in 1928, was, firstly that the Soviet Union was no longer living through 'the great break', the bitter struggle to impose collectivisation on the peasants and build the foundations of an advanced socialist industrialised state.[9] The question of full *khozraschet* emerged on to the historical agenda after the 22nd Congress, when the ideas of those economists concerned with the effecient allocation of resources became relevant to the real situation which existed in the country and to the policy options open to the party, in a way which was not so in 1929—61. Secondly, those who are so concerned with the efficient allocation of resources really were able, in the 1960s, to help improve the efficiency of planning, and demonstrated this convincingly in practice. Whereas in *Economic problems of socialism in the USSR* Stalin expressed his scepticism about the very existence of a problem of the efficient allocation of resources, at the present time the authorities do recognise the existence of this problem. This is shown by the facilities with which TSEMI and other institutes have been provided for the calculation of optimal plans, and the views of TSEMI are heard when policies for reforming the economic mechanism are being worked out.

Given the objectives of the party, it makes little sense to criticise the authorities for ignoring the views of those who advocated full *khozraschet* at the time of the grain crisis, explained the merits of *khozraschet* during the Great Patriotic War [a] , advocated greater reliance on profit in 1955—65, and who, when the reform ran into difficulties, recommended the implementation of a three level planning scheme. On the other hand, it is clear that the authorities are open to serious criticism for being extremely dilatory in the large scale application of techniques for ensuring the efficient allocation of resources. Although linear programming was discovered in the 1930s by a Soviet mathematician in order to solve a production scheduling problem, the first large scale application of linear programming to production scheduling in the USSR was three decades later, and followed, rather than preceded, similar work in the United States. Similarly, it is clear that the problems of the administrative economy are serious problems, and that measures are required to overcome them. Shortages are a great nuisance, and Novozhilov was quite right to argue that they are not inevitable, that by suitable measures of economic policy they can be overcome.

The work done in the Soviet Union in working out the theory and practice of an optimally functioning economic system can conveniently be considered under six heads, abstract theoretical work designed to deepen understanding of the properties of optimal economic systems, the application of the theory of optimal planning and functioning to working out planning methods, the application of operational research to particular economic problems, the calculation of numerical planning models, the introduction of computers into the work of the planning and statistical organs, the ministries and enterprises, and the application of the theory of the optimally functioning economy to the economic mechanism.

The first kind of work is likely to continue, (for a good example see Makarov's paper on the asymptotic behaviour of optimal growth paths [10]) and

(a) The 'Great Patriotic War' is the Soviet phrase for the Soviet—German war 1941—45.

186

to be as irrelevant for understanding the problems of the Soviet economy as similar American work is irrelevant for understanding the problems of the American economy. It may lead to important contributions to economics. The second type of work is likely to continue and is likely to have an influence on planning practice, although practical planners may well continue to be sceptical of the relevance of the ideas of academic economists and mathematicians who are inclined to 'solve' problems by ignoring the difficulties. An example of this influence is provided by the impact of TSEMI's ideas on the new method for the pricing of new industrial commodities. (In 1968 TSEMI and other institutes worked out a method for the pricing of new industrial products which was approved by the bureau of the Economics Section of the Academy of Sciences and recommended to the Committee on prices for practical implementation.[11]) Similarly, the ideas of Novozhilov and Lur'e have not been without influence on the official method for ranking investment projects. The application of operational research to particular economic problems is likely to be developed further, and continue to be marked by a certain tension between the research workers who do the calculations and the officials responsible for implementing them (a phenomenon familiar in other countries). Examples of this type of work were provided in chapter 9. The calculation of numerical planning models for current and perspective planning and long term forecasting, to improve the information available to decision makers, will continue and become increasingly sophisticated. Examples of this type of work were given in chapter 6. The introduction of computers into the work of the planning and statistical organs, the ministries and enterprises, will continue. This will lead to the replacement of manual methods by electronic data processing, the operational computer control of industrial processes, and will open up new possibilities for planning, e.g. optimal production scheduling and the control of large construction projects by network planning.[12] It seems likely however, that while proposals for reforming the economic mechanism based on the application to it of the theory of the optimally functioning economy will continue to be made, policy makers will continue to adopt a sceptical attitude towards them. The reasons for this appear to be threefold, that they are unfeasible, theoretically incorrect, and politically unacceptable.

The ideas of Kantorovich and TSEMI on optimal functioning (as opposed to optimal planning) are widely thought, by practical administrators, to be quite unfeasible, and it is indeed difficult to visualise either Kantorovich's ideas about an optimally functioning steel industry, or TSEMI's three level planning scheme, ever being put into practice. Chapter 8 made clear the gulf between the problems of the enterprise incentive funds system, such as the type of incentive system, the stability of the norms, and the division of the net income between profit and turnover tax, and the theories propounded by Kantorovich and TSEMI.

The theoretical correctness or otherwise of TSEMI's position turns on the issue of whether it is correct to derive policy conclusions from a study of the conditions for the efficient allocation of resources, or whether, per contra, correct policy conclusions can be derived only by applying a

Marxist–Leninist perspective to concrete economic problems. More specifically, the question is whether 'growth' is more important than 'choice'.

In *Economic problems of socialism in the USSR* Stalin argued that it was
quite wrong to suppose that economic policy should be determined by considerations arising from the organisation of production. 'It is not true ...
that communism means the rational organisation of the productive forces,
that the rational organisation of the productive forces is the beginning and
the end of the communist system, that it is only necessary to organise the
productive forces rationally and the transition to communism will take place
without any particular difficulty ... This is a profound error and reveals a
complete lack of understanding of the laws of economic development of
socialism'. Seventeen years later the same point was made by Bachurin, a
deputy chairman of Gosplan USSR, in the course of a critique of the work of
Academician Fedorenko, the Director of TSEMI. [13]

> 'With all the significance of economic-mathematical methods and con-
> temporary computer technology in the improvement of planning and the
> management of production, in providing optimal solutions, they cannot
> themselves determine the scientific methodology of planning but are only
> an auxiliary means for the realisation of the basic principles of scien-
> tific planning. The wide utilization of economic-mathematical methods
> simplifies the working out of optimal plans, the determination of the most
> efficient structure of social production and economic proportions. The
> scientific principles of planning the economy, however, were formed in
> the past and will develop further on the basis of Marxist–Leninist
> political economy and the creative application of its various points to the
> practical problems of the building of communism.'

Bachurin continued by comparing Fedorenko's formulation of the national-
economic optimality criterion adversely with the formulation of the basic
economic law of socialism offered in *Economic problems of socialism in the
USSR* [a] and went on to observe that:

(a) Stalin's formulation of the basic economic law of socialism is, 'the securing of
the maximum satisfaction of the constantly rising material and cultural requirements of the whole of society through the continuous expansion and perfection
of socialist production on the basis of higher techniques.' Fedorenko has argued
that 'the logical basis for constructing the optimality criterion is the assumption
that the behaviour of the consumer reflects his conscious or unconscious striving
for the fullest possible satisfaction of his needs.' (*Diskussiya ob optimal'nom
planirovanii* (1968) p. 10). Petrakov, a research worker at TSEMI, has explained
that the basic economic law of socialism is 'the maximum satisfaction of the
needs of society'. (*Novyi Mir* 1970 No. 8, p. 182.) TSEMI's mistake is that it has
retained the first half of Stalin's formulation but omitted the second half, thus
focussing attention on consumer satisfaction, and treating production, growth,
and technical progress as secondary, which represents an abandonment of the
Marxist–Leninist standpoint that production, growth, technical progress and the
rate of increase of labour productivity are primary, and the increased satisfaction
of consumers only one aspect of the growth process, for the chief thesis of the
subjective school of political economy, the proposition that the striving by the
individual consumer in the market to maximise his utility should be the starting
point of economic analysis.

188

'Attempting to create a theory of optimal planning, some research workers base themselves primarily on mathematical apparatus and not on economic theory. This is a serious error.'

The decisive importance of growth was also stressed by Stalin in *Economic problems of socialism in the USSR*. 'It is necessary', he wrote, 'to ensure not a mythical "rational organisation" of the productive forces, but a continuous expansion of all social production, with a relatively higher rate of expansion of production of the means of production'. The idea that 'growth' was more important than 'choice' had earlier been argued by Schumpeter,[14] and was subsequently argued by Wiles[15] and Pasinetti.[16] This argument has recently been taken up by Karagedov, of the Institute of Economics and the Organisation of Industrial Production, who in the course of a critique of the idea that profit is a unique measure of efficiency has attacked the model of competitive equilibrium on which this policy conclusion is based. He quoted with approval Shackle's observation that 'the natural condition of an efficient economy is not a static optimum, the best utilisation of given resources, but growth, the ever better utilisation of continually increasing resources'.[17] This type of debate, now going on in the Soviet Union, between those who extend the problem of the efficient allocation of resources to the whole economy, and draw policy conclusions from it, and those who regard this as wholly illegitimate, is familiar to all economists, and some aspects of the underlying theoretical issues were briefly discussed in chapters 3 and 4 of this study. The points of view being expressed in the USSR range from the argument that Kantorovich's work is purely static,[18] to the argument that 'growth' may have an undesirable effect on 'choice'. [19]

Both of the theoretical objections to the concept of the optimally functioning economic system as understood by TSEMI (that economic policy must be derived from Marxist—Leninist political economy and not from a study of the conditions for the efficient allocation of resources, and more specifically, that the decisive test of any suggestions for improving the economic mechanism is its effect, not on allocative efficiency but on economic growth) were recently combined by a deputy chairman of Gosplan. He explained yet again to a conference of economists held to discuss the economic reform a few days before the December (1969) Plenum, that the views of those economists who emphasised the need to expand the independence of enterprises and the sphere of market relations were incorrect, both because they contradicted Leninist principles and because this conception 'does not promise the development of the productive forces' as is demonstrated both by Soviet experience and by the experience of the capitalist countries. [20]

The reasons for the political unacceptability of 'market socialism', 'a major change in the productive relations of socialism comparable to the transition from War Communism to NEP', a 'new economic mechanism', 'the *khozraschet* economy' and kindred ideas, is that the experience of the new economic model in other countries suggests that it might bring unemployment and open inflation, accentuate regional disparities, have adverse effects on the distribution of income, and above all that it might weaken the role of the socialist state and the party of the working class in the management of the economy. TSEMI, of course, is not advocating a new economic mechanism, but is concerned with the optimisation of planning. Nevertheless, to the extent that TSEMI's proposals have elements in common with the unacceptable theories (wholesale trade, emphasis on value relations as guides to efficiency) they too may turn out to be unacceptable.

It would clearly be an exaggeration to state that Soviet mathematical economics has been imported, lock stock and barrel, from the West, as a number of Western economists are inclined to do. This not only ignores the early Soviet work on input-output and linear programming, but also by the fact that the evolution of economic cybernetics in the USSR has been profoundly influenced by the Soviet economic mechanism, the methods of economic calculation used in the Soviet Union, and the official doctrine of the USSR — Marxism—Leninism. The influence of the economic mechanism is shown in the work of those, such as Novozhilov, Kantorovich, Terekhov, Volkonsky and TSEMI, who have emphasised the allocative function of prices, the desirability of charges for the use of natural resources and capital goods, and of wholesale trade, and the advantages of equilibrium prices in the retail market. The discussion of local optimality criteria and the use of profit as a synthetic success indicator can only be understood against the background of the administrative economy and its problems. The influence of the methods of economic calculation is shown, for example, by Dudkin's optimal material balances, the work done by Aganbegyan, I.Ya. Birman and others on optimal plans for the development and location of industries, and the work done by TsSU in compiling a capital stock matrix for the USSR. As a result of the latter the data on the Soviet capital stock published in the Soviet official statistics is now substantially better than the data on the US capital stock published in the US official statistics, and the data on the UK capital stock published in the UK official statistics. The influence of Marxism—Leninism is shown, for example, in the work of Novozhilov, who has devoted great efforts to demonstrating that the theory of optimal planning fits into Marxist—Leninist political economy. In the USA economists working on modern planning techniques have to argue that their work fits into Walrasian orthodoxy and far from being incompatible with the free enterprise system actually helps to increase profits. In the USSR economists working on modern planning techniques have to argue that their work fits into Marxist—Leninist orthodoxy and far from being incompatible with socialist planning actually helps to raise its efficiency.

On the other hand, it is undoubtedly true that Soviet work in this field has been heavily influenced by Western work. This is not an isolated phenomenon. One finds the same in other fields, such as sociology. Western mathematical economics is, of course, deeply impregnated with liberal ideology, and in taking over some techniques from the West some Soviet economists have taken over ideas which are no more valid in their new setting than they were in the old. According to Fedorenko, the 'logical

basis for constructing the optimality criterion' (for the national economy)
'is the assumption that the behaviour of the consumer reflects his conscious
or unconscious striving for the fullest possible satisfaction of his needs',
a formulation which has a familiar ring. Novozhilov is not the only economist
to find the concept of 'consumer sovereignty' unsatisfactory.[21] All too often,
Soviet economists, in understandable reaction to the poverty of Marxism–
Leninism, adopt ideas and techniques for no better reason than that they
are fashionable in the West. It is encouraging to see that not all Soviet
specialists in economic cybernetics have succumbed to the fashion for
Western ideas, and that some, such as Lur'e, Gerchuk and Val'tukh have
rejected ideas which are orthodox in many universities and journals in the
West.

In the late 1960s 'the price mechanism' was a fashionable phrase at
TSEMI. Excessive emphasis on the allocative function of prices contributes
neither to the understanding of capitalism nor to the formulation of relevant
policy proposals. What made liberal capitalism into such a dynamic system
was the energy and drive of tens of thousands of individuals striving to enrich themselves. What makes managerial capitalism into such a dynamic
force is the energy and drive of tens of thousands of individuals striving to
enrich themselves, the dynamic of the large companies, and the actions of
the state. Schumpeter had much more insight into the capitalist system than
Walras. It is encouraging to see that not only D. Gale, *The theory of linear
economic models*, but also J. Galbraith, *The new industrial state*, has been
translated into Russian. When thinking about possible improvements in the
Soviet economic mechanism, excessive emphasis on the role of optimal
prices ignores the policy objectives of the state, the social structure of the
USSR, and the importance for the success or failure of any economic policy
of the attitudes and behaviour of tens of millions of workers and consumers.
The reason why the Soviet government has persistently, over a period of
more than 40 years, rejected the views of those economists who have
argued for equilibrium prices in the retail market, is not that the government
is 'irrational', nor that it suffers from 'bureaucratic conservatism'. Partly it
is because in an economy where the main aim of production planning is to
provide for the needs of the defence, space and investment programmes,
suppressed inflation makes it easier to sell the consumer goods that are
produced. Partly it is because in an economy where administrative privilege
is decisive for access to the good things of private consumption, top people
are not affected by shortages. Partly it is because higher prices might
bring strikes in the factories and riots in the cities.

The discussion of optimal planning in the 1960s provided a striking
demonstration of the importance of ideology in economics. In part, the
challenge posed by economic cybernetics to political economy represented
a clash between the ideology of Soviet society and the ideology of capitalism adapted to Soviet conditions by writers such as Volkonsky. The fact
that a debate of this kind could take place is a tribute to the open nature of
the political situation in 1962–67. (The emergence of economic cybernetics
after the 20th Congress, and the creation of TSEMI after the 22nd Congress,

191

were not accidental.) This debate was an ideological reflection of the real issue at stake in the discussion of economic reform, whether or not Soviet society should continue to evolve within the framework of the social order which has existed in the USSR since 1929.

Summary

Since before the creation of the administrative economy there have existed in the Soviet Union economists who have rejected the argument that a socialist planned economy is bound to be more efficient than capitalism. They have agreed that socialism creates the possibility of a more efficient allocation of resources than is possible under capitalism, by eliminating the conflict between the productive forces and the productive relations which characterises capitalism. They have argued, however, that this possibility will only become a reality when the appropriate economic mechanism has been established and the appropriate methods of economic calculation are used.

Stalin ignored this line of argument in practice, and rejected it in theory. After the 20th Congress a new direction, the economic-mathematical direction, rapidly developed within Soviet economic science. The economic cyberneticians have already made three important contributions to Soviet economic thought and planning practice. First, they have provided a theoretical basis for full *khozraschet*. Secondly, they have provided a new method of economic calculation, the input-output table. Thirdly, they have actually solved a number of the problems of the efficient allocation of resources, and thus contributed to raising the efficiency of Soviet planning. Their work is continuing and is likely to make a useful contribution to Soviet planning in fields as diverse as production scheduling, investment planning, and the replacement of manual methods by electronic data processing in the planning and statistical organs.

As well as improving the methods of economic calculation the economic cyberneticians also put forward proposals for improving the economic mechanism. Kantorovich tried to introduce an optimally functioning economic system in the steel industry, and TSEMI put forward proposals for an optimally functioning economic system in the economy as a whole. The purpose of introducing an optimally functioning economic system is to ensure the efficient allocation of resources. There are also in the USSR economists who agree with the supporters of the theory of an optimally functioning economic system that reforms are necessary in order to bring about the efficient allocation of resources, but who are sceptical about the relevance for economic policy of this theory, and advocate the transition to the *khozraschet* economy.

The ideas of the economic cyberneticians about the economic mechanism have not been accepted, although in certain limited areas, such as the recognition of capital intensity as a factor in price formation, the introduc-

192

tion of payments for the use of natural resources, and the development of wholesale trade, their ideas have not been entirely rejected and may become more influential in the future.

The appropriate way of deriving the economic mechanism is either from considerations of economic strategy or from social objectives. In the latter case the conditions for the efficient allocation of resources may be useful for ideological purposes. In the 1920s the problem of ensuring the efficient allocation of given investment resources (Yushkov's problem), though important, was much less important for the economic mechanism than the problem of sharply increasing the share of investment in the national income (Preobrazhensky's problem). In the 1960s people concerned with deepening the line of the 20th and 22nd Congresses used ideas developed twenty years earlier by a mathematician to provide a 'scientific' basis for their objectives in the field both of economic strategy (e.g. to improve the position of personal consumption) and of the social order (e.g. to reduce the role of government officials in the life of society). Up till now the economic strategy which has been pursued in the USSR since 1929 and the social order which sustains it have proved stronger than the social groups which challenge them. Hence the optimal planners are confined to the solution of particular planning problems, and of the transition to the optimally functioning socialist economy there are few signs.

References

Note

Books in Russian are published in Moscow unless otherwise stated.

Books in English are published in London unless otherwise stated.

Introduction

1. L. Walras, *Elements of pure economics* (1954) p. 255. This is the English translation of a book the first edition of which was published in Lausanne in 1874.

2. Barone's paper was published in English in F. Hayek (ed.) *Collectivist economic planning* (1935).

3. Von Mises' paper was published in English in F. Hayek (ed.) *Collectivist economic planning* (1935). Von Mises repeated this argument in his book *Socialism* (1936).

4. L. Robbins, *The great depression* (1934) pp. 154–156. (One footnote omitted.) For a contemporary Soviet elaboration of the 'millions of equations' argument see A. and N. Kobrinskii, *Mnogo li cheloveku nuzhno?* (1969) passim especially p. 199.

5. L.P. Yushkov, Osnovnoi vopros planovoi metodologii (The basic question of planning methodology) *Vestnik Finansov* 1928 No. 10. This article was printed with a note to say that it was a discussion article, i.e. that the views expressed in it were the responsibility of the author alone.

    Yushkov is not just a forgotten forerunner of later developments. His article is referred to in their books by Kantorovich (*Ekonomicheskii raschet nailuchshego ispol'zovaniya resursov* (1960) p. 261), Lur'e (*O matematicheskikh metodakh resheniya zadach na optimum pri planirovanii sotsialisticheskogo khozyaistva* (1964) p. 222), Bogachev (*Srok okupaemosti* (1966) pp. 56–58), and Zalesski (*Sravnitel'naya otsenka khozyaistvennykh reshenii* (1968) p. 4 and p. 10).

    The importance of Yushkov's paper was noticed by Collette. (J.M. Collette, *Politique des investissements et calcul economique: L'experience sovietique* (Paris 1965) pp. 40–41.) Collette however, and following after him Zauberman (*Soviet Studies* vol. 18, p. 91), treat

Yushkov as a precursor of linear programming, an interpretation which the present author finds rather strained, and play down Yushkov's emphasis on the necessity for full *khozraschet* for the efficient allocation of resources in a socialist planned economy.

6. L.V. Kantorovich, *Matematicheskie metody organizatsiya i planirovaniya proizvodstva* (Leningrad 1939). This work was reprinted with minor changes in V.S. Nemchinov (ed.) *Primenenie matematiki v ekonomicheskikh issledovaniyakh* (1959). For an English translation see *Management Science* July 1960.

Kantorovich's achievement, in this and subsequent writings, was that he realised that the problem of the efficient allocation of resources is a general problem of production planning with a large number of applications, that he provided an algorithm for deriving numerical solutions, and that he provided a mathematical analysis of the problem emphasising the economic significance of the optimality conditions. The importance of the problem of the efficient allocation of resources, within the field of railway freight transport, was already familiar to Soviet planners, and methods for achieving it had been worked out. See *Planirovanie perevozok* (1930) a collection of papers based on the work of the Interdepartmental office for the planning and rationalisation of transport; A.N. Tolstoi, *Sotsialisticheskii transport* 1939 No. 9; and A.N. Tolstoi, *Metody ustraneniya neratsional'nykh perevozok pri sostavlenii operativnykh planov* (1941).

7. *Voprosy ekonomiki* 1968 No. 4.

Chapter 1

The use of mathematics in Soviet economics — an historical survey.

1. *Ekonomisty i matematiki za kruglym stolom* (1965) p. 9.

2. See the Soviet essays of the 1920s collected and translated in Spulber (ed.) *Foundations of Soviet strategy for economic growth* (Bloomington, Indiana, 1964).

The first Russian mathematical economist was V.K. Dmitriev, whose main work was V.K. Dmitriev, *Ekonomicheskie ocherki* (1904). There is a French translation, V.K. Dmitriev, *Essais Economiques* (Paris 1968). For a contemporary tribute to Dmitriev see N.N. Shaposhnikov, *Pervyi russki ekonomist-matematik Vladimir Karpovich Dmitriev* (1914).

3. L.P. Yushkov, *Vestnik Finansov* 1928 No. 10.

4. J. Stalin, *Sochineniya* vol. 12 (1955) pp. 141–172.

5. V.V. Novozhilov, Metody soizmereniya narodnokhozyaistvennogo

effektivnosti planovykh i proektnykh variantov, *Trudy Leningradskogo Industrial'nogo instituta* 1939 No. 4; V.V. Novozhilov, Prakticheskie metody soizmereniya sebestoimosti i vlozhenii, *Trudy Leningradskogo Politekhnicheskogo instituta* 1941; V.V. Novozhilov, Metody nakhozhdeniya minimuma zatrat v sotsialisticheskom khozyaistve, *Trudy Leningradskogo Politekhnicheskogo instituta* 1946; and subsequent papers. The 1946 paper and part of the 1939 paper are translated into English in *International Economic Papers* 1956 No. 6. Novozhilov's main work is *Problemy izmereniya zatrat i rezul'tatov pri optimal'nom planirovanii* (1967). There is an English translation, V.V. Novozhilov, *Problems of cost-benefit analysis in optimal planning* (New York 1970).

6. For some historical details see V.S. Nemchinov, *Izbrannye proizvedeniya* vol. 1 (1967) pp. 20–23 and 28–32.

7. See for example, V.S. Nemchinov, Statisticheskie i ekonomicheskie voprosy postroeniya balansa narodnogo khozyaistva, *Uchenie zapiski po statistike* vol. 3, *Voprosy balansa narodnogo khozyaistva i proizvoditel'nosti truda* (1957).

8. The English translation is A. Nove (ed.) *The use of mathematics in economics* (Edinburgh 1964).

9. The English translation is L.V. Kantorovich, *The best use of economic resources* (Oxford 1965).

10. For this and other historical information see Vainshtein's essay commemorating the 25th anniversary of linear programming in L.E. Mints (ed.) *Ekonomiko-matematicheskie metody*: vol. 3, *Ekonomiko – matematicheskie modeli narodnogo khozyaistva* (1966) p. 25.

11. See *Planovoe khozyaistvo* 1960 No. 1, *Kommunist* 1960 No. 15, and *Voprosy ekonomiki* 1960 No. 5 and 1961 No. 2.

12. V.S. Nemchinov (ed.) *Trudy nauchnogo soveshaniya o primenenii matematicheskikh metodov v ekonomicheskikh issledovaniyakh i planirovanii* (4–8 aprelya 1960 goda) in 7 volumes.

13. *Planovoe khozyaistvo* 1960 No. 1 p. 95.

14. See for example Campbell's article in *Slavic Review* October 1961; Johansen's articles in *Monthly Review* January 1963 and in *Economics of Planning* vol. 3, 1963, No. 2; Dickinson's rebuttal ibid December 1963; A.A. Konius, Trudovaya teoriya stoimosti i ekonometrika, *On political economy and econometrics*: Essays in

honour of Oskar Lange (Warsaw 1964); *Ekonomisty i matematiki za kruglym stolom* (1965).

15. L.V. Kantorovich, *The best use of economic resources* (Oxford 1965) p. 218.

16. V.S. Nemchinov (ed.) *Matematicheskii analiz rasshirennogo vosproizvodstva* (1962) − vol. 2 of the *trudy* of the April 1960 conference − pp. 20−22. One footnote omitted.

17. *Ekonomicheskie nauki* 1970, No. 7, pp. 40−50.
   The legitimacy of the distinction between scarce and reproducible goods is, of course, the crucial issue which divides Ricardians and Walrasians, as Walras was well aware. For his denial of the legitimacy of the Ricardian dichotomy see L. Walras, *Elements of pure economics* (1954) lesson 38.
   The problem of efficient allocation is not just relevant to the pricing of Old Masters. It is also relevant, as Kantorovich showed, to the organisation of production.

18. *Ekonomika i matematicheskie metody* 1966, No. 3, p. 336.

19. Ya.P. Gerchuk, *Granitsy primeneniya lineinogo programmirovaniya* (1965).

20. A.L. Lur'e, *Ekonomika i matematicheskie metody* 1969, No. 3, pp. 366−377.

21. V.V. Novozhilov, *Izmerenie zatrat i rezul'tatov pri optimal'nom planirovanii* (1967) p. 356.

22. N.P. Fedorenko, *O razrabotke sistemy optimal'nogo funktsionirovaniya ekonomiki* (1968) p. 7.

23. The proceedings of this conference were reported in *Diskussiya ob optimal'nom planirovanii* (1968) compilers L.Ya. Kazakevich and L.V. Levshin. For earlier reports see *Voprosy ekonomiki* 1967, No. 5, pp. 148−155; *Ekonomicheskie nauki* 1967, No. 2, pp. 96−98; *Ekonomika i matematicheskie metody* 1967, No. 2, pp. 317−324.

24. *Izvestiya*, 4 December 1964.

25. *Diskussiya ob optimal'nom planirovanii* (1968) pp. 120−121.

26. B.V. Rakitskii, *Formy khozyaistvennogo rukovodstva predpriyatiyami* (1968).

27. Ya.G. Liberman, *Gosudarstvennyi byudzhet SSSR v novykh usloviyakh khozyaistvovaniya* (1970).

28. N.P. Fedorenko, *O razrabotke sistemy optimal'nogo funktsionirovaniya ekonomiki* (1968) p. 7.

29. ibid p. 16.

30. Fedorenko, Bunich and Shatalin (eds.), *Sotsialisticheskie printsipy khozyaistvovaniya i effektivnost' obshchestvennogo proizvodstva* (1970). The author of the first chapter does not belong to the economic-mathematical direction in Soviet economic science.

31. *Vestnik Akademii Nauk SSSR* 1970, No. 2, pp. 13–20.

32. M.Z. Bor and V.K. Poltorygin (eds.) *Planirovanie i khozyaistvennogo reforma* (1969) p. 5.

33. M.Z. Bor, Ekonomicheskaya reforma i voprosy teorii planirovaniya narodnogo khozyaistva, in M.Z. Bor and V.K. Poltorygin (eds.) *Planirovanie i khozyaistvennaya reforma* (1969). The quotation is from p. 7.

34. A. Bachurin, *Planovoe khozyaistvo* 1969, No. 11.

35. *Planovoe khozyaistvo* 1970, No. 5. An earlier article by Kovalev (*Voprosy ekonomiki* 1964, No. 2) was criticised by a number of TSEMI authors (*Voprosy ekonomiki* 1965, No. 1).

36. I.Ya. Birman (ed.) *Optimal'nyi plan otrasli* (1970) p. 5.

Chapter 2

Optimal planning and functioning – a theory of economic reform and improved methods of economic calculation.

1. L.Ya. Kazakevich and L.V. Levshin (compilers) *Diskussiya ob optimal'nom planirovanii* (1968) pp. 7–9.

2. Ya.G. Liberman, *Ekonomika i matematicheskie metody* 1968, No. 5, pp. 691–692. This article carries a note from the editors to the effect that the views expressed in the article represent the opinions of the author only and have no official standing.

3. The phrase is Batyrev's. See *Diskussiya ob optimal'nom planirovanii* (1968) p. 190.

4. N.P. Fedorenko, *O razrabotke sistemy optimal'nogo funktsionirovaniya ekonomiki* (1968) p. 43.

5. A.G. Aganbegyan in *Diskussiya ob optimal'nom planirovanii* (1968) p 39.

6. A.I. Katsenelinboigen and E.Yu. Faerman, *Ekonomika i matematicheskie metody* 1967, No. 3, p. 331.

7. For a comparison of the points of view of these three institutes see the article by I. Siroyezhin (a leading Soviet operational researcher) in *Management Science* 1968, vol. 15, No. 2.

8. D. Allakhverdyan, *Pravda* 26 September 1969.

9. V. Chernyavsky, *Voprosy ekonomiki* 1969, No. 7, p. 86.

10. TSEMI's policy ideas are set out in Fedorenko, Bunich and Shatalin (eds.), *Sotsialisticheskie printsipy khozyaistvovaniya i effecktivnost' obshchestvennogo proizvodstva* (1970).

11. V.A. Volkonskii, *Model'* *optimal'nogo planirovaniya i vzaimosvyazi ekonomicheskikh pokazatelei* (1967) p. 8.

12. *Ekonomika i matematicheskie metody* 1970, No. 4, p. 491.

13. I.Ya. Birman, *Optimal'noe programmirovanie* (1968) p. 163.
    This book is controversial. It was well reviewed in *Novyi Mir* (1968 No. 5), and severely criticised in *Voprosy ekonomiki* (1969, No. 4, p. 108) by Ya.P. Gerchuk. According to the reviewer in *Ekonomicheskie nauki* (1969, No. 2, p. 118) 'It is impossible to agree fully with all the statements of the author about the economic function of the system of shadow prices. His position on many issues is questionable ... Evidently it is necessary to examine the question of the optimal national economic plan in a more thorough and detailed way.'

14. I.Ya. Birman op cit p. 222.

15. V.F. Pugachev, *Optimizatsiya planirovaniya* (1968) pp. 20–21.

16. A.I. Berg and E. Kol'man (eds.), *Kibernetika ozhidaemaya i kibernetika neozhidannaya* (1968) p. 145. Italics added.

17. *Ekonomika i matematicheskie metody* 1969, No. 5, p. 791.

18. I. Friss, *Acta Oeconomica* 1970, Fasc 1–2, pp. 41–42.

19. S. Kavčič (Prime Minister of Slovenia) *Teorija in praksa* (Ljubljana) 1968, No. 2.

20. V.A. Volkonsky, *Model' optimal'nogo planirovaniya i vzaimosvyazi ekonomicheskikh pokazatelei* (1967) p. 140.

21. V. Chernyavsky, *Effektivnaya ekonomika* (1967) pp. 4–5.

Chapter 3

What is the most useful economic interpretation of the linear programming problem?

1. *Management Science* July 1960, p. 367.

2. Ya.P. Gerchuk, *Granitsy primeneniya lineinogo programmirovaniya* (1965) p. 27.

3. A.L. Vainshtein, Voznikovenie i razvitie primeneniya lineinogo programmirovaniya v SSSR (k 25—letiyu lineinogo programmirovaniya), in L.E. Mints (ed.) *Ekonomiko-matematicheskie metody*, vol. 3, *Ekonomiko-matematicheskie modeli narodnogo khozyaistva* (1966) p. 30.

4. See for example the paper by Lur'e in *Optimal'noe planirovanie i sovershenstvovanie upravleniya narodnym khozyaistvom* (1969), and the paper by Granberg in, Aganbegyan and Val'tukh (eds.) *Problemy narodnokhozyaistvennogo optimuma* (Novosibirsk 1966).

5. V.S. Nemchinov (ed.) *Primenenie matematiki v ekonomicheskikh issledovaniyakh*, vol. 3 (1965) p. 57.

6. J. Schmookler, *American Economic Review* 1965 Papers and proceedings p. 335.

Chapter 4

How the study of linear programming leads to proposals for reforming the economic mechanism

1. *Economic Journal* 1960, pp. 706–707.

2. V.A. Volkonsky, *Model' optimal'nogo planirovaniya i vzaimosvyazi ekonomicheskikh pokazatelei* (1967) p. 10. Bracketed passage added.

3. L.V. Kantorovich, A new method of solving some classes of extremal problems, *Comptes Rendues (Doklady) de l'Academie des Sciences de l'USSR* 1940, vol. 28, No. 3, pp. 211–214.

4.   L.V. Kantorovich, *The best use of economic resources* (Oxford 1965)
     pp. 274–275. For an earlier formulation see L.V. Kantorovich, O
     metodakh analiza nekotorykh ekstremal'nykh planovo-proizvodstvennykh
     zadach, *Doklady Akademii Nauk SSSR* 1957, No. 3, p. 442.

5.   A.I. Katsenelinboigen, I.L. Lakhman, Yu.V. Ovsienko, Optimal'noe
     upravlenie i tsennostnoi mekhanizm (Optimal control and the price
     mechanism), *Ekonomika i matematicheski metody* 1969, No. 4.

6.   For this example see L.V. Kantorovich, *The best use of economic
     resources* (Oxford 1965) pp. 1–33.

7.   L.V. Kantorovich and A.B. Gorstko, *Matematicheskoe optimal'noe
     programmirovanie v ekonomike* (1968) p. 25.

8.   N.E. Kobrinskii and A.M. Matlin, *Ekonomiko-matematicheskie modeli
     v planirovanii* (1968) p. 106 and p. 21.

9.   L.L. Terekhov, *Otsenki v optimal'nom plane* (1967) p. 66. For a sim-
     ilar formulation see V.A. Volkonskii, *Model' optimal'nogo planirovaniya
     i vzaimosvyazi ekonomicheskikh pokazatelei* (1967) pp. 123–126.

10. See for example Kantorovich's comments in *Ekonomicheskaya Gazeta*
     1965, No. 45, p. 9.

11. For this example see Terekhov op cit pp. 60–64. The subsequent
     quotations are all from here.

12. A.M. Rumyantsev and P.G. Bunich (eds.) *Ekonomicheskaya reforma:
     yeyo osushestvlenie i problemy* (1969) p. 151 (Aganbegyan).

13. For this example see L.K. Kantorovich, *The best use of economic
     resources* (Oxford 1965) pp. 76–79.

14. Kantorovich op cit p. 80.

15. L.L. Terekhov, *Otsenki v optimal'nom plane* (1967) p. 58.

16. Kantorovich op cit pp. 62–68.

17. *Trud* 12 May 1968.

18. J.V. Stalin, *Sochineniya* vol. 10 (1950) p. 119.

19. *Matematicheskie modeli i metody optimal'nogo planirovaniya*
     (Novosibirsk 1966) p. 119.

20.   Kantorovich, *The best use of economic resources*, pp. 124–137.

21.   See *Tipovaya metodika opredeleniya ekonomicheskoi effecktivnosti kapital'nykh vlozhenii i novoi tekhniki v narodnom khozyaistve SSSR*, 1st ed. 1960, 2nd ed. 1969.

22.   L.L. Terekhov, *Otsenki v optimal'nom plane* (1967) p. 112. cf E. Malinvaud, The analogy between atemporal and intertemporal theories of resource allocation, *Review of Economic Studies*, vol. 28.

23.   Kantorovich op cit pp. 191–193.

24.   T.C. Koopmans, *Three essays on the state of economic science* (New York 1957) pp. 12–13.

25.   V.A. Volkonskii, *Model' optimal'nogo planirovaniya i vzaimosvyazi ekonomicheskikh pokazatelei* (1967) p. 60.

26.   G.B. Dantzig and P. Wolfe, The decomposition algorithm for linear programming, *Econometrica*, 1961.

27.   C. Almon, Central planning without complete information at the centre, in G. Dantzig, *Linear programming and extensions* (Princeton 1963).

28.   A.I. Katsenelinboigen, Yu.V. Ovsienko, E.Yu. Faerman, in *Problemy funktsionirovaniya bol'shikh ekonomicheskikh sistem* (1969) p. 19.

29.   K.Kouba, The Plan and the Market in a Socialist economy, *Czechoslovak Economic Papers* 11 (1969) pp. 37–38. Italics added.

30.   This diagram is taken from Dorfman, Samuelson and Solow, *Linear programming and economic analysis* (New York 1958) p. 35.

Chapter 5

A risk or a help?

1.   A. and N. Kobrinskii, *Mnogo li cheloveku nuzhno?* (1969) p. 173.

2.   *Soviet Studies*, vol. 14, p. 69.

3.   T. Koopmans, *Three essays on the state of economic science* (New York 1957) p. 41.

4.   Dorfman, Samuelson and Solow, *Linear programming and economic analysis* (New York 1958) p. 410.

5. Cf Mandeville, *The fable of the bees* (1732).

6. K. Arrow, *Social choice and individual values* (New York 1951) p. 18.

7. A.K. Sen, Optimising the rate of saving, *Economic Journal* September 1961.

8. Sen and Runciman, Games, Justice and the General Will, *Mind* 1965.

9. E.H. Carr, *The Soviet impact on the Western World* (1946) pp. 5–19; and J.L. Talmon, *The origins of totalitarian democracy* (1955), *Political messianism: the romantic phase* (1960), and *Utopianism and politics* (1957).

10. For some examples designed to suggest that this conclusion is not only valid but also interesting, see Part 2 of Michael Ellman, Individual preferences and the market, *Economics of Planning*, 1966, No. 3.

Chapter 6

The consistency of the current plans

1. *Byulleten' oppozitsii*, No. 31, November 1932, p. 8.

2. For a description of the *tekhpromfinplan* see A.M. Kovalevskii, *Tekhpromfinplan v novykh usloviyakh i tipovaya metodika ego razrabotki* (1968). For a description of the process by which enterprise operating plans are drawn up, see B. Richman, Formulation of enterprise operating plans in Soviet industry, *Soviet Studies*, vol. 15.

3. V.S. Nemchinov, *O dal'neishem sovershenstvovanii planirovaniya i upravleniya narodnym khozyaistvom* (2nd ed. 1965) p. 56.

4. The standard English language description of this process is H.S. Levine's contribution to, Joint Economic Committee of Congress, *Comparisons of the United States and Soviet economies* (Washington 1959).

5. N.V. Ivanov, E.Yu. Lokshin, and G.M. Demichev, *Ekonomika i planirovanie material'no-tekhnicheskogo snabzheniya* (1969) p. 338.

6. V.F. Kotov, *Planirovanie realizatsii produktsii, pribyli i rentabel'nosti v promyshlennosti* (1969) p. 41.

7. See for example S.I. Grigor'ev and K.M. Skovoroda, *Planirovanie fondov tovarov narodnogo potrebleniya* (1969).

8. This figure is taken from L.I. Istomin and D.T. Novikov, *Matematicheskie metody v praktike upravleniya material'no-tekhnicheskim snabzheniem i sbytom* (1966) p. 23.

9. A.N. Lebed', M.Sh. Dovetov, Yu.M. Aristakov, *Material'no-tekhnicheskoe snabzhenie i sbyt v sovremennykh usloviyakh* (1969) p. 54.

10. I.A. Tanchuk, *Pravoe regulirovanie material'no-tekhnicheskogo snabzheniya promyshlennosti* (1965) pp. 80–81.

11. A.G. Aganbegyan, *Vestnik Akademii Nauk SSSR* 1964, No. 6, p. 66.

12. *Reforma stavit problemy* (1968) compilers Yu.V. Yakovlets and L.S. Blyakhman p. 152. Emdin makes the same point. See A.Ya. Emdin, *Metodologiya planirovaniya i organizatsiya material'no-tekhnicheskogo snabzheniya* (1966) pp. 5–6.

13. V.F. Kotov, *Planirovanie realizatsii produktsii, pribyli, i rentabel'nosti v promyshlennosti* (1969) p. 43.

14. ibid pp. 43–44.

15. A.A. Zakruzhnyi, *Organizatsiya i planirovanie material'no-tekhnicheskogo snabzheniya* (Minsk 1966) p. 53.

16. ibid p. 86.

17. *Ekonomika material'no-tekhnicheskogo snabzheniya* 2nd ed. (1963) p. 313.

18. This figure is taken from N.V. Gukov, *Organizatsiya material'no-tekhnicheskogo snabzheniya predpriyatii bytovogo obsluzhivaniya naseleniya* (1969) p. 108.

19. For an account of the use of material balances in planning, see Yu.I. Koldomasov, *Metod material'nykh balansov v planirovanii narodnogo khozyaistva* (1959); G.I. Grebtsov and P.P. Karpov (eds.) *Material'nye balansy v narodnokhozyaistvennom plane* (1960); _.M. Montias, Planning with material balances in Soviet type economies, *American Economic Review*, 1959; and N.K. Chandra, *Some problems of investment planning in a socialist economy with special reference to the USSR and Poland* (PhD thesis London 1965) especially chapter 5.

20. A.N. Efimov and L.Ya. Berri (eds.) *Metody planirovaniya mezhotraslevykh proportsii* (1965) p. 8.

21. For this contrast see B.L. Isaev, *Int egrirovannye balansovy e sistemy v analize i plani rovani i ekonomiki* (1969) p. 271.

22. A.N. Efimov, *Perestroika upravleni y a promy shlennostiy u stroitel' stvom* (1957) p. 107.

23. Kvasha and Krasovski, *Voprosy Ekonomiki*, 1961, No. 8.

24. See J.M. Montias, *Cent ral Planni ng in Poland* (New Haven 1962) pp. 339–345, and J.M. Montias, On the consistency and efficiency of central plans, *Review of Economic Studies*, October 1962.

25. Attention has been drawn to this by Dobb. See M. Dobb, *Soviet economic developmen t* (1966) p. 359.

26. V.F. Kotov, *Planirovanie realizatsii produktsii, pri by li i rentabel' nosti v promy shlennosti* (1969) p. 44.

27. Baranov, Klotsvog, Shatalin and Eidel'man, *Ekonomika i matematicheskie metody* 1967, No. 5, p. 686.

28. Popov P.I. (ed.) *Balans narodnogo khozy aistva SSSR 1923/24 goda* (1926) TsSU USSR.

29. He reviewed some of it in a German journal. For a contemporary Russian translation of his review see W.W. Leontief, Balans narodnogo khozyaistva SSSR; metodologicheskii obzor raboty TsSU, *Planovoy e Khozy aistvo* 1925, No. 12. There is an English translation in Spulber (ed.) *Foundations of Soviet strategy for economic growth* (Bloomington, Indiana 1964) pp. 88–94.

30. 'It would be incorrect to suppose that the input-output table can fully substi tute itself for the existing system of plan calculations. Its task is simply that of combining the totality of these calculations into a single whole.' *Ekonomika i matematicheskie metody* 1969, No. 1, p. 35.

31. A.G. Aganbegyan and A.G. Granberg, *Ekonomiko-matemati cheskii analiz mezhotraslevogo balansa SSSR* (1968) pp. 13–15.

32. M.R. Eidelman, *Mezhotraslevoi balans obshchestvennogo produkta* (1966) p. 85.

33. ibid pp. 85–134 are devoted to the methods used in Soviet sample survey s for input-output purposes.

    'One of the chief obstacles to the construction of input-output tables is the inadequacy of the official statistics, which creates the need for cumbersome sample survey s. Much has been said by now about the necessity for altering the statistical reporting, but nothing has been done in this direction.'

L.E. Mints (ed.) *Mezhotraslevye issledovaniya v ekonomicheskikh raionakh (opy t raboty po pribaltiskomu ekonomicheskomu raionu)* (1967) p. 28.

34.   R. Stone, *Input-output and national accounts* (Paris 1961) pp. 34–35.

35.   ibid pp. 35–36.

36.   L.E. Mints (ed.) *Mezhotraslevye issledovaniya v ekonomicheskikh raionakh* (1967) p. 27.

37.   See Eidelman M.R., *Mezhotraslevoi balans obshchestvennogo produkta* (1966) pp. 220–229; Efimov A.N. and Berri L.Ya. (eds.) *Metody planirovaniya mezhotraslevy kh proportsii* (1965) pp. 159–170; and V.V. Kossov (ed.) *Mezhotraslevoi balans proizvodstva i raspredeleniy a produktsii ekonomicheskogo raiona* (1964) pp. 65–69.

38.   A.G. Granberg, *Problemy planovogo mezhotraslevogo balansa v natural'nom virazhenii* (Unpublished thesis, Moscow 1963) p. 34.

39.   ibid p. 35.

40.   V.V. Kossov and V.S. Dadayan, *Balans ekonomicheskogo raiona kak sredstvo planovykh raschetov* (1962) p. 38; and H.B. Chenery and P.G. Clark, *Interindustry economics* (New York 1966) p. 144.

41.   For a description of the construction of the 24×24 transactions matrices for Estonia for 1961 and 1970 which separated out the non-proportional inputs see Kukke's article in *Ekonomiko-maticheskie issledovaniya narodnogo khozyaistva estonskoi SSR* (Tallinn 1968).

42.   Yu.M. Shvirkov in *Ocherky po sovremennoi sovetskoi i zarubezhnoi ekonomika*, vol. 3 (1962) ed. A.N. Oznobin p. 29. The reference is to the 1959 all-Union table in value terms.

43.   A.N. Efimov and L.Ya. Berri (eds.) *Metody planirovaniya mezhotraslevkh proportsii* (1965) pp. 156–157.

44.   See *Journal of Development Planning* 1969, No. 1, pp. 79–80, and *Metodicheskie ukazaniya k sostavleniy u gosudarstvennogo plana razvitiy a narodnogo khozy aistva SSSR* (1969) p. 598.

45.   A.N. Efimov (ed.) *Mezhotraslevoi balans i proportsii narodnogo*

khozvaistva (1969) p. 31. See also chapter 15 of A.P. Carter and
A. Bródy (eds.) *Application of input-output analysis* (Amsterdam and
London 1970).

46.   A.N. Efimov (ed.) op cit p. 81.

47.   This is Vainshtein's estimate. See his article in *Ekonomika i
matematicheskie metody* 1967, No. 1.

48.   See the articles by Mikhalevsky in *Ekonomika i matematicheskie
metody* 1966, No. 6; 1967, No. 2; 1967, No. 5 and 1968, No. 1.

49.   A.G. Aganbegyan (ed.) *Problemy narodnokhozyaistvennogo optimuma*
(Novosibirsk 1966) pp. 10–18.

50.   This diagram is taken from E.F. Baranov, *Osobennosty razrabotki
raionykh mezhotraslevykh balansov i metody raschetov na ikh osnove
(na opyte rabot po Latviiskoi, Litovskoi i Estonskoi SSR)*
(Unpublished thesis Moscow 1964) p. 209.

51.   B.A. Volchkov, *Ekonomika i matematicheskie metody* 1966, No. 3,
p. 436.

52.   See the article by Klotsvog, Ageeva and Buzunov in *Ekonomika i
matematicheskie metody* 1969, No. 1.

53.   L.E. Mints, V.V. Kossov and E.F. Baranov, *Mezhotraslevoi balans
ekonomicheskogo raiona* (1967) p. 264 and appendix 4. For a discussion
of some of the differences between the indices of an input-output
table and the plan, see the papers by Meerovich and Chernikova in
Planovyi mezhotraslevoi balans soyuznoi respubliki (1968).

54.   B.A. Volchkov op cit p. 436.

55.   Yu.M. Shvirkov op cit p. 35.

56.   Granberg A.G. op cit pp. 193–194.

57.   A. Modin, Mezhotraslevoi balans i sistema matrichnykh modelei,
Voprosy Ekonomiki 1964, No. 1; and N.V. Makhrov, Metod
mezhotraslevogo balansa – osnova svoda nizovykh planov, in V.S.
Nemchinov (ed.) *Primenenie matematiki v ekonomicheskykh
issledovaniyakh* vol. 3 (1965).

58.   Granberg A.G. op cit pp. 214–220. Attention was drawn to this point
by Treml. See J.P. Hardt et al (eds.) *Mathematics and computers in
Soviet economic planning* (New Haven and London 1967). p. 113.

59. M. Lemeshev, *Mezhotraslevye svyazi sel'skogo khozyaista* (1968). For reviews of this controversial book see *Ekonomika sel'skogo khozyaistva* 1969, No. 6 and *Ekonomika i matematicheskie metody* 1969, No. 5.

60. For these tables see A.N. Efimov (ed.) *Mezhotraslevoi balans i planirovaniya v stranakh − chlenakh SEV* (1969) pp. 109–111.

61. A.N. Efimov (ed.) *Mezhotraslevoi balans i proportsii narodnogo khozyaistva* (1969) p. 6.

62. *Planovyi mezhotralslevoi balans soyuznoi respubliki* (1968) p. 8.

63. V.V. Kossov and V.S. Dadayan op cit p. 9.

64. For a comparison of material balances and input-output as techniques for arriving at a consistent plan see S.S. Ahluwalia, Balancing versus input-output techniques in ensuring the internal consistency of a plan, in *Essays on planning and economic development* (Warsaw 1965).

65. N.E. Kobrinskii and A.M. Matlin, *Ekonomiko-matematicheskie modeli v planirovanii* (1968) p. 17.

66. E.O. Kaitsa, *Snabzhenie i proizvodstvenno-khozyaistvennaya deyatel' nost' promyshlennogo predpriyatiya* (Tartu 1965) p. 6.

67. *Khozyaistvennaya reforma i problemy realizatsii* (1968) p. 36.

68. See chapter 5, part 3, of M. Lemeshev, *Mezhotraslevye svyazi sel'skogo khozyaistva* (1968).

69. J.C. Emery, *Organisational Planning and Control Systems* (1969) pp. 24–28.

70. N.I. Bukharin, Zametki ekonomista, *Pravda* 30 September 1928.

71. A.E. Probst, Znachenie rezervov dlya narodnokhozyaistvennogo planirovaniya, *Sovershenstvovanie planirovaniya i upravleniya narodnym khozyaistvom* (the Strumilin *festschrift*) (1967).
    Probst considers that the well known calculations of Campbell (*American Economic Review* September 1958) according to which the Soviet inventory/output ratio is higher than the American one, are erroneous.

72. B.M. Smekhov (ed.) *Problemy sovershenstvovaniya planirovaniya* (1968) (vol. 59 of the *Trudy* of the Plekharov Insitute).

73. P. Krylov, deputy departmental head Gosplan USSR, *Ekonomicheskaya Gazeta* 1969, No. 45, p. 9.

74. This decree is reprinted in *khozyaistvennaya reforma v SSSR* (1969) (the *Ekonomicheskaya Gazeta* book) pp. 159–166. The importance of reserves is recognised in 1 (c). Chapter 4 of V.M. Lagutkin (ed.) *Nekotorye problemy sovershenstovovaniya material'no-tekhnicheskogo snabsheniya* (1970) is devoted to the question of stocks.

75. N.V. Ivanov, E.Yu. Lokshin and G.M. Demichev, *Ekonomiki i planirovanie material'no-tekhnicheskoe snabzheniya promyshlennosti* (1969) p. 340; and N.V. Gukov, *Organizatsiya material'no tecknicheskogc snabzheniya predpriyatii bytovogo obsluzhivaniya naseleniya* (1969) p. 79.

76. M. Lemeshev, *Mezhotraslevye svyazi sel'skogo khozyaistva* (1968) p. 228.

77. A.N. Lebed', M.Sh. Dovetov, and Yu.M. Aristakov, *Material'no-tekhnicheskoe snabzhenie i sbyt v sovremennykh usloviyakh* (1969) p. 54; and *Material'no-tekhnicheskoe snabzhenie* 1970, No. 5, p. 93.

78. V.M. Lagutkin (ed.) *Nekotorye problemy sovershenstvovaniya material'no-tekhnicheskoe snabzheniya* (1970) chapter 6, section 2.

79. L. Dudkin and E. Yershov, *Planovoe khozyaistvo* 1965, No. 5; L.M. Dudkin, *Optimalny material'ny balans narodnogo khozyaistva* (1966); Dudkin's article in N.P. Fedorenko (ed.) *Ekonomicheskie problemy razvitiya i razmeshcheniya khimicheskoi promyshlennosti* (1968); and Shchennikov's article in *Ekonomika i matematicheskie metody* (1966). No. 5.

80. I.Ya. Birman (ed.) *Optimal'nyi plan otrasli* (1970) p. 143.

81. A.N. Lebed', M.Sh. Dovetov and Yu.M. Aristakov op cit p. 61.

82. A.M. Matlin, *Tseny i ekonomicheskaya effektivnost' mashin* (1968) chapter 6.

Chapter 6 Appendix 1

Aggregation as a cause of inconsistent plans

1. See A.G. Granberg, *Problemy planovogo mezhotraslevogo balansa v natural'nom virazheniya* (unpublished thesis, Moscow 1963) pp. 34–41.

2. See A. Nove, Principal problems of Soviet planning, *Was Stalin really necessary?* (1964).

Chapter 6 Appendix 3

The use of input-output in regional economic planning

1. *Ekonomika i matematicheskie metody* 1966, No. 4, p. 620.

2. Institute of Economics of the Estonian Academy of Sciences, *Metody sostavleniya i analiza planovogo mezhotraslevogo balansa respubliki* (Tallinn 1966) p. 45.

3. Ibid p. 46.

4. L.E. Mints, V.V. Kossov and E.F. Baranov (eds.), *Mezhotraslevoi balans ekonomicheskogo raiona* (1967) pp. 237–241; E.F. Baranov, *Osobennosti razrabotki raionykh mezhotraslevykh balansov i metody raschetov na ikh osnove (na opyte rabot po Latviiskoi, Litovskoi i Estonskoi SSR)* (unpublished thesis, Moscow 1964) pp. 159–198.

5. L.E. Mints, V.V. Kossov and E.F. Baranov (eds.) *Mezhotraslevoi balans ekonomicheskogo raiona* (1967) p. 243; E.F. Baranov, *Osobennosti...* pp. 198–205.

6. M. Belov, *Planovoe khozyaistvo* 1964, No. 5; and Belov's article in *Planovyi mezhotraslevoi balans soyuznoi respubliki* (1968) pp. 5–15.

7. *Ekonomika i matematicheskie metody* 1966, No. 4, pp. 619–622.

8. L.E. Mints, V.V. Kossov, E.F. Baranov (eds.) *Mezhotraslevoi balans ekonomicheskogo raiona* (1967) p. 244.

9. E.N. Utrobin and R.N. Shniper, *Planirovanie khozyaistva krupnogo ekonomicheskogo raiona* (1966).

10. Utrobin and Shniper op cit p. 43. Italics added.

11. V.V. Kossov and L.E. Mints, *Vestnik Statistiki* 1964, No. 6.

12. L. Mints (ed.) *Mezhotraslevye issledovaniya v ekonomicheskikh raionakh (opyt raboty po pribaltiskomu ekonomicheskomu raionu)* (1967) p. 20.

13. C.B. Tilanus, *Input-output experiments: the Netherlands 1948–1961* (Rotterdam 1966).

Chapter 6 Appendix 4

Input-output tables compiled in the USSR

1. This table was partially published, together with derived data, in

Narodnoe khozyaistvo SSSR v 1960 g (1961). A reconstruction of the entire table is in V.G. Treml, The 1959 Soviet input-output table, Joint Economic Committee of Congress, *New directions in the Soviet economy* (Washington 1966).

2. *Narodnoe khozyaistvo SSSR v 1967 g* (1968).

3. This table was partially published in *Narodnoe khozyaistvo SSSR v 1961 g* (1962).

4. *Narodnoe khozyaistvo SSSR v 1968 g* (1969).

5. *Narodnoe khozyaistvo SSSR v 1968 g* (1969).

6. Excluding exports and imports and error. Of the 13 columns, 3 were for accumulation and 10 for consumption.

7. Excluding competitive imports and including amortisation.

8. This table was compiled under the aegis of the Laboratory of Economic-Mathematical methods which subsequently became TSEMI.

9. See Yu.I. Cherniak, Osnovnye cherty mezhotraslevogo balansa ekonomicheskogo raiona, in V.S. Nemchinov (ed.) *Mezhotraslevoi balans proizvodstva i raspredeleniya produktsii v narodnom khozyaistve* (1962).

10. Excluding exports and imports and error. Of the 11 columns, 2 were for accumulation and 9 for consumption.

11. According to V.V. Kossov *Mezhotralevoi balans proizvodstva i raspredeleniya produktsii ekonomicheskogo raiona* (1964) p. 68.

12. Excluding exports and imports and error. Of the 6 columns 4 were for accumulation and 2 for consumption.

13. Of the 109, six were non-productive branches of the economy, such as medical care, passenger transport, education, science and adminstration. See the article by Kolpakov and Semenov in *Voprosy Ekonomiki* 1970, No. 1.

14. For the Georgian table a 3 fold classification was used. 119 was the number of industries distinguished in the most aggregated of the classifications. See M.V. Kekelidze, *Analiz mezhotraslevykh svyazei respubliki* (1968) pp. 19–24.

Chapter 7

Some problems of current planning

1. *Optimal'noe planirovanie i sovershenstvovanie upravlenie narodnym khozyaistvom* (1969) p. 32.

2. N.E. Kobrinskii and A.M. Matlin, *Ekonomiko-matematicheskie modeli v planirovanii* (1968) pp. 19–21.

3. I. Friss (ed.) *Reform of the economic mechanism in Hungary* (Budapest 1969) p. 11.

4. See for example E.G. Liberman, *Khozyaistvennyi raschet mashinostroitel'nogo zavoda* (1950).

5. B. Kuz'michev, *Pravda* 3 June 1968.

6. G.V. Bazarova, *Pribyl' v ekonomicheskom stimulirovanii proizvodstva* (1968) p. 138.

7. B. Kuz'michev op cit.

8. A.N. Efimov, *Sovetskaya industriya* (1967) pp. 248–249.

9. This example is taken from the review article, Ekonomicheskii rost i vybor (Economic growth and choice), *Novyi Mir* 1967, No. 12.

10. For a striking example of this see Sely uni n's article in *Ekonomicheskaya Gazeta* 1968, No. 25, p. 14.

11. For a discussion of the instability of Soviet plans see B.M. Smekhov, Khozyaistvennay a reforma i stabil'nost' planov, in B.M. Smekhov (ed.) *Problemy sovershenstovovaniya planirovaniya* (1968) (vol. 59 of the *Trudy* of the Plekhanov Institute). Numerous examples can be found by reading *Sotsialisticheskaya Industriya*.

12. For a description of the traditional price system see S.K. Stoly arov, *O tsenakh i tsenoobrazovanii v SSSR* (1963); R. W. Campbell, Accounting for cost control in the Soviet economy , *Review of Economics and Statistics* February 1958; M. Boornstein, The Soviet price system, *American Economic Review* March 1962; M. Boornstein, Soviet price theory and policy, Joint Economic Committee of Congress, *New directions in the Soviet economy* (Washington 1966).

13. N. Fedorenko, Ob ekonomicheskoi otsenka prirodnikh resursov, *Voprosy Ekonomiki* 1968, No. 3, p. 102.

14. *Pravda* 6 December 1968.

15. V.V. Novozhilov, Nedostatok tovarov, *Vestnik Finansov* 1926, No. 2.

16. V.S. Nemchinov (ed.) *Primenenie matematiki v ekonomicheskikh issledovaniyakh* (1959) pp. 199–200.

17. A. Bachurin, *Planovoye Khozyaistvo* 1969, No. 11, p. 15.

18. *Sotsialisticheskaya Industriya* 16 August 1970, p. 2, and ibid 15 September 1970, p. 3.

19. I.T. Luchinsky, *Vestnik Akademii Nauk SSSR* 1968, No. 12.

20. A.I. Lyovin, *Ekonomicheskoe regulirovanie vnutrennogo rynka* (1967) p. 74.

21. J. Kuron and K. Modzelewski, *An open letter to the party* (n. d. 1968?) pp. 34–35.

22. O. Lange, On the economic theory of socialism, *Review of Economic Studies* February 1937, pp. 127–128.

23. See B. Horvat, *Towards a theory of planned economy* (Belgrade 1964) p. 225; J. Kornai, *Overcentralisation in economic administration* (1959) chapter 5 ('Excessive cent r alisation as a socio-political problem').

24. cf A. Downs, *Inside bureaucracy* (Boston 1967).

25. For a striking example of this, see the letter from V. Yudina in *Novyi Mir* 1969, No. 9, pp. 270–275.

26. J. Kornai, *Overcentralisation in economic administration* (1959) p. 121.

27. J.C. Emery, *Organisational planning and control systems* (1969) p. 121.

28. As Lichfield has observed, 'Externalities exist only because of the institutional limitations on the costs and benefits which the decision makers choose to take into their reckoning.' J. Margolis (ed.) *The public economy of urban communities* (Washington 1965) p. 247.
    For a discussion of this point see A. Nove, Internal economies,

Economic Journal December 1969.

29.   Kornai op cit pp. 225–226.

Chapter 7 Appendix

The optimal value of an enterprise output plan — a suggestion for behavioural research.

1.   E. Ames, *Soviet economic processes* (Homewood, Illinois 1965); R.D. Portes, The enterprise under central planning, *Review of Economic Studies* April 1969.

2.   P. Samuelson, *Foundation of economic analysis* (Cambridge, Mass. 1947) chapter 4.

3.   E. Devons, *Planning in practice* (1950) pp. 27–42.

4.   G.H. Hofstede, *The game of budget control* (1968) chapter 8.

5.   For a US experiment on the effect of budget levels on performance see A.C. Stedry and E. Kay, *The effects of goal difficulty on performance: A field experiment* (Sloan School of Management, MIT, 1964).

Chapter 8

Can the optimal planners help improve the economic mechanism?

1.   L.V. Kantorovich and A.B. Gorstko, *Matematicheskoe optimal'noe programmirovanie v ekonomike* (1968) p. 95.

2.   V.F. Kotov, *Planirovanie realizatsii, produktsii, prybyli i rentabel' nosti v promyshlennosti* (1969) pp. 182–189.

3.   *Planovoe Khozyaistvo* 1969, No. 12, p. 58. cf Ivanchenko's article in *Ekonomicheskaya Gazeta* 1969, No. 50, p. 15.

4.   V.V. Sitnin, *Problemy pribyli i khozyaistvennogo rascheta v promy shlennosti* (1969) p. 109.

5.   L.I. Malyshev and V.A. Malich, *Analiz fondov ekonomicheskogo stimulirovaniya predpriyatii* (1968) p. 8.

6.   *Narodnoe Khozyaistvo SSSR v 1968 g* (1969) p. 772.

7.   N.E. Drogichinsky and D.I. Tsarev, *Khozyaistvennaya reforma: opyt*

perspektivy (1968) pp. 241–242. Drogichinsky is the head of Gosplan USSR's department for the introduction of the new methods of planning and economic incentives.

8. *Ekonomika i organizatsiya promyshlennogo proizvodstva* 1970, No. 1, p. 105.

9. Drogichinsky and Tsarev op cit p. 136.

10. V.P. Karamkin (ed.) *Khozraschetnye stimuly raboty predpriyatii* (1969) p. 5.

11. Drogichinsky and Tsarev op cit p. 137.

12. Sitnin op cit p. 146.

13. Drogichinsky and Tsarev op cit p. 137. Sitnin concurs. See Sitnin op cit p. 118.

14. V.M. Ivanchenko, *Khozy aistvennay a reforma segodnya i zavtra* (1969) p. 45. Ivanchenko is an official of the department of Gosplan USSR charged with implementing the reform.

15. N.P. Fedorenko, *O razrabotke sistemy optimal'nogo funktsionirovaniya ekonomiki* (1968) p. 54.

16. cf G.C. Harcourt, The account ant in a golden age, *Oxford Economic Papers* 1965, and S.S. Alexander, Income measurement in a dynamic economy, W.T. Baxter and S. Davidson, *Studies in accounting theory* 2nd ed. (1962).

17. See Ivanchenko's article in *Ekonomicheskaya Gazeta* 1969, No. 50 pp. 15–16.

18. It is entitled 'On the procedure and periods for working out and confirming stable norms for deductions from profits into the economic incentive funds' and is published in *Ekonomicheskaya Gazeta* 1969, No. 16, p. 11. It is explained by two officials of Gosplan USSR in *Planovoe Khozyaistvo* 1969, No. 8, pp. 29–36 (the example which follows is taken from here) and by another official of Gosplan USSR in *Finansy SSSR* 1969, No. 10, pp. 80–84.

19. Sitnin op cit p. 138.

20. V.D. Belkin and V.V. Ivanter, *Ekonomicheskoe upravlenie i bank* (1969) p. 4.

21. N.V. Garetovskii (ed.) *Finansy i kredit v usloviyakh khozyaistvennoi reformy* (1969) p. 148. For the quotation which follows see ibid p. 153.

22. G.A. Yegiazaryan and L.S. Kheifets, *Problemy material'nogo stimulirovaniya v promyshlennosti* (1970) pp. 5–6.

23. Sitnin op cit. p. 166.

24. *Pravda* 14 January 1969 article by Ivanchenko.

25. V.V. Novozhilov, *Izmerenie zatrat i rezul'tatov pri optimal'nom plani rovani i* (1967) p. 14, footnote 1.

26. M.Z. Bor and A.G. Kulikov (eds.) *Tempy, proportsii, kriterii effektivnosti* (1968) p. 122.

27. *Ekonomika i matematicheskie metody* 1968, No. 5, p. 694.

28. M.Z. Bor and I.Kh. Bairamukov (eds.) *Sovershenstvovani e planirovani ya i upravleni ya proizvodstvom* (1969) p. 165.

29. Ya.G. Liberman, *Gosudarstvennyi byudzhet SSSR v novy kh usloviyakh khozyaistvovani ya* (1970).

30. N.Ya. Petrakov, *Rent abel'nost' i tsena* (1964) p. 45.

31. D.D. Kondrashev and G.D. Kondrashev, *Priby l', tsena khozraschet* (1969) p. 209.

32. Kotov op cit pp. 172–173.

33. F. Veselkov, *Voprosy ekonomiki* 1969, No. 12, p. 42.

34. See Karagedov's article in *Izvestiya sibirskogo otdeleniya akademii nauk SSSR: seriya obshchestvennykh nauk* 1970, No. 1.

35. *Ekonomicheskay a Gazeta* 1969, No. 45, p. 8.

36. V.F. Pugachev, *Optimizatsiya plani rovaniya* (1968) chapter 3, section 3.

37. *Voprosy ekonomiki* 1970, No. 5.

38. Karagedov op cit, and his article in *Planovoe Khozyaistvo* 1970, No. 9.

39. G.Khanin, Logika ekonomicheskogo mekhanizma (The logic of the economic mechanism) *Novyi Mir* 1970, No. 5, pp. 270–274.

40. *Diskussiya ob optimal'nom planirovanii* (1968) compilers L.Ya. Kazakevich and L.V. Levshin p. 120.

41. *Voprosy ekonomiki* 1970, No. 3.

42. *Planovoe khozyaistvo* 1967, No. 4, p. 14.

43. Ya.G. Liberman, *Gosudarstvennyi byudzhet SSSR v novykh usloviyakh khozyaistvovaniya* (1970) pp. 65–71.

44. *Diskussiya ob optimal'nom planirovanii* (1968) pp. 190–191.

45. *Voprosy ekonomiki* 1967, No. 10, p. 23.

46. N. Fedorenko (ed.) *Ekonomiko-matematicheskie modeli* (1969) pp. 499–500. One footnote omitted.

47. Arrow and Hurwicz, Decentralization and computation in resource allocation, in Pfouts (ed.) *Essays in economics and econometrics* (Chapel Hill n. d.); E. Malinvaud, Decentralized procedures for planning, in E. Malinvaud and M. Bacharach, *Activity analysis in the theory of growth and planning* (1967); Kornai and Liptak, Two level planning,, *Econometrica* 1965; Novozhilov and Gdalevich, Khozraschetnaya sistema planirovaniya, *Optimal'noe planirovanie i sovershenstvovanie upravleniya narodnym khozyaistvom* (1969).

Chapter 9

Can the optimal planners help improve the methods of economic calculation?

1. V.S. Nemchinov (ed.) *Primenenie matematiki v ekonomicheskikh issledovaniyakh* (1959) p. 276.

2. *Management Science* July 1960, pp. 410–419.

3. L.V. Kantorovich and A.B. Gorstko, *Matematicheskoe optimal'noe programmirovanie v ekonomike* (1968) pp. 48–53. For this application of linear programming see also Kantorovich's article in *Material'no-tekhnicheskoe snabzhenie* 1970, No. 4, and V.M. Lagutkin (ed.) *Nekotorye problemy sovershenstvovaniya material'no-tekhnicheskogo snabzheniya* (1970) pp. 26–30.

4. Z.I. Loginov and L.Yu. Astanskii, Skhema optimal'nogo razmeshcheniya tsementnoi promyshlennosti, *Primenenie matematicheskikh metodov v razmeshchenii proizvodstva* (1968) pp. 28–29. The description of the work in the text is based on this paper.

5. I.Ya. Birman (ed.) *Optimal'nyi plan otrasli* (1970) p. 327.

6. ibid p. 306.

7. Ya.P. Gerchuk, *Granitsy primeneniya lineinogo programmirovaniya* (1965) section 7, and Gerchuk's article in *Voprosy ekonomiki* 1969 No. 4.

8. I.Ya. Birman (ed.) *Optimal'nyi plan otrasli* (1970) p. 327.

9. *Izvestiya* 20 January 1968.

Chapter 10

Conclusion

1. *Vestnik Finansov* 1928, No. 10, pp. 32–33.

2. L.V. Kantorovich, *Ekonomicheskii raschet nailuchshego ispol'zovaniye resursov* (1960) p. 200.

3. For English language surveys of this discussion see A. Zauberman, Law of value and price formation, in G.Grossman (ed.) *Value and plan* (Berkeley 1960); and pp. 149–155 of M. Dobb, *Papers on capitalism, development and planning* (1967).

4. B. Ward, *The socialist economy* (New York 1967) p. 16.

5. K. Popper, *The open society and its enemies* (1962) p. 304.

6. M. Friedman, *Capitalism and freedom* (Chicago 1962) p. 12.

7. *Novyi Mir* 1968, No. 12, p. 187.

8. *The Banker* September and October 1939.

9. 'The year of the great break' was Stalin's description of the year 1929. See J. Stalin, *Sochineniya* vol. 12, (1955). pp. 118–135.

10. *Sibirskii matematicheskii zhurnal* 1966, No. 7.

11. *Voprosy ekonomiki* 1969, No. 5, p. 149.

12. For Soviet work in these fields see B.A. Volchkov, *Avtomatizirovannaya sistema planovykh raschetov* (1970); and N.P. Fedorenko (ed) *Voprosy proektirovaniya otraslevykh avtomatizirovannykh sistem upravleniya* (1970).

13. *Planovoe khozyaistvo* 1969, No. 11.

14. J. Schumpeter, *Capitalism, socialism and democracy* (1950) p. 83.

15. P. Wiles, Growth versus choice, *Economic Journal* June 1956.

16. L.L. Pasinetti, A new theoretical approach to the problems of economic growth, in Pontifical Academy of Sciences, *Study week on the econometric approach to development planning* (Amsterdam and Chicago 1965) p. 694.

17. *Izvestiya sibirskogo otdeleniya akademii nauk SSSR: seriya obshchestvennykh nauk* 1970, No. 1.

18. A.I. Kats, *Dinamicheskii ekonomicheskii optimum* (1970).

19. Ekonomicheskii rost i vybor (Economic growth and choice) *Novyi Mir* 1967, No. 12.

20. *Izvestiya AN SSSR: Seriya ekonomicheskaya* 1970, No. 2, p. 155.

21. V.V. Novozhilov, *Problems of cost-benefit analysis in optimal planning* (New York 1970) pp. 301–302.